ADAPTING TO
WEB STANDARDS

CSS and Ajax for Big Sites

Christopher Schmitt, Kimberly Blessing, Rob Cherny,
Meryl K. Evans, Kevin Lawver, and Mark Trammell

New
Riders

VOICES THAT MATTER™

Adapting to Web Standards: CSS and Ajax for Big Sites

Christopher Schmitt

Kimberly Blessing
Rob Cherny
Meryl K. Evans
Kevin Lawver
Mark Trammell

New Riders
1249 Eighth Street
Berkeley, CA 94710
510/524-2178
510/524-2221 (fax)

Find us on the World Wide Web at: www.newriders.com
To report errors, please send a note to errata@peachpit.com

New Riders is an imprint of Peachpit, a division of Pearson Education

Project Editor: Victor Gavenda
Production Editor: Hilal Sala
Development Editor: Wendy Katz
Copyeditor: Doug Adrianson
Tech Editor: Molly Holzschlag
Proofreader: Doug Adrianson
Compositor: Kim Scott, Bumpy Design
Indexer: Emily Glossbrenner
Cover design: Charlene Charles-Will
Interior design: Kim Scott, Bumpy Design

ISBN-13:   978-0-321-50182-0
ISBN   0-321-50182-9

9 8 7 6 5 4 3 2 1

Printed and bound in the United States of America

Acknowledgements

Adapting to Web Standards tackles the very real problems of reaching out and teaching people about Web standards, but also how to incorporate those technologies into everyday workflows when swift and frequent deadlines often crush progress.

Written to empower the individual designer and the large organizations to start working in the correct direction, *Adapting to Web Standards* required the involvement the hands of a great number of professionals.

If you know Rob Cherny, you know a *true* Web specialist. He seems to cover every aspect of the DOM. His presence is felt in the core of this book from the introduction up through the fourth chapter.

I'm not sure how Kimberly Blessing came into the book project. I believe it was during one of those mad, late night pushes to get edits and reviews out the proverbial door when she chimed in to offered to write about managing Web standards. That turned into Chapter 5 of the current book. I'm grateful for her time and support for this project.

Special thanks go to Meryl K. Evans, the content maven. She stepped in at the right moment to help tackle the Tori Amos chapter.

I was honored when I talked to Kevin Lawver about building off his panel idea and turning into a book, he not only supported it, but also wanted to be a part of the process. He did an amazing job in capturing a small part of the Web standards process at AOL.

Thanks to the illustrator Rebecca Gunter for the illustrations for Kimberly's chapter. You can find more of her work at http://soap-committee.deviantart.com/.

Many thanks go to Molly E. Holzschlag for doing the technical editing chores of the book. Not sure how she had the time to do this among her various other activities, but I'm sure someone who has written thirty-plus books on Web development like she has could find the way. See http://molly.com.

Wendy Katz and Doug Adrianson helped guide the creation of the book with their timely questions and editing skills.

Thanks to Victor Gavenda and Michael Nolan from Peachpit Press/New Riders for guiding the book from concept to reality.

As anyone who has ever written a chapter for a book, it's not easy. It's a commitment demanding time and focus that keeps people away from weekend getaways or get-togethers with friends and loved ones. I want to let the ones closest to me know that I'm looking forward to our seeing you all and not boring you with talk about Web standards.

For a while, at least.

Christopher Schmitt
christopherschmitt.com
Lead Author

About the Authors

Christopher Schmitt is the founder of Heatvision.com, Inc., a small new media publishing and design firm based in Cincinnati, Ohio.

An award-winning web designer who has been working with the Web since 1993, Christopher interned for both David Siegel and Lynda Weinman in the mid 90s while he was an undergraduate at Florida State University working on a Fine Arts degree with an emphasis on Graphic Design. Afterwards, he earned a Masters in Communication for Interactive and New Communication Technologies while obtaining a graduate certificate in Project Management from FSU's College of Communication.

In 2000, he led a team to victory in the Cool Site in a Day competition, where he and five other talented developers built a fully functional, well-designed Web site for a nonprofit organization in eight hours.

He is the author of *CSS Cookbook*, which was named Best Web Design Book of 2006, and one of the first books that looked at CSS-enabled designs, *Designing CSS Web Pages* (New Riders). He is also the co-author of Professional CSS (Wrox), *Photoshop in 10 Steps or Less* (Wiley) and *Dreamweaver Design Projects* (glasshaus) and contributed four chapters to *XML, HTML, XHTML Magic* (NewRiders). Christopher has also written for New Architect Magazine, A List Apart, Digital Web and Web Reference.

At conferences and workshops such as Train the Trainer, Web Visions and SXSW, Christopher demonstrates the use and benefits of accessible and standards-based designs. He is the list moderator for Babble (www.babblelist.com), a mailing list community devoted to advanced web design and development topics.

On his personal web site, www.christopher.org, Christopher shows his true colors and most recent activities. He is 6' 7" and doesn't play professional basketball but wouldn't mind a good game of chess.

Kimberly Blessing is a computer scientist, technical leader, and Web standards evangelist. At PayPal she leads the Web Development Platform Team, which is responsible for driving the creation and adoption of standards through training and process. She co-leads The Web Standards Project, a grass-roots organization that advocates standards-compliance and use to browser manufacturers and developers alike. A graduate of Bryn Mawr College's Computer Science program, Kimberly is also passionate about increasing the number of women in technology. Her on-line presence is at www.kimberlyblessing.com.

Rob Cherny is the Lead Web Developer at Washington DC-based Web user experience consulting firm, NavigationArts. He has 11 years experience implementing Web sites, content management, and Web-based applications, typically filling an ambiguous space between the creative and technical teams.

Rob has introduced Web standards-based solutions as both an employee and a consultant for a broad range of clients including Sallie Mae, Sunrise Senior Living, the American Red Cross, Discovery, Weatherbug, Marriott, Freddie Mac, GEICO, the US Department of Health and Human Services, and the US State Department.

He lives outside Boston, Massachusetts with his wife, two dogs, and three cats. While not obsessively multitasking online in front of his computer he enjoys movies and hikes with his wife and dogs. He periodically blogs about Web design and development on his personal Web site, www.cherny.com.

Rob holds a Bachelor of Arts in History degree from Towson State University in Maryland.

Meryl K. Evans is a content maven and the author of *Brilliant Outlook Pocketbook*. She has written many articles and contributed to books covering Web design, business, and writing. Meryl has also written and edited for *The Dallas Morning News*, Digital Web Magazine, MarketingProfs.com, *PC Today*, O'Reilly, Pearson, Penguin, Sams, Wiley, and WROX. You can contact the native Texan through her Web site at www.meryl.net.

Kevin Lawver has worked for AOL for over twelve years, building all manner of web applications. He is a passionate advocate for standards-based development and is currently AOL's representative to the W3C Advisory Council and a member of the CSS Working Group. He spends his time writing code, blogging, preaching the gospel of web standards, and speaking at conferences about standards, mashups, best practices and Ruby on Rails. You'll find Kevin on the Web at http://lawver.net.

Mark Trammell has been chasing function and usability as a standard for Web design since 1995. Mark has served as Web Standards Evangelist at PayPal and directed the Web presence of the University of Florida. In his tenure at UF, Mark led a widely acclaimed standards-based rebuilding of www.ufl.edu. To download Mark's interview with Jimmy Byrum, who is the Web developer at Yahoo! responsible for the home page at yahoo.com, be sure to register this book online at www.webstandardsbook.com.

Contents

Constructing Standards-Based Web Sites

Part **1**

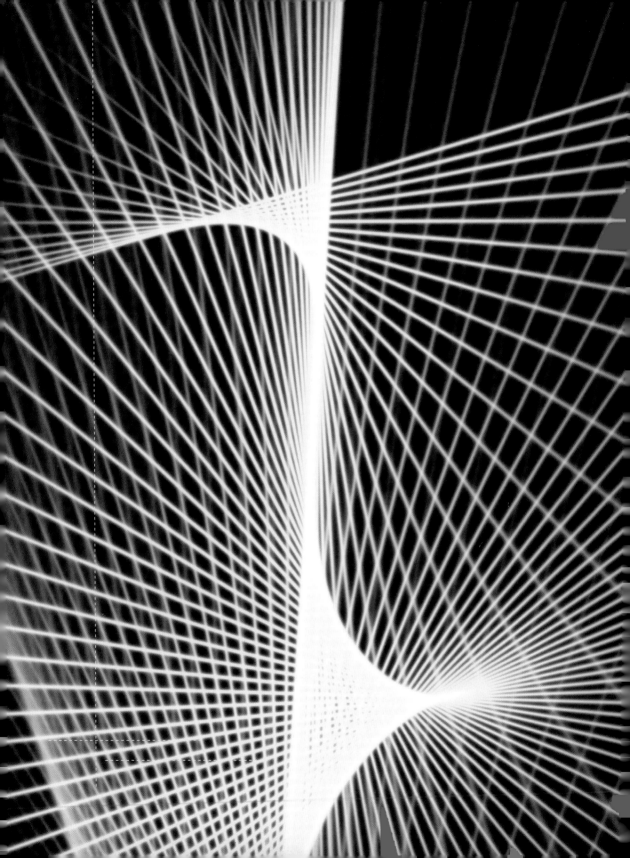

Introduction

Building Web sites has changed, and someone forgot to tell the architects. Web browsers' support for modern techniques has allowed a new degree of discipline and control in coding the front end of a Web site. These new best practices are those dictated in what is commonly referred to as "Web standards-based" design or development.

A Web standards-based approach has countless benefits. The larger or more complex a Web presence, the more critical Web standards become. This is particularly true for an enterprise with many different properties, channels, or brand considerations. Add to this the prospect of critical Web-based applications and content management, and it becomes a mandate to ensure a high level of quality at every tier of an online presence.

To embrace standards is only the start. Some planning must occur to create a standards strategy that will endure over time, be applied gracefully, and scale within an organization, team, or enterprise. A solid foundation should be created by getting back to the basics and building with deliberate choices instead of accidental decisions.

This book will help a Web team reexamine why they are creating standards-based Web sites and how best to do it. It will help evaluate what is in place now as well as the impact of Web standards on a team or a Web site as a whole. It will also assist with staying organized over time and in finding ways to improve stability and reduce risk in Web applications. It will help create techniques that leverage the unique strengths of Web standards in a CMS (Content Management System). Finally, this book will finish by examining some process and staffing considerations of Web standards.

What Are Web Standards?

Web standards is a term used to mean Web pages built using the open and compatible recommendations from the World Wide Web Consortium (W3C) and other standards bodies as opposed to closed, proprietary, corporate feature sets. These recommendations, combined with modern best practices, exploit the standardized power of the modern Web browsers that dominate the market today, as opposed to out-of-date browsers that were feature-rich but inconsistent and often incompatible. Placing a graphic that reads "This site designed for Netscape Navigator" on the main page of a Web site should be a thing of the past.

Web standards fail gracefully when encountered by out-of-date browsers. The standards are also intended to provide greater benefit for accessibility and for other types of media. These techniques are built with intentional side effects that can benefit users, the company, and the team responsible for creating the sites. Whole books have been written on the subject.

Basic Benefits of Web Standards

Sites built with Web standards have many benefits, right out of the box, virtually without robust technique or experience. These include

❖ Style and script reuse and consistency

❖ Reduced bandwidth use and caching of style and script files

❖ Faster rendering of pages

❖ Cleaner, easier-to-maintain code

❖ Easier to make accessible for assistive technologies

❖ Easier to make search engine-optimized

❖ Increased compatibility between browser vendors

❖ Improved chances of document legibility for the next generation of browsers

❖ Increased readership for your site!

Web User Interfaces

In simple software terms, the front end of a Web site can be referred to as its user interface (UI) layer. The UI layer of a Web site includes all the artwork, text, formatting commands, interaction instructions, and controls sent from a Web server over the Internet to be viewed by a user inside a Web browser. A user may interact or "interface" with the resulting Web page UI by clicking objects or typing, thus providing input for a new request, which is then sent back over the Internet to the Web server to start the cycle again (**Figure in.1**).

Contrast this front end to server-side programming, which includes business logic and direct interactions with databases or other data stores. Oftentimes a server-side program must render a UI layer. By the same token, the UI layer can send

User Interface (UI) Layer

UI of <Web Page>
in Browser

JavaScript Behavior Layer

CSS Presentation Layer

(X)HTML Content & Structure

INTERNET

Web Server:
server-side scripts,
databases,
business logic

User Actions
and Input

Figure in.1 The user interface of a Web page is composed of several layers of technologies.

directives or input to a server-side program and may contain some business logic. This demonstrates how pervasive a UI is and how it touches every aspect of Web sites, from the simplest static marketing page to intricate business logic.

When Web authors build a modern UI layer, they may include complex instructions or share code between pages and server-side programs to be more efficient. Therefore, a redesign, or modifications to the UI, can get complicated or far-reaching. Or both.

How can this code be managed in an effective manner, shared among large teams, and remain efficient from a productivity standpoint over time?

User Interface Planning

The 1990s dot-com boom introduced horrible UI practices that led to bloated, unstructured, risky, and inefficient construction of Web sites. The structure of a simple Web page became an ugly mess referred to as "tag soup"—a virtual train wreck of nested HTML tables and single-pixel transparent spacer GIFs that had to be designed before work could begin on the page's content or an application (**Figure in.2**).

Massive HTML documents were the norm, weighing down the user experience and making the slightest modifications difficult. To enable user interaction via

Figure in.2 An example of old-school HTML code featuring inline presentation, event handlers, `<font>` tags—the usual suspects.

```
<td align=center width=107>
<a href="#272"
onMouseOver="define('etwo5b'); window.status='Electronic Reporting';return true;"
onMouseOut="define('prblnk4a');">
<img src="images/ 272icon.gif" width=107 height=25 border=0 alt=" "></a><br>
<td align=left width=246>
<a href="#cash"
onMouseOver="define('cash6b'); window.status='Cash Information';return true;"
onMouseOut="define('prblnk4a');">
<img src="images/cashicon.gif" width=107 height=25 border=0 alt=" "></a><br>
<tr>
<td colspan=3 align=center>
<img src="images/prnavbotm.gif" width=321 height=27 border=0 alt=" "><br>
</table>
<center>
<table width=380 cellspacing=2 border=0>
<td valign=bottom width=125>
<center>
<font face="Arial, Helvetica" size="-2">
To utilize or learn <br>
about a specific <br>
payment / reporting<br>
<br><br>
</font>
</center>
<td rowspan=4 align=center width=2>
<img src="images/grypixel.gif" width=1 height=600 border=0 alt=" ">
<td width=50%>
<font face="Arial, Helvetica" size="-1">
<font face="Times New Roman" size=+2>T</font>he Management is
<p><font face="Times New Roman" size=+2>I</font>n keeping with tradition,
```

JavaScript was also a hack, with embedded event handling and code forks based on proprietary browser techniques. Finally, to control any of the output on your Web site or application required intertwining your content, presentation, and application logic all together in layers, which introduced business risk and management hassles.

Web Site Planning Today

The vast majority of the effort and project planning on large-scale Web projects today trivializes the UI layer and treats it as an afterthought, when in fact it can deeply impact content management, Web applications, search engine optimization (SEO), bandwidth costs, site performance, and maintenance efforts. Plans typically start with the back-end software and only touch on the UI in terms of design.

Fortunately, there are ways to pare down the long-term risks and remove the constraints of traditional Web coding. Embracing modern techniques starts with the W3C and its recommendations, often called Web standards.

The issue should be considered not only in terms of your design, but also where the content management, applications, and other dynamic systems are concerned. If a Web site is to reap the benefits of a Web standards-based UI, it needs to be considered at all levels, and plans should be introduced that will allow the site to grow intelligently.

The Keys to Web Standards

What, exactly, changes when you're planning a site with a Web standards-based approach?

First, on the UI layer, conforming to Web standards means 100% separation of presentation from content and structure, as well as the scripting behavior of UI elements. Second, on the back end, this means limiting the mixing of UI code in the Web applications and CMS code that may need periodic updates, and applying the same strict separation as to any other static screen.

The distinct areas to concentrate on are

❖ Content and structure—the markup layer, usually made up of HTML (Hyper-Text Markup Language) or XHTML (eXtensible HyperText Markup Language)

❖ The presentation layer—consisting of CSS (Cascading Style Sheets), which is referenced from the markup and the sites scripts

❖ The behavior layer—the JavaScript elements that enable user events and interactions

❖ The software and CMS layers—these have a UI of their own and often produce the above UI layers

❖ The teams and processes that help to build all of the above

It is not difficult to attain UI layer separation in a static setting devoid of software or large teams. The key is that the Web software needs to respect these distinctions as well, and the project plans need to consider the UI layer as a first-class citizen that needs to interact with all systems in an intelligent and thoughtful way, not as a second-class citizen that is simply an afterthought.

Software Architecture Patterns

Layers of code serving different purposes are not a new concept for the software industry. In fact, there are numerous examples of architectural design patterns that software students have been studying for years. A good list with links to examples of architectural design patterns can be found on Wikipedia at http://en.wikipedia.org/wiki/Architectural_pattern_%28computer_science%29.

An example of a popular pattern called "model-view-controller" is, in simple terms, something like the following:

❖ **Model:** Logical meanings of raw data used for various business purposes. Think of the model layer as an application program interface (API) for other parts of a program to connect with it. This layer is responsible for the computational footwork we rely on computers to do for us, like adding up the cost of items in a shopping cart or determining if today is our wedding anniversary.

❖ **View:** This is the eye candy one sees when the model is rendered into a UI layer or part of the UI layer. Think of an HTML+CSS web page from a Web application as the view.

❖ **Controller:** Frequently event driven, it interprets and responds to user actions and may drive changes to the model. Think of this as the layer responsible for handling user actions which include, but are not limited to, mouse clicks or Web-based form submissions.

To extend this model to Web software and Web standards, some have labeled the UI layer separation of content, presentation, and behavior as a parallel to this pattern, using the model (content and structure), the view (presentation), and the controller (behavior). Experienced software architects are often quite eager to embrace a layered front end whether they are familiar with Web design or not.

A New Approach: UI Architecture Plans

A traditional plan starts with back-end requirements and then builds on a UI layer code as an afterthought. Today, using a modern Web standards-based approach, teams should ask themselves the following:

- ❖ Is the UI layer built and structured for easy maintenance?
- ❖ How does the UI layer impact SEO?
- ❖ How does the UI layer interact with the site's content management system (CMS)?
- ❖ Is it possible to redesign or make simple design changes without deep CMS impact or the need for CMS staff?
- ❖ What happens when it comes time to modify or enhance the UI?
- ❖ How do you integrate a UI with a Web application?
- ❖ What happens when the application logic changes?
- ❖ How risky is a design change to an application?
- ❖ Should mission-critical applications buckle under the pressure of needlessly risky design, simple content, or script changes?

A well-planned Web standards approach will mitigate these risks at two levels: first, the front-end code; and second, where the back end meets the front end.

Over time, for any site, these questions become big issues. Larger enterprises often have a Web presence in place, and mass change will not be possible or will be too difficult to achieve overnight. Incremental change may be required. Where the line is drawn will be different in almost every case.

When planning for change, first figure out what needs to be designed, whether it's marketing content or an application, and how it needs to be rendered in the browser. Second, make reasoned decisions based on the pros and cons of each option. Finally, figure out how to get a site to its standards-compliance goals and how to keep it that way.

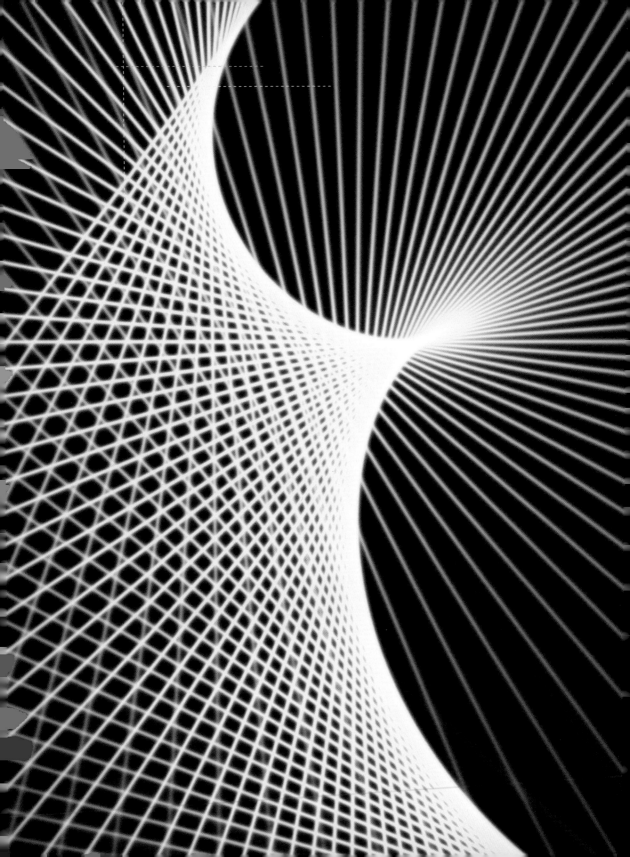

1

Coding the Front End

Advocates of Web standards tend to be passionate, but far from unanimous. Disagreement is nothing new. The concept of "Web standards-based" Web sites means different things to different people. Web standards is the subject of many an argument online, and, to some, almost a religious crusade. This is in part because there are many myths that surround Web standards. To those who think they know what Web standards are all about, it's important to filter truth from all the noise.

The most important aspects of Web standards-based Web sites are the separation of content and structure (HTML or XHTML) from presentation (CSS) and behavior (JavaScript). These key characteristics are by far the most critical ones, and will help provide most of the advantages of standards-based code, in particular easier site maintenance.

One of the most intensely debated subjects within the realm of standards is the myth that all code must be validated. Validation is seen as a critical aspect of Web standards-based development, with its noble purpose of ensuring compliance and compatibility, and providing help with debugging. Although no one would ever suggest that the creation of invalid documents is a good thing, realities need to mitigate this process, and be tempered with project priorities as necessary. Both the advantages of easier maintenance and the realities of external factors that impact validation may occur (and therefore conflict) in any development environment.

Separation can coexist with legacy content and applications that are migrating to a more standards-based approach, often preventing pure validation.

While this perhaps should be true in an idealistic sense, in reality Web standards need not be all or nothing. Web teams can ease into standards and have them coexist with legacy content and applications. It's all really just about improving your code. If legacy content exists or is full of markup that contains presentation attributes, it doesn't mean that new code needs to be the same way. Fix what can be fixed and move forward in a methodical way. Some environments may not be able to validate right away; that's just fine, and is to be expected during any transition. Transitional specifications exist for those very reasons.

Other myths or exaggerations are that Web standards-based development means not ever using tables and that design can be only "DIV-based." This is a gross simplification. Tables can be perfectly valid, and a bunch of DIVs in a document can likewise be perfectly invalid and just used wrongly. Web standards-based markup means using elements and attributes for what they were intended to be used for: Tables are for tabular data, not for layout; headers are content headers; paragraphs are paragraphs; and presentation of all elements should be controlled with CSS. The truth of standards is in using code as it was intended to be. The project's success depends on being realistic.

There is no standards on-off switch for a Web team. Technique is everything, and that discussion starts now. Looking deeper, there actually *is* a standards on-off switch: It's built into the Web browser. To learn about that, keep reading.

Where To Start

A Web standards strategy needs to start at the markup level, since that's where the offense of mixing HTML markup with presentation details is usually committed. Allowing a team to evaluate existing code and look at Web standards for direction will shed light on what the ultimate standards strategy should be. The more complex a site, the more barriers to an absolute pure standards approach may exist. This may lead to compromises and a phased approach that moves to standards over time. Such compromises are not ideal but sometimes they are unavoidable.

Document Structure: Markup Language Choices

Back in the day, building Web sites meant only one thing: using HTML. Over time, some who took notice might have included features from HTML 3.2, 4.0, or even 4.01.

Creative techniques were invented using HTML to design high-end sites involving single-pixel GIFs and massive amounts of nested tables, which resulted in bloated and inefficient front-end code. These techniques worked but were difficult to maintain, because the technology was being used for things it was never intended to do. Basic layouts and design treatments were effectively code hacks. Today these hacks have been worked into marketing Web sites, Web software applications, and content management alike. Web browsers today can support a more modern and disciplined approach that can help simplify all of these environments through the adoption of Web standards-based code.

A Web standards-based approach means creating markup that conforms to the spec as closely as can be accomplished. This typically means well-formed, correctly nested tags; accurate quoting of attributes; and properly structured code. At first, these parameters sometimes put off Web authors who are caught off guard by them, but oftentimes they find that following the guidelines actually sets them free.

Choosing a markup language can be a tough decision, because there are multiple options and some aspects are subjective at best, but in the end it is still technique that matters.

HTML vs. XHTML

Today, the two basic choices are HTML 4.01 or XHTML 1.0. Both specifications have gone a long way to improve the structure of Web markup and move presentation information out of the markup and into separate files. Both languages are recommended by the W3C and fully acceptable for producing Web sites. In fact, the two languages are not that different, with the exception of some attributes, deprecation of presentational elements, and XHTML's adherence to XML syntax.

HTML vs. XHTML Syntax Differences

There are a number of differences between HTML and XHTML. The bottom line is that XHTML uses a stronger, XML-like syntax, whereas HTML is more forgiving with optional elements. Assuming the document is valid:

- XHTML is XML, as well as being XSLT and XML tool-compatible.

- XHTML elements are lowercase.

- XHTML attribute names are lowercase.

- XHTML is case sensitive.

- XHTML elements match CSS selectors on a case-sensitive basis.

- XHTML attribute values are quoted, with single or double quotes.

- XHTML elements are all closed, including single, empty (also known as "replaced") tags with a trailing slash such as **
** and **<img />**

- XHTML requires that all non-empty tags, such as **<td>**, **<p>**, **<li>**, have corresponding closing tags **</td>**, **</p>**, **</li>**.

- XHTML block-level elements generally do not appear inside inline elements.

- XHTML optional elements such as **tbody** are not represented in the DOM unless they are actually in the document.

- XHTML features XML's "well-formedness," meaning that tags are correctly nested in a tree structure where starting and ending tags do not overlap out of order.

- XHTML empty (single-tag or singleton) elements are closed with a trailing slash preceded by a space for compatibility reasons (e.g., **
, **<hr />, etc.).

- XHTML attributes may not use HTML attribute minimization; rather attributes must be fully specified and quoted like others (e.g., selected="selected").

- XHTML elements are returned and specified in DOM JavaScripts in their correct case, whereas in HTML they are always uppercase.

- XHTML 1.0 and HTML 4.01 Strict deprecate a number of tags and attributes that are allowed in transitional varieties.

- XHTML-embedded CSS and JavaScript blocks are considered #PCDATA, and their content may need to be wrapped in XML CDATA blocks; consider external scripts and style sheets.

- XHTML can, under some circumstances, force JavaScript to behave much differently than in HTML (e.g., document.write sometimes will not work, etc.).

- XHTML **name** attributes are deprecated; use id attributes instead of, or in addition to, the **name** attribute, depending on the need.

For more information, please see the W3C: www.w3.org/TR/xhtml1/#diffs.

NOTE

XHTML 1.1 has been defined; however, by the specification it must conform so closely to XML that the majority-share Web browser today has significant trouble with it. This is, of course, Microsoft Internet Explorer, which has incomplete support for XML. That leaves HTML 4.01 and XHTML 1.0 as the most realistic options.

For years, many Web standards advocates insisted that XHTML was the next logical step for the Web and that it should be used for all markup. Some still feel strongly that this is the case. Exceptions among experts exist, and in fact many of the creators of browser software today favor HTML and consider most of the XHTML on the Web to be invalid due to its being served from Web servers in an incorrect manner (see sidebar "Controversy and the History and Future of XHTML"). Everyone has an opinion, and a developer should always weigh the pros and cons against the goals of his or her particular project.

Whatever option is subscribed to, HTML is here to stay, and it will be a very long time before any Web browsers drop support for it. In the end, though, what really matters is *how* a developer codes her or his language of choice, and in particular how it relates to presentation and behavior.

Pros and Cons of HTML vs. XHTML

Here are a few of the many opinions about HTML and XHTML, starting with some pros of HTML:

❖ HTML has an established authoring base with a smaller learning curve than other markup languages. Most content authors understand the basics of HTML syntax and need only learn the subtle nuances of using CSS as opposed to presentational HTML. They need to unlearn a few bad habits and stop thinking that elements and tags look a certain way because this will be controlled via CSS. They will also need to learn to code the markup in a semantic style, which will be explained further later.

❖ HTML is easier to integrate with legacy systems' markup. This is a compelling case in a large-scale enterprise environment that has lots of legacy code. Some software simply will not produce valid XHTML and in situations like this, HTML may be the only way to go.

CONTROVERSY AND THE HISTORY AND FUTURE OF XHTML

The specification for XHTML states that since XHTML is XML it should be served over HTTP by Web servers as `application/xhtml+xml`. Now, the major browser on the market, Microsoft Internet Explorer, does not support XHTML served as XML and will only accept it served as `text/html`, like traditional HTML. For this reason many advocates of XHTML promote something called "content negotiation," which means serving the content with the types the browser says it accepts. This is all fine, but others point out that there are XHTML/HTML compatibility guidelines in the XHTML specification that will allow XHTML to be served as HTML. It is important to note that in these cases the browser sees the XHTML content as nothing more than HTML with invalid attributes that are ignored, not as XHTML. A search online for "XHTML considered harmful" will yield many results and much debate on the matter.

In the meantime, HTML was left years ago without much of a future at the W3C, XHTML was defined and embraced by standards advocates everywhere, and then XHTML 2 came along, breaking every imaginable rule of backwards compatibility. It was practically ignored.

In 2004, staff at several browser companies, including Apple, the Mozilla Foundation, and Opera, formed the WHATWG (Web Hypertext Application Technology Working Group) when it seemed that the W3C was no longer interested in a future for HTML. The WHATWG began to define a specification called HTML 5 (and XHTML 5, not to confuse anyone) as well as extensions to the way forms and Web applications might work in the future. The W3C did not really comment on the new working group for several years.

Fast forward to 2006, when the W3C finally announced a new HTML working group of its own to help address the future of HTML and XHTML. The WHATWG has offered up its specification, which blurs the lines between HTML and XHTML considerably. The specification has been accepted by the W3C as a starting point, and the debate has begun on the future of both HTML and XHTML. Only time will tell.

For more information on both working groups:

www.w3.org/html/wg/
www.whatwg.org

Anyone can participate in either of these groups.

Some cons of HTML might be:

❖ Some consider HTML less robust and more prone to error due to its more relaxed syntax requirements. This can lead to bad practices and confusion.

❖ Extraction, parsing, or manipulation of HTML content from existing documents or systems for other purposes is more difficult than with XHTML because of the unpredictable nature of the markup.

❖ Staying with HTML as opposed to XHTML might indirectly discourage some content production authors from learning more strict standards and adopting best practices.

Some pros of XHTML are:

❖ XHTML is an XML-ready language. It follows the rules of XML and is therefore compatible with XML-compatible tools, such as XSL parsers or other software used to syndicate, parse, or manipulate the content.

❖ The rules that XHTML uses are often easier to learn and remember than those of HTML; consistent XML rules are less prone to error than the flexible rules of HTML, and XHTML has no optional closing tags or attributes.

❖ XHTML syntax is close to the XHTML-MP (Mobile Profile) and XHTML Basic used by many mobile or handheld devices.

❖ Most authoring tools today support creation of valid XHTML.

And finally, some cons of XHTML might be:

❖ While some portions of the syntax are easier, other aspects, such as character encoding and entities, are more difficult to grasp.

❖ Some find the controversy over mime-types not worth the trouble or too difficult to deal with (see sidebar "Controversy and the History and Future of XHTML").

❖ Strict HTTP serving of XHTML as XML introduces issues that will catch some authors off guard, such as JavaScript `document.write` statements not working, different interpretations of CSS, link `target` attributes being obsolete, and `IFRAME` not being supported.

❖ XHTML may not be an option for legacy content stores in CMS tools or content being served by third parties such as advertising servers (banner ads and so forth). However, an author may opt for transitional code in some of these cases.

❖ XHTML 2.0 has called into question the "future proofing" of XHTML as a language. This specification is hotly debated and may be radically reworked or even abandoned (see sidebar "Controversy and the History and Future of XHTML").

Transitional vs. Strict Flavors

Both HTML and XHTML have two "flavors" called Transitional and Strict, with significant differences in syntax. The language and version flavor is specified at the start of the document by a Document Type Definition (DTD) that identifies which language the document is written in.

Transitional language versions:

❖ Include more presentation attributes and elements than the Strict, because the intention is that in a strict mode the presentation information is fully pushed out to the CSS files.

❖ Are considered to be a transitional bridge specification intended to move from the lax rules to the more specific ones in the strict variation.

❖ May be used when there is legacy code that can't be made fully Strict.

A common issue in an organization is that content is marked up with atrocious code in a CMS because it has been around for years. The important thing to note is that just because the legacy content stored in a CMS is a wreck, it doesn't mean new code needs to be. This should apply even with a transitional DTD: Just because the presentational attributes and elements are valid, it does not mean developers should use these presentational attributes and elements. Any new code should use CSS. This begins a migration path where any new code is using the strict rules.

The following table outlines attributes and elements that are invalid in strict documents.

TABLE 1.1 Strict vs. Transitional Attributes and Elements

Strict Elements Deprecated	Strict Attributes Deprecated
applet	align (except tables)
basefont	alink
center	background
dir	bgcolor
font	border (except tables)
isindex	color
iframe	height
noframes	hspace

continued on next page

Strict Elements Deprecated	Strict Attributes Deprecated
listing	language
menu	link
plaintext	name (allowed in HTML Strict)
s	noshade
strike	nowrap
u	size
	start
	target
	text
	type
	vspace
	width (except images, objects, tables—except td)

Picking the language is the difficult part of the decision, but it's important to make a reasoned comparison of strict or transitional against the nature of the destination environment.

NOTE

Some organizations will invest effort or time in using or writing software to parse legacy content in HTML to convert it over to XHTML. With careful execution, these techniques can also strip `<font>` tags and other presentational elements. This can be done typically through generous usage of regular expressions or other string-parsing algorithms. Results may vary with this approach, however, and great care should be used.

DOCTYPE Switching and Browser Rendering Modes

Something that often comes as a surprise to Web authors switching to Web standards is that modern Web browsers have different rendering modes. This means that based on the DTD, or Document Type Definition, the browser calculates and interprets Web pages differently.

DOCTYPE Presence

DOCTYPE presence, commonly called the "DOCTYPE switch" or "DOCTYPE sniffing," is the ability to assess and change the browser mode. In order to snap a browser out of its old methods of rendering Web documents and into standards-compliant rendering mode, the placement of valid DOCTYPE within a Web document becomes exceptionally important.

Starting back in 2000 with Internet Explorer 5 for the Macintosh, the rendering engines of most browsers toggle between what is commonly referred to as "quirks mode" and "standards mode." Netscape, Mozilla, Safari, Konqueror, Opera, and Internet Explorer (for the PC above version 6.0) all have this feature built into their rendering engines.

Any of the following will cause standards-compliant rendering in most browsers today:

```
<!DOCTYPE HTML PUBLIC "-//W3C//DTD HTML 4.01//EN"
    "http://www.w3.org/TR/html4/strict.dtd">
```

```
<!DOCTYPE html PUBLIC "-//W3C//DTD XHTML 1.0 Transitional//EN"
    "http://www.w3.org/TR/xhtml1/DTD/xhtml1-transitional.dtd">
```

```
<!DOCTYPE html PUBLIC "-//W3C//DTD XHTML 1.0 Strict//EN"
    "http://www.w3.org/TR/xhtml1/DTD/xhtml1-strict.dtd">
```

Quirks mode is intended to use the less strict parsing rules and to be more forgiving of code mistakes that were common in the 1990s. Authors have come to know and expect certain subtle quirks (hence the name) that are actually invalid behaviors.

Standards mode, on the other hand, introduces more rigid understandings of the specifications. Based on further research of the standards, browser manufacturers have attempted to get closer to the strict exactitude of the specifications. This has had the effect of changing what Web authors had come to expect in many cases.

The typical practice in a Web standards-based approach is to strive to keep the browser in standards mode at all times for more consistent behavior across browsers and across platforms.

Determining the Browser Rendering Mode

Web authors can be sure they are in standards mode by using the DOCTYPEs with URIs, as specified above. However, sometimes layout issues may arise because an HTML element or comment is inserted prior to the DTD or due to other unpredictable scenarios—which may trigger quirks mode. There are several ways to tell which rendering mode the browser is using. One easy way is to open the page in Mozilla Firefox, right-click (or Control-click on Mac) and select "View Page Info." The resulting dialog displays a number of pieces of useful information, including the browser's current render mode (**Figure 1.1**).

Figure 1.1 In Mozilla Firefox, the Page Info dialog shows the render mode for the currently visible page.

There are subtle differences in DOCTYPE switching methods that force some browsers into quirks mode while others are still in standards mode. At the code level for most browsers, including IE, JavaScript can also be used to display the rendering mode of the browser. Try out the following code:

```
function testRenderMode(){
    alert(document.compatMode);
}
window.onload = testRenderMode;
```

The possible values resulting from this code include "BackCompat" for quirks mode and "CSS1Compat" for standards mode.

Oops, the Wrong Rendering Mode Broke the Page

It is not unusual to have a site or a series of templates built in a carefully crafted Web standards-based structure, and then something just goes wrong, pushing the browser into the wrong rendering mode. The result is an entire page or series of pages with widespread layout and alignment issues that were not there a moment ago.

This can leave a whole team scratching their heads wondering what is going on. Usually something has happened in terms of the design being incorporated with some software backend or a CMS tool, or someone just inserted an HTML comment before the DTD without realizing it.

Take, for example, the popular CSS gallery site CSS Beauty, designed, built, and maintained by designer Alex Giron (**FIGURE 1.2**).

FIGURE 1.2 Alex Giron's cssbeauty.com serves as an inspiration portal and a Web standards resource.

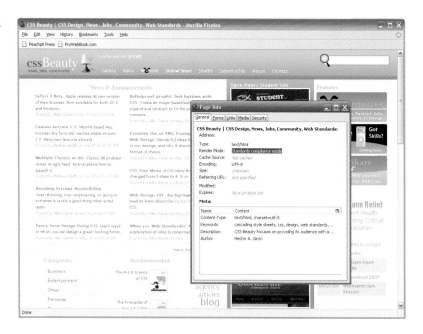

CSS Beauty is coded to XHTML 1.0 Strict, and features a wide variety of carefully aligned Web standards-related content featuring XHTML that starts out this way:

```
<!DOCTYPE html PUBLIC "-//W3C//DTD XHTML 1.0 Strict//EN" "http://www.
w3.org/TR/xhtml1/DTD/xhtml1-strict.dtd">
<html xmlns="http://www.w3.org/1999/xhtml" xml:lang="en" lang="en">

<head>

<title>CSS Beauty | CSS Design, News,  Jobs, Community, Web
Standards</title>
```

```
<meta http-equiv="Content-Type" content="text/html;
charset=utf-8" />
```

For the sake of argument, assume for a moment that a mistake is made, and the DOCTYPE declaration is removed from the site in its development environment (this would never happen in production, unless he was editing live, which should always be avoided). This would leave the document starting out raw with the HTML element rather than the DOCTYPE.

```
<head>
```

```
<title>CSS Beauty | CSS Design, News,  Jobs, Community, Web
Standards</title>
```

```
<meta http-equiv="Content-Type" content="text/html;
charset=utf-8" />
```

Alex would see something that was close to his normally appearing site for the most part; however, a number of rendering issues would spring up (**FIGURE 1.3**).

The result is an oddly mixed-up layout with changes all over the place, as opposed to in one small area. How the introduction of quirks mode will affect page rendering will vary from site to site. Similarly, switching to standards mode from quirks can also yield unpredictable results.

FIGURE 1.3 cssbeauty. com breaks if the DTD is removed and the browser enters quirks mode.

For starters, there are extra background graphics behind the headers at the top of the page. Additionally, the layout seems to have shifted up the page slightly and the "Recommended" column is way off in the middle left compared to its usual symmetrical alignment. Scrolling down the page, things get even worse. The entire information bar at the bottom of the page has lost its background color, except on hover, and the font sizes are off (**FIGURE 1.4**).

FIGURE 1.4 In quirks mode, the information footer on the home page of cssbeauty.com is broken.

Adding back the DOCTYPE declaration is a simple thing in this case, but the lesson to be learned is that when widespread layout issues start happening, these problems are often symptomatic of a document-wide issue, such as the rendering mode, styles not being linked correctly, or missing tags in a sensitive location. Quirks mode in particular can wreak havoc on a well-structured page. Using a validation tool to check the syntax of the page can be a huge help in cases like this.

There are specific documented issues, some of which will be discussed below, that exist for quirks and standards rendering modes. These often surface when code is being mixed with legacy markup, when browsers are reviewed, or when new designs are being produced. This is particularly an issue when looking at Internet Explorer 5.0 and 5.5 because although they do not feature multiple rendering modes, they are essentially always in "quirks" mode. This means designs will display differently than even in IE 6.0 as compared to 5.5 when working in a "standards" mode document because they are interpreted differently.

Legacy Markup and DOCTYPE Switching

In the 1990s Web authors often ignored the DOCTYPE declaration, since at that time it was largely meaningless to Web browsers and was used simply for validating the document. Yet only a select few were doing this because the languages were being used in odd ways, and much energy was being expended on catering to the proprietary features of browsers. Most Web authors either misunderstood or ignored the DOCTYPE, which in today's world is in fact one of the most critical parts of the document. So now, many of those authors spend their time dealing with migrating from legacy markup to semantic markup.

Several common scenarios may come up while migrating to Web standards in environments where legacy content and valid markup are mixed:

❖ Web standards means switching a Web site's UI templates from an often complicated HTML TABLE structure to a layout using clean tagged elements without presentation attributes and CSS for positioning. However, some authors might insert a new, valid DTD at the top of an existing page whose design uses sliced images and a TABLE structure, only to discover that their layout shatters.

❖ New CMS templates might be introduced using modern layout code for the page wrapper containing the branding, main, and global navigation. Then, when this is applied to content areas coming out of the CMS, that content can break.

❖ Web application developers might be using a new CSS-based design template with a strict DTD for their application pages, and find that integration of these pages with the new design template might break existing HTML.

The Boxes Were Measured All Wrong

When IE 4 came out in 1997, and when IE 5 for the Macintosh came out in 2000, Microsoft seemed to be doing fairly well with its Web browsers. Not that they were great, but in terms of CSS support and user adoption, they were simply doing much better than Netscape 4 had fared. Netscape 6 was poorly received, and Microsoft had essentially won the so-called "Browser War." With Internet Explorer 5 and 5.5 (the only games in town for many Web authors), it was assumed by most developers that the CSS support that they were getting used to was in fact correct. But just because something's better or more popular doesn't mean it's correct.

Building a CSS-based layout using the building blocks contained in IE 4 and IE 5.x was misleading. A layout on a Web page is described with elements and tags representing a series of boxes and objects on a canvas—the document body. A CSS layout is defined by a box composed of an element that has a content area;

padding around the top, right, bottom, and left; borders around the same areas; followed by margins around the object as well.

The width of an object is technically defined by the content area alone; however, these older versions of IE defined the width incorrectly, so any CSS object set with a width is actually measured incorrectly. This can wreak serious havoc on layouts, since the measurements for the dimensions of objects on pages are all wrong. IE 6.0 in "standards" mode fixed this. However, it is now different from Internet Explorer 4 and 5, so Web authors have to deal with more than one measurement model while laying out pages using CSS (**FIGURE 1.5**).

FIGURE 1.5 In Internet Explorer versions 4, 5, 5.5, and version 6 in "quirks" mode, the width of a box is calculated to include the size of its content plus its border and padding. The CSS layout box model, on the other hand, measures the box and padding separately from the content.

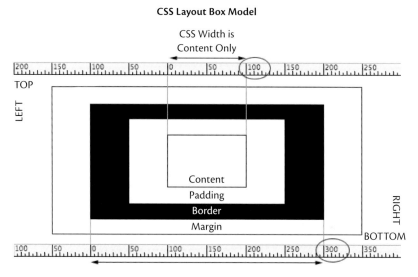

What Microsoft did was define the width as including the content, padding, and borders. To help correct this problem, Microsoft introduced the DOCTYPE switch and "standards" and "quirks" modes that measure differently. However, their box model was different previously, so the "standards" and "quirks" differences are greater than many other Web browsers' differences in these two modes. Other browsers have smaller nuances that happen in "quirks" mode, but they need to be watched for as well.

Web authors new to building Web standards-based layouts, but who may have built pages using Internet Explorer 5.x's CSS box model, are in for a surprise when other browsers render the pages differently. Oftentimes, the belief is that other browsers were getting it wrong, or something broke in IE 6.0. The truth is, something was fixed, and the other guys had it right.

Unfortunately for the industry as a whole, the majority browser is Internet Explorer, and so everyone suffers from different measurements, leading many to believe that CSS support is hopelessly broken. There are ways to cope with these differences, from sending different style sheets to IE 4 and 5 to creating special selector "hacks" to be read only by specified browsers.

TIP

There are many, many references for quirks and standards modes in browsers, but this is a good one:

www.cs.tut.fi/~jkorpela/quirks-mode.html

A Web search for "CSS box model hack" will yield many techniques for providing different measurements to different browsers.

A preferred method today for serving different styles to IE is using Conditional Comments, described in the next chapter.

MSDN published an excellent document on the CSS changes in Internet Explorer 6.0, which were significant and introduced the correct box model: http://msdn2.microsoft.com/en-us/library/bb250395.aspx

---

The Table Gap

Another major area where the change to standards-based layout can cause significant confusion is where TABLEs are being used for layout—they no longer behave in the old, expected manner. CSS guru Eric Meyer has explained some TABLE and image layout scenarios in an article online called "Images, Tables, and Mysterious Gaps" (http://developer.mozilla.org/en/docs/ Images,_Tables,_and_Mysterious_Gaps).

In particular, he describes the trouble that can happen when a Web author takes a site that originally used tables for layouts and converts it to strict mode with XHTML or HTML. This usually results in some of the tables and images having gaps where they used to be flush against one another.

The reason is that the correct default bottom alignment for images is on the baseline of the text, leaving room beneath for the descenders (such as the letter "y") that hang below the line of text. When it was common to build Web sites with images sliced up and set flush in tables against one another, Web browsers were actually interpreting the specification and images behavior incorrectly by leaving out this space. By default, images are inline elements intended to align with text.

Here is an example of a table with two rows, with a 50px by 50px black graphic set in a table with the cells set to be flush using a 50px height and all the spacing removed, much like graphics were frequently set back in the day:

```
<html>
<head>
    <title>Table in Quirks Mode</title>
    <style type="text/css">
    <!--
    table { border: 1px solid #000; }
    td { font-size: 200%; height: 50px; }
    -->
    </style>
</head>

<body>

<table border="0" cellspacing="0" cellpadding="0">
<tr>
    <td>The quick brown fox jumped over the lazy...</td>
    <td><img src="quirks-block.gif" width="50" height="50" alt="">
    </td>
</tr>
<tr>
    <td>The quick brown fox jumped over the lazy...</td>
    <td><img src="quirks-block.gif" width="50" height="50" alt="">
    </td>
</tr>
</table>

</body>
</html>
```

The document above renders in quirks mode because it lacks a DOCTYPE declaration, and has the graphics flush against one another, row to row (**FIGURE 1.6**).

FIGURE 1.6 A common technique in the 1990s was to use tables to place graphic elements flush against each other.

Taking that very same document without any modifications and slapping a strict DOCTYPE declaration on the top of the file switches the document to be rendered in standards mode in today's browsers:

```
<!DOCTYPE HTML PUBLIC "-//W3C//DTD HTML 4.01//EN" "http://www.w3.org/
TR/html4/strict.dtd">
<html>
<head><title>...
```

Opening up the file in a standards-compliant browser yields some surprising results that include extra gaps appearing under the graphics in each row, blowing out the carefully crafted and beautiful black square boxes (**FIGURE 1.7**).

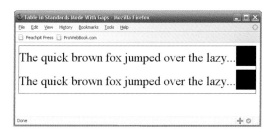

FIGURE 1.7 A browser in standards mode can create gaps between artwork in table cells.

The quick and dirty lesson here is that a few simple rules in the CSS can address these problems:

```
td img { vertical-align: bottom; }
```

Or even:

```
td img { display: block; }
```

Which solution is appropriate depends on the circumstances, and sometimes it's easiest to simply use both. In the end, however, these treatments are quite a common scenario in a standards migration, which is exceptionally tricky to debug unless the developer is intimately familiar with box model and alignment characteristics from the specifications. Fortunately for everyone, experts like Eric Meyer are around. With the small corrections applied by Meyer's technique, the table and graphics' layout and rendering is fixed (**FIGURE 1.8**).

FIGURE 1.8 Table artwork gaps are easily fixed with a little CSS.

The bottom line is, when mixing legacy and modern code, be aware that the unexpected can happen, and you may have to do some debugging to get around the oddities that spring up.

To Validate or Not To Validate Markup

Correct code syntax is extremely important, particularly where XML, accessibility, or alternative browsing devices are concerned. For a Web developer just starting to use Web standards, a validation service is a great way to debug the code and help achieve validation. Plus, it will help ensure the code will display consistently in any browser that supports Web standards.

The W3C makes several validation tools available online:

❖ Markup Validation Service for HTML and XHTML (**Figure 1.9**):

http://validator.w3.org/

❖ CSS Validation Service

http://jigsaw.w3.org/css-validator/

Figure 1.9 The Web-based validation services offered by the W3C are excellent resources.

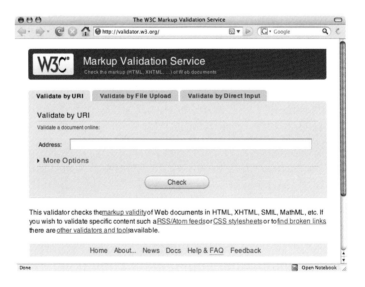

Additionally, several tools exist to help Web authors validate their code right from their Web browser:

❖ The Firefox browser Web Developer Extension from Chris Pederick

http://chrispederick.com/work/webdeveloper/

❖ The Microsoft Internet Explorer Developer Toolbar

  http://channel9.msdn.com/wiki/default.aspx/
  Channel9.InternetExplorerDevToolbar

With the benefits of validation in mind, it is also important to note that validation is a goal at one end of a spectrum running from transitional to strict code and is much easier to achieve in smaller and controlled environments. The usual practice with a Web standards-based approach is to strive for strict validation.

In larger companies with a multitude of systems, staff, software, internal, external, and other unknown conditions, complete validation may simply have to wait. Probably the most common scenario is to work from valid templates; then the errors that crop up in the full site are likely to stem from external sources that may be difficult to correct. In fact, in larger organizations validation can be nearly impossible to achieve due to all of the external factors that may impact what is ultimately being served up:

❖ Advertising servers

❖ Embedded third-party software, such as Web statistic tracking tools

❖ Content management tools

❖ Content management tools' WYSIWYG editors

❖ Application code from software frameworks or development tools

❖ Staff skill levels or lazy developers who may be difficult to rein in

❖ Application service provider (ASP) hosted software, which may accept an organization's templates and styles but not generate validated code for their portion of the software

In these cases, a Web team must determine what the appropriate tradeoff level of validation is—strict vs. transitional DTDs, external vs. internal code, and so forth.

Particularly on an initial launch, there may be pressures and scheduling issues that make tasks other than validation a higher priority when the site renders correctly in all the major browsers. Validation of a Web site's code, free from errors, is something that authors should strive for regardless of external realities, but typically has to be weighed against project realities.

In general, validation will be easier to get with a complete redesign that has fewer external forces or small applications, but it matters most where portions of a site's content need to be reused or integrated with a service that expects to get, for instance, valid code in an XML format. This can often mean the individual pieces, such as content in the CMS, are the most important aspects to make valid.

Content and Structure: Design to Execution

You never want to plan last. Knowing what needs to be built will help inform your decisions while planning a site build. This means the teams responsible for the design and those building the site, CMS, and applications need to begin to collaborate as early as possible in order to plan ahead.

Taking Inventory and Templates

Most design teams will have a series of graphics files that visually describe the look and feel of the site based on all the project requirements. An inventory of the designs, their similarities, and differences is a great place to start and will quickly reveal the sheer volume of what needs to be built. Fortunately, with a Web standards-based approach this will be easier to manage than in the past, and organizations will likely need fewer templates than before.

Each unique design represents a grid and potentially a UI template that can be applied as needed. Grouping similar derivatives of designs can create a hierarchy and determine how many templates will need to be built to get an understanding of the level of effort involved.

In a CSS and XHTML world, templates that are derivatives may have the same exact underlying markup structure but have CSS that provides slight tweaks. When putting templates into groups, Web authors should concentrate on layout. Color changes can be addressed with CSS tricks, and the underlying structure should be addressed in the CMS templates—just concentrate on the layout! Each set of templates will have corresponding specifications from the UI design and any application or CMS rules that may have been created. It may involve parts of the grid coming and going, or possibly collapsing when an element is not present. When dealing with potentially dozens or even several dozens of designs on a massive Web site, pausing to collect and organize what really needs to be built is immensely helpful (**FIGURE 1.10**). This will also help as new pages are added later.

A UI template inventory is simply an exercise in grouping similar designs together so Web authors will know what needs to be built. Some organizations find it valuable to literally print out all the designs and tape them to a wall in groups, labeling them by number (or name) for easy reference. The subtle changes that don't necessarily require a new template might engender variants labeled, say, "template 3" and "template 3a."

Once again, this is a simple exercise in helping determine the complexity and level of effort required, and to literally give the "big picture." This is why frequently a "big picture" on a big wall can actually help. It may sometimes be helpful to formally document these groupings. In some cases, the inventory can be leveraged when creating a style guide later.

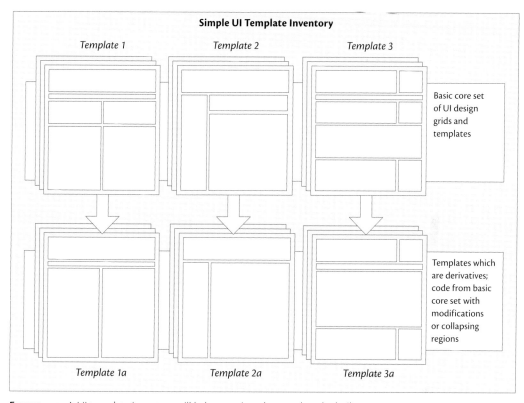

FIGURE 1.10   A UI template inventory will help organize what needs to be built.

Naming Conventions for IDs and Layout Blocks

Continuing to the next step, one of the obvious first decisions that must be made when planning to break up artwork into markup and CSS is the structure of the HTML documents. The old way of laying out a Web page involved complex nested tables and bloated code, which was difficult to run through and understand at a glance.

In a standards-based solution, the layout of the page is controlled with CSS, but the structure of the page becomes a simple series of HTML elements. Since the basic structure is typically a series of elements with ID attributes, creating a naming system for the IDs organizes the code. Mapping the naming system back to the template inventory will help the whole Web team.

At some point, in a CMS phase for instance, developers may break the code up into separate files. In these cases, it is very useful to have logical naming conventions that describe the relative location of the DIV elements in the code, because they may be seen out of context.

One way of doing this is to use a hyphenated hierarchy to indicate locations in the document:

```
<div id="nav">
   ...
   <ul id="nav-main">
   ...
   </ul>
   <ul id="nav-sub">
   ...
   </ul>
</div>
<div id="content">
   <div id="content-section">
   ...
   </div>
   <div id="content-main">
   ...
   </div>
   <div id="content-related">
   ...
   </div>
</div>
```

Note that nav-main is inside nav and content-section is inside content. The naming convention strongly conveys this information.

In larger teams, it may be a good idea to document the outline hierarchy of the each template's structure as part of the template inventory:

```
body
   div#nav
      div#nav-main
      ul#nav-sub
   div#content
      div#content-section
      div#content-main
      div#content-related
```

> **NOTE**
>
> Where it can be done, the usage of meaningful elements is preferable such as with the usage of the `<ul>` elements above. This is because a `<div>` may be unnecessary, as the styles can be applied to the `<ul>` element just as easily.

When naming the IDs and classes in a document, keep in mind that the goal at all times is to separate content and structure from presentation. This means that for classes and IDs it is best to call out what the item is or does, as opposed to what it looks like. Note that in the example above, the content IDs were not named `left-rail`, `middle-column`, or `right-rail`, as that would have merely reflected their location on the page, rather than their function.

The W3C has an excellent note on its Web site discussing meaningful classes here (www.w3.org/QA/Tips/goodclassnames). This discussion also introduces the concept of semantics or meaning in markup.

Consider the following:

```
<style type="text/css">
p.rederror {color: red;}
p.bolduser { font-weight: bold; }
</style>

<p class="rederror">Warning: Username not found!</p>
<p class="bolduser"><label for="username">Username:</label>
<input type="text" id="username" name="username" /></p>
```

There are two things wrong with this from a best practices standpoint. Both have to do with the naming of the classes on the `<p>` elements: `rederror` and `bolduser` both convey presentation information that implies what those elements look like. The standard practice is to avoid basing a name on a description of a "physical" or visual characteristic.

A better solution might be:

```
<style type="text/css">
p.errormessage {color: red;}
p.userfield { font-weight: bold; }
</style>

<p class="errormessage">Warning: Username not found!</p>
<p class="userfield"><label for="username">Username:</label>
<input type="text" id="username" name="username" /></p>
```

Note that this removes from the markup any indication what the element looks like, so that when the site is redesigned the classes are still relevant and the markup does not need to be updated. These also identify what the objects are, as opposed to what they look like. This is especially important on a large-scale site and where CSS is being used for layout—when changes happen in a redesign, the CSS class names are of vital importance to an easy transition, and their meaning should not be lost or confused because of a poor naming system that contradicts what each object actually is.

IDs Names Are Unique in a Document

A common mistake made by newcomers to CSS and modern markup is something like the following:

```
<div id="content">This is my content on the right side.</div>
<div id="main">This is my content.</div>
<div id="content">This is also my content.</div>
```

That's invalid code, because it calls out the same ID name multiple times in the same document. It is important to note that IDs are always unique in an HTML or XHTML document. This means that there is only one single instance of an ID per page. An ID can exist once and only once in a document, despite what some Web browsers might allow. The preceding example will have unpredictable results, particularly when scripting is attached to the document.

Semantic Markup To Give Meaning

Once a Web team has selected a markup language and DTD strategy, the style of XHTML or HTML markup is *everything*. In the Web standards world, Web authors should immediately forget what the elements look like and start thinking about what they mean in terms of "semantic markup." "Semantic" means that the documents are marked up in a way that conveys information about what the content *is*, as opposed to how it looks (which, remember, should be defined in the CSS). Authors can begin to think of HTML and XHTML as lightweight XML to help get their head around this concept.

Here is a screen that uses classic, old-school HTML to lay out a page (**FIGURE 1.11**).

Examine the source for that simple article:

```
<font face=arial size=4><b>My Online Article Title</b></font><p>
<font face=arial size=3><b>May, 2007</b></font><p>
Hey everybody, welcome to my article. Today we're going to be
talking about:<p>
Web standards-based markup<br>
```

```
Cascading Style Sheets<br>
XHTML<br><br>
Let's get started!
<br>
<br>
<table cellpadding=3 cellspacing=0 border=1 width=400>
<tr><td>
<i>About the author:</i><br><br>
<a href="http://navigationarts.com">Rob Cherny</a><br>
Lead Developer<br>
NavigationArts, LLC<br>
7901 Jones Branch Road<br>
McLean, VA, 22102 United States of America<br>
703.584.8920
</table>
```

This code, common from the 1990s, does not follow a separation of content from presentation in any way. It's littered with presentation information and doesn't give meaning to any of the content elements.

FIGURE 1.11 A simple article document. There is a right way and a wrong way to mark up a simple structure like this.

What about the following:

```
<span class=bigHeader>My Online Article Title</span><p>
<span class=dateentry>May, 2007</span><p>
<span class=regulartext>Hey everybody, welcome to my article. Today
we're going to be talking about:<p>
<span class=list>
Web standards-based markup<br>
Cascading Style Sheets<br>
XHTML</span><br><br>
Let's get started!
<table class="box">
<tr><td>
<span class="italics">About the author:</span><br><br>
<a href="http://navigationarts.com" class=authorHeader>Rob Cherny</
a><br>
Lead Developer<br>
NavigationArts, LLC<br>
7901 Jones Branch Road<br>
McLean, VA, 22102 United States of America<br>
703.584.8920
</td></tr>
</table>
```

This code uses CSS and pulls content and presentation information apart. So what's wrong with it and the first example? For starters, in both these examples, the code as it relates to the content is meaningless.

Even more so:

❖ The first example uses the <font>, <b>, and <i> presentation elements, all of which are deprecated.

❖ The second example features usage of <span> elements around all the content items, which does not convey that the information is a header, paragraph text, or list.

❖ With the <span> elements, the usage of the bigHeader class implies presentation information in its name.

❖ The <p> tags are being used at the end of each line and do not explain what a paragraph is in the document so much as demonstrate what its presentation attributes might do: create a double line break. The list class on the last <span> is just odd when there are perfectly good XHTML elements for lists: <ol> and <ul>.

❖ The double break at the end of the list is completely devoid of meaning in setting up the text of the article following the list.

❖ Finally, both examples use a table to draw a box around the contact information, when there is no actual tabular data.

POSH, or Plain Old Semantic HTML

The usage of clean, intelligent, semantic (X)HTML code has been called POSH, or Plain Old Semantic HTML (http://microformats.org/wiki/posh) and is a fundamental building block of modern markup. The essential goal is clean, meaningful markup without presentation elements or attributes. The elements used should convey information about the structure of the content.

Contrast the code in the previous examples with the following (**FIGURE 1.12**), and note that superficially it looks virtually the same as the first.

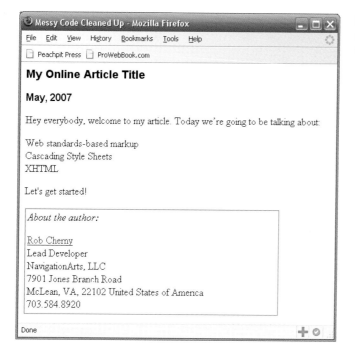

FIGURE 1.12 The simple article document, coded with Web standards.

But note also that it conveys much more information in the markup itself:

```
<div class="article">
    <h1>My Online Article Title</h1>
    <h2>May, 2007</h2>
    <p>
```

```
        Hey everybody, welcome to my article. Today we're going to
        be talking about:
    </p>
    <ol>
        <li>Web standards-based markup</li>
        <li>Cascading Style Sheets</li>
        <li>XHTML</li>
    </ol>
    <p>Let's get started!</p>
</div>
<div class="credit">
<h3>About the author:</h3>
<h4><a href="http://navigationarts.com">Rob Cherny</a><br>
    Lead Developer</h4>
<p>
NavigationArts, LLC<br>
7901 Jones Branch Road<br>
McLean, VA, 22102 United States of America<br>
703.584.8920
</p>
</div>
```

The first two examples in the previous section are similar to many others commonly found online. The second of the two comes from a Web author who thinks he is doing the right thing by pulling presentation information into CSS classes. It is a good start, but it does not convey structure or meaning. It also continues to rely on the presentation aspects of the <p> tag without marking any text as a paragraph.

The third example is superior in many ways:

❖ The content is easier to read in the code.

❖ The article is surrounded by a <div> element with a class of article, and the credit section is surrounded by a class of credit. This breaks the portions of the code up from others and allows the usage of CSS, which does not need extra classes added to the markup. A single class per section is easier to remember, use, and document than several.

❖ Presentation elements such as the bold <b> tag have been dropped in favor of meaningful code. Additionally, usage of <em> for emphasis as opposed to italics is preferred.

❖ The article title is marked up in an <h1> header element, indicating its importance above all the other content.

❖ The date is an <h2> second level header, demonstrating its position as second most important on the page, but can still be given a unique CSS format in the form of a CSS rule such as the following:

```
.article h2 {
    font: bold 16px Arial, Helvetica, Sans-Serif; margin-top: 0;
}
```

❖ Paragraph tags surround (and therefore identify) actual paragraphs of text, rather than show up at the end of the lines of text.

❖ The list is marked up as a proper XHTML list, accurately identifying the list of elements as such.

❖ The final sentence following the list is set off as a real paragraph, separate from the list that precedes it.

❖ By identifying certain text as headers, on which many search engines place importance, the cause of search engine optimization (SEO) is aided.

❖ Because each content element is marked up according to its function, the page is made more accessible. For instance, assistive technologies contain tools to help users navigate through headers on a page.

❖ The meaningless table has been replaced by a <div> with a class of credit, which has CSS applied to create a border and set the width and padding.

Plain old semantic HTML (POSH) markup is a fundamental principle of Web standards-based markup and will aid an organization in fully reaping the benefits of modern best practices. It is "plain old" not because of its age, rather because it is devoid of presentation aspects—which, again, are (or should be) handled by the CSS.

POSH code brings meaning to content. Where authors can do it, they should begin to introduce meaning to markup in order to convey as much information about the content as possible. By its nature, it also means that all presentation information is outside the document.

The wonderful thing about it is that with POSH you or a Web development team can clarify, identify, or isolate the meaning of the content. This can also be used with other technologies and techniques, such as microformats (discussed in the next section), which are built on top of POSH.

TIP

Web designer Dan Cederholm at SimpleBits.com has published an excellent set of articles on his Web site that examine and discuss almost endless ways to mark up different types of pieces of information in XHTML documents. He called his series the "SimpleQuiz" (www.simplebits.com/notebook/simplequiz/index.html).

Markup Wrap Up

Once a team has determined its markup language and its DTD, established how many templates are needed, and begun to describe how the markup will be coded, the next step is to apply styles to the markup.

The importance of this foundation of understanding and setting up valid markup cannot be overstated. The markup is interconnected to all Web software on a site; acts as a delivery mechanism for syndication; and is essential for accessibility, backwards compatibility, SEO, CMS template structure, and Web site performance. All CSS and JavaScript is keyed off the decisions in the markup. For any and all of these other technologies and components to work, valid markup needs to be in place.

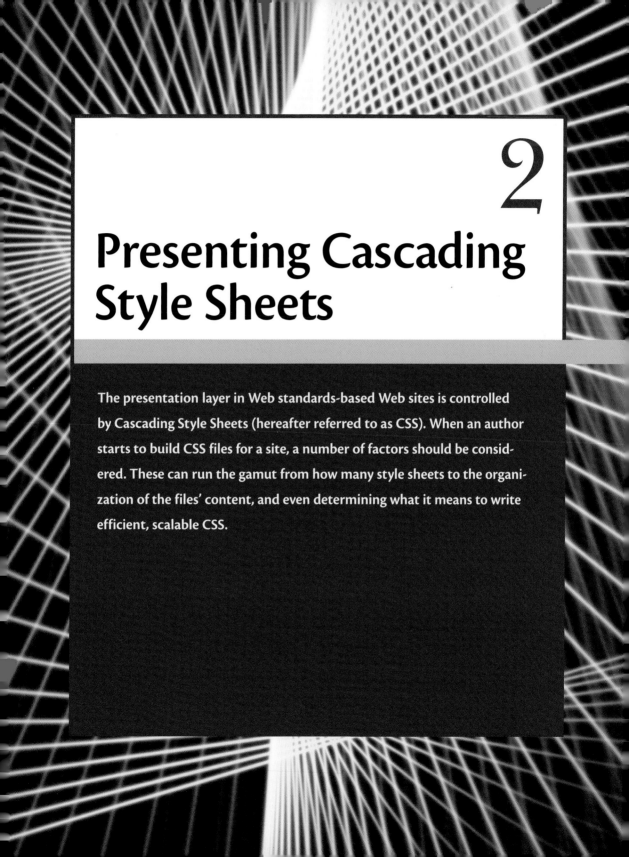

2

Presenting Cascading Style Sheets

The presentation layer in Web standards-based Web sites is controlled by Cascading Style Sheets (hereafter referred to as CSS). When an author starts to build CSS files for a site, a number of factors should be considered. These can run the gamut from how many style sheets to the organization of the files' content, and even determining what it means to write efficient, scalable CSS.

How Many CSS Files?

One of the hardest questions is how many CSS files a project will need. This depends entirely on the needs and size of a Web site. The answer, frankly, is: as many as are needed (and this may evolve as the site is built). Some sites may need a single style sheet, while others may need many. In larger sites, it may not make sense to load all the CSS rules that are required on every page. One of the major strengths of CSS is the rule cascade and how multiple files and sets of rules can be merged by applying multiple sources of CSS to a single document. The challenge is to structure the files in an intelligent way that scales well.

Designers and developers are commonly tempted to break CSS files up into function based on the types of rules. An example breakup is as follows:

❖ `typography.css`

❖ `theme.css` (or `colors.css`)

❖ `layout.css`

At our company, we've tried this approach and found it to be fundamentally not worth the effort, with the negatives far outweighing the positives. With this technique, a Web team could easily switch out the colors or the type styles by using alternate style sheets. Sounds good, but in reality the maintenance issues, particularly over time, skyrocket with this approach and are simply not worth it in most cases. There needs to be a good reason to do this.

The issues that come up with broken-up CSS files include

❖ Debugging becomes difficult and time-consuming because each selector is spread out among many files.

❖ Hidden dependencies between files begin to surface or even get lost.

❖ Less disciplined team members may violate the breakup of rules, resulting in inconsistent distinctions between files.

❖ Debugging by editing multiple files becomes a hassle or debugging begins in a single file and then solutions need to be broken up between files; sometimes this last step does not happen, either on purpose or by accident.

❖ The CSS cascade and specificity is more difficult to manage.

❖ Increased overall size of the CSS for a site; each selector is repeated in each file.

❖ Web authors can be confused as to the nature of different rules and what files the rules belong to. For instance, some rules, such as borders, provide both layout and color.

❖ Broken-up CSS files require additional HTTP requests for a full set of style sheets—an unnecessary burden on both the Web browser and server.

The only time that this is a good idea is when there is in fact a solid requirement for this approach, and even then, alternatives might exist.

For instance, a site may feature a JavaScript text-resizing widget. In this case, a different style sheet for a different set of typography-related style rules may be a good idea. However, it is important to note that even in this case a different approach could be taken, and the extra file may not be required. Instead of using a full alternative style sheet, consider applying a new class to a parent element such as the <body> element or a content area. Resetting the base <body> text size can be highly effective if designers are using relative font sizes and em- or percentage-based units. Additionally, a single extra class on a parent element can affect the font size of an entire <div> element or the entire document.

A JavaScript file may include the following:

```
var x = document.getElementsByTagName("body")[0];
    x.className = "altText";
```

Where the style sheet contains rules such as this:

```
body {font-size: 1em;}
body.altText {font-size: 1.3em;}
```

The bottom line is, Web authors should be selective as to what rules are pulled into different files, and consider the reasons for doing so as well as any alternatives. Also, don't create additional files for the heck of it when other techniques—such as using a script, like above, rather than switching style sheets—may create savings or keep the code cohesive.

CSS File and Linking Strategies

There are several different ways to construct a flexible and scalable CSS file structure. In all cases, there are tradeoffs between performance, modularity, and ease of maintenance.

Linking a single CSS file will place all rules in a single location that is easy to manage, and you can use string searches to find appropriate rules and easily edit the files. At the same time, a single CSS file can be enormous and difficult to manage across an enterprise with a multitude of business channels, requirements of branding or functionality, or a growing team.

An exceptionally flexible approach is using modular sets of CSS files that serve different purposes. Using a series of linking CSS files, developers can easily mix and match sets of @import rules of CSS files that serve different purposes.

Take a moment to consider the following structure. If XHTML template #1 contains the following CSS link element:

```
<link href="css/global.css" rel="stylesheet" type="text/css" />
```

Then, in the global.css file, the file contains no rules, but rather uses the @import CSS command to bring in external CSS files (**FIGURE 2.1**) for global pages on the site:

```
@import url(styles.css);
@import url(nav-bar.css);
@import url(content.css);
```

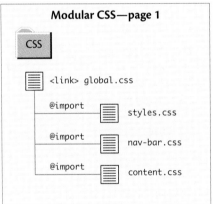

FIGURE 2.1 A modular CSS linking structure for sharing CSS files.

Elsewhere on the site, XHTML template #2, which contains some applications and forms, contains the following:

```
<link href="css/global-apps.css" rel="stylesheet" type="text/css" />
```

Then, the global-apps.css file contains import statements for the following:

```
@import url(styles.css);
@import url(forms-brand.css);
@import url(forms.css);
```

Note that the link file allows for a modular inclusion of different CSS files based on need (**FIGURE 2.2**). Both files include styles.css as the core CSS. The styles for forms in forms-brand.css and forms.css are not needed in the global pages,

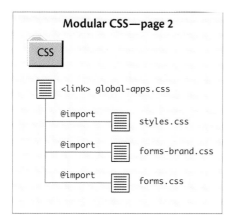

FIGURE 2.2 The same modular CSS link structure for another page uses some of the same files.

and therefore those CSS files are not included on the global pages; however, they can be linked locally from an application.

This has both advantages and disadvantages. The technique is a powerful approach from a maintenance and distributed-team standpoint, where multiple teams may need to import CSS files that are from a parent brand or some similar scenario. Additionally, from a CMS or template-based site structure, this has the added benefit of being able to add new CSS files without updating the XHTML site templates, because only a change to the CSS link files is required. Also, from a performance standpoint, if the forms rules are large in size, users do not need to download that data before it's needed.

However, this performance consideration should be carefully considered, because there are also performance downsides. Essentially, for a given page a Web browser and a server are going to have to create and execute lots of HTTP requests. To load a single page with the second example above, four HTTP requests are issued—which puts added burdens on both the client Web browser and the Web server. Multiply that by the full number of users hitting a site at a given moment and the number grows exponentially. This is one demonstration of how the CSS setup alone can impact page load times and site performance. The pros and cons of this type of approach should be carefully considered before being implemented.

NOTE

Performance and load-time considerations will be examined more thoroughly in Appendix C.

Site Section and Directory-Based CSS Files

A more conservative approach that scales well over a large Web presence is a well-thought-out, directory-based setup for linking style sheets. A typical large-scale Web site has global presentation-layer needs, and also, quite often, site-section and even page-level needs. From these needs you can create a CSS directory structure that will scale and can be easy to manage. The directory structure could include:

❖ Global CSS folder/files

❖ Site-section or channel CSS folder/files

❖ Page-level CSS folder/files (includes home page)

❖ Media CSS folder/files (print, mobile, etc.)

❖ Internationalization CSS files (folders for en_US/, es_ES/, fr_FR/, etc. Note each of these items consists of a language code followed by an underscore, followed by the region.)

Most Web pages will only require the global and possibly site-section CSS files (**FIGURE 2.3**). Based on unique needs, authors can link page-specific CSS files, and so forth. The biggest downside is that the site templates will require additional <link> elements in the document's <head> element depending on what section of the site is being styled.

FIGURE 2.3 Using a directory-based CSS structure rather than a modular structure provides a more robust and scalable CSS linking structure.

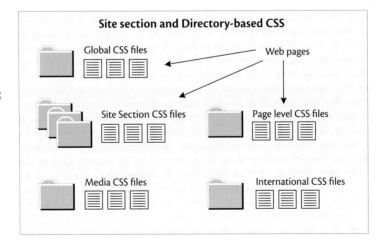

Using this approach and routine evaluations of page-level files, authors can push the rules up to site sections and then ultimately to the global files. This approach will be examined more thoroughly in the upcoming section.

This structure scales well and is easy for Web teams to manage. There are also fewer questions on the maintenance side as to where to put, as well as where to find, rules. Finally, there will be fewer HTTP requests than with multiple layers of linked CSS files.

Merging Multiple CSS files

Another technique worth consideration is merging multiple CSS files. This can be done during a build, deployment, or publishing process, or even in real time as the files are served to the browser. Merging has the added benefit of allowing multiple files to be managed by different teams, yet reducing the performance drag when a single request is used. This technique has to be carefully planned and executed, keeping all sites that might reference the CSS files in mind.

As a quick example, imagine a site that included these files in the documents' `<head>` element:

```
<link rel="stylesheet" href="main.css" type="text/css" />
<link rel="stylesheet" href="page.css" type="text/css" />
```

Assume `main.css` contained the following:

```
body {font: bold 1.2em Sans-serif;}
.special { color: red; }
#content { font-size: 1em; }
```

Then, `page.css` had the following:

```
.other { color: green; }
#content { font-size: 1.2em; }
#content h1 { font-size: 1.5em; }
```

Obviously these are simple files for demonstration purposes only. Different teams or team members could easily manage `main.css` and `page.css` separately, and it would be easier to locate rules as needed in smaller files. However, before production, a process might create a file called `styles.css` and link it to the document:

```
<link rel="stylesheet" href="main.css" type="text/css" />
```

During deployment or even upon dynamic generation of the CSS, the files would be merged. Keep in mind, if there are rules that depend on the cascade so they should be in a certain order, then they should be merged in order as appropriate.

```
/* main.css */
body {font: bold 1.2em sans-serif;}
.special { color: red; }
#content { font-size: 1em; }
```

```
/* page.css */
.other { color: green; }
#content { font-size: 1.2em; }
#content h1 { font-size: 1.5em; }
```

Fewer files are downloaded and linked. In this case, the effort would not be worth it; however, with large sets of files for many properties, disparate teams, site sections, or micro-sites, then the benefit can help simplify the code in the actual pages when deployed.

Conditional Comments for CSS and Internet Explorer

Microsoft Internet Explorer (IE) features some proprietary extensions that can be helpful when dealing with some oddities in its CSS features. In particular, IE's "conditional comments" are useful when linking CSS files for IE. Check out the following:

```
<!--[if lte IE 5.5]>
<link rel="stylesheet" href="patches/ie5.css" type="text/css" />
<![endif]-->
```

Basically, this code is ignored by most browsers because the code wrapping the <link> element looks like a standard XHTML comment. However, the expression in the square brackets [if lte IE 5.5] means "if less than or equal to IE 5.5," and therefore IE's parser knows to include this code, but only if the version number of the browser is 5.5 or below. This can be useful when dealing with issues such as the different box model measurements between IE 5.x and 6.x.

There is some controversy around code such as conditional comments, because code is being introduced that is meaningless to anything but Internet Explorer. Ideally, we should avoid targeting a specific browser whenever possible, even IE, since this can lead to problems when new versions come out. Sometimes finding alternative ways to code something might eliminate the need altogether.

Conventions for Files and Selector Case

Naming rules for CSS files themselves can be just about anything, so long as an organization can agree to a system and keep it consistent. What matters more is that the usage is consistent and makes sense.

Moving deeper into the CSS files' content, an important aspect worth mentioning is that CSS class names and IDs are case sensitive. Consider the following:

```
<style type="text/css">
.myRules { font-size: 1em; }
</style>
```

```
<p class="myrules">
   My text will NOT be 1em because the case is not right.
</p>
```

Some Web browsers are more forgiving than others, but for cross-browser com-patibility it is best at all times to remain true to CSS names being case sensitive.

CLASS CONVENTIONS

Remember that IDs and CSS classes should honor the rules of proper separa-tion of content from presentation; they should describe what an object does or the purpose it serves, not what it looks like. If the presentation attributes ever change, the names might become disconnected or mismatched from the actual attributes—not a pretty sight.

See Chapter 1 for CSS class naming-convention guidelines.

Microformats for Conventions, Meaning, and Utility

Good news for authors who might be trying to decide what to call a CSS class: There are protocols being established in the industry. A group of Web technolo-gists have begun to collaborate and define best practices for defining, in a con-sistent way, certain types of information that might be classified in CSS. These nascent protocols for classifying objects and collections of information support application programming interfaces (APIs) and data-mining activities, but also establish simple models for those looking for naming conventions. Some of these protocols have been called *microformats*.

Microformats, on microformats.org (**FIGURE 2.4**), are defined as:

"Simple conventions for embedding semantic markup … that normalize exist-ing content usage patterns using brief, descriptive class names often based on existing interoperable standards to enable decentralized development of resources, tools, and services."
—www.microformats.org/wiki/what-are-microformats

Most expert Web standards-aware designers and developers today consider microformats to be an excellent protocol to use for coming up with meaningful naming conventions for some types of information on a Web site.

FIGURE 2.4 The home page for microformats. org.

Microformats and POSH

Microformats are built on top of POSH to help deliver real meaning in HTML. So POSH is an integral and critical part of a microformat.

Taking the example from the POSH section in Chapter 1 (see Figure 1.12), where the document displayed an article introduction and the information about the author of the article. The code looked like this:

```
<div class="article">
    <h1>My Online Article Title</h1>
    <h2>May, 2007</h2>
    <p>
        Hey everybody, welcome to my article. Today we're going to
        be talking about:
    </p>
    <ol>
        <li>Web standards-based markup</li>
        <li>Cascading Style Sheets</li>
        <li>XHTML</li>
    </ol>
    <p>Let's get started!</p>
</div>
<div class="credit">
    <h3>About the author:</h3>
    <h4><a href="http://navigationarts.com">Rob Cherny</a><br>
        Lead Developer</h4>
```

MICROFORMATS

The specifications being created at microformats.org are not only an excellent source of inspiration for class names, but they may pave the way to a more semantic Web. By marking up content of certain types in POSH and standardized ways, the content is given meaning. Tools embedded in Web browsers today (there are extensions for Mozilla Firefox already) can call out that information and enable users to do useful things with it, such as adding appointments to their calendar software or adding users' contact information to their address books.

Future tools may do even more. Search aggregators that mine for data such as reviews of products, resumes, or even syndication of articles are a distinct possibility.

There are a number of microformats already standardized, and more in development every day. Some of these include

- hCalendar format for date and time (appointment) type information
- hCard format for contact information
- XOXO format for outlines
- hAtom format for syndication of blog articles
- hResume format for resumés
- hReview format for reviews

```
<p>
    NavigationArts, LLC<br>
    7901 Jones Branch Road<br>
    McLean, VA, 22102 United States of America<br>
    703.584.8920
</p>
</div>
```

Concentrating on the credit portion, this bit of POSH code can be enhanced with even greater meaning by overlaying a microformat. For instance, one way to assign classes and pieces of information to the credit information might be:

```
<div id="hcard-Robert-M-Cherny" class="vcard">
    <h3>About the author:</h3>
    <h4><a class="url fn n" href="http://navigationarts.com">
    <span class="given-name">Rob</span>
        <span class="family-name">Cherny</span></a><br>
```

```
      <span class="title">Lead Developer</span></h4>
  <p>
    <span class="org">NavigationArts, LLC</span><br>
    <span class="adr">
    <span class="street-address">
    7901 Jones Branch Road</span><br>
    <span class="locality">McLean</span>,
    <span class="region">VA</span>,
    <span class="postal-code">22102</span>
    <span class="country-name">
      United States of America</span><br>
    <span class="tel">703.584.8920</span>
    </span>
  </p>
</div>
```

This example adopts the hCard microformat defined at microformats.org. The classes defined for vcard, given-name, additional-name, family-name, org, adr, and so forth identify key pieces of information. While on the markup-heavy side, it does, in a very granular way, specify the meaning of each element, which is of potentially great use.

In XML, tags give meaning to each field of information. With microformats, valid class and other attribute information can be added to the POSH code to enable understanding of the granular pieces of information.

Pulling Information from a Page with Microformats

Using the hCard example above and an extension add-on for the Mozilla Firefox browser, it is possible to demonstrate a simple example of how powerful microformats can be. Michael Kaply at IBM has created an excellent extension called Operator, which you can download and install from the Mozilla Add-ons site: https://addons.mozilla.org/en-US/firefox/addon/4106

Once the extension is installed, users have either a new toolbar or a status bar icon that becomes active when visiting a Web page with data embedded in a microformat. The toolbar allows a multitude of ways to interact with a variety of microformats (**FIGURE 2.5**).

Since this example is an hCard, the Operator extension allows the user to export the embedded contact information to a vCard file, which can be imported into any software package that accepts that format, such as Microsoft Outlook. It is an incredibly easy and powerful way to add information to an address book directly from a Web page, particularly in a business environment (**FIGURE 2.6**).

For a breakdown of CSS selectors, see Appendix D.

FIGURE 2.5 An hCard microformat being exported using the Operator add-on for Firefox.

FIGURE 2.6 A vCard being imported to Outlook from a Web page via a microformat and Operator.

Too Much Class

Web standards purists have coined the term *classitis*, which means putting too many classes in a Web site's markup and CSS. The term is a funny word for a valid concern. Having dozens and dozens of CSS classes to remember, document, and reference is difficult for Web authors and business users alike.

In the long run, a more practical, graceful, and scalable solution is to use element and descendant CSS selectors. These selectors automatically apply styles to XHTML elements without having to apply classes to every item.

Classic Classitis

Descendent selectors match any element inside another element having a space between the two elements.

```
div p {color: red;}
```

In this example, any <p> element that descends from a <div>element will be red. This technique also works with classes and IDs. Using this simple technique, authors can begin to remove the complexity from their CSS code.

Here is an example of classitis at work (**FIGURE 2.7**). Note that styles are embedded in the document for convenience alone, as this is not necessarily a best practice.

FIGURE 2.7 Superficially, a document suffering from "classitis" looks just like any other.

```
<!DOCTYPE html PUBLIC "-//W3C//DTD XHTML 1.0 Strict//EN"
      "http://www.w3.org/TR/xhtml1/DTD/xhtml1-strict.dtd">

<html xmlns="http://www.w3.org/1999/xhtml" xml:lang="en" lang="en">
<head>
   <title>Classitis Example</title>
   <meta http-equiv="Content-Type"
      content="text/html;charset=utf-8" />
   <style type="text/css">
   /* elements */
   body { font-size: .9em; }
   /* main styles */
   .main { width: 200px; float:left; margin-right: 15px;}
   .main-header { text-decoration: underline; color:
      green; font-size: 1.2em; }
   .content { color: #666; font-size: 1em; }
   .main-list { list-style-type: square; color: #f60; }
   /* related styles */
   .main-related { width: 200px; float: left; }
```

```
    .rel-header { border-bottom: 1px dashed #f60; font-size: 1.2em; }
    .rel-content { color: maroon; font-size: .85em; }
    .rel-list { list-style-type: square; color: #666;
      font-size: .85em; }
    </style>
</head>
<body>
    <div class="main">
        <h1 class="main-header">My Header</h1>
        <p><span class="main-content">
          My content goes here.
        </span></p>
        <ul>
            <li class="main-list">Item one</li>
            <li class="main-list">Item two</li>
            <li class="main-list">Item three</li>
        </ul>
    </div>
    <div class="main-related">
        <h1 class="rel-header">My Related Header</h1>
        <p><span class="rel-content">
          My content goes here.
        </span></p>
        <ul>
            <li class="rel-list">Item one</li>
            <li class="rel-list">Item two</li>
            <li class="rel-list">Item three</li>
        </ul>
    </div>
</body>
</html>
```

Curing Classitis

Examination of the above document reveals a number of areas that could be improved upon. The code references an army of CSS classes that simply do not need to be there. The author of this document has defined classes for each <div>, all the headers, text, and list styles for each column in this simple two-column document. All the classes make the document difficult to read and increase the page weight needlessly. Most experts agree that classes should be reserved for exceptions to the basic rules that are being set up for elements in a document.

Now look at an alternative example, which provides the same design in a more graceful way (**FIGURE 2.8**).

FIGURE 2.8 Here is the same page using more efficient markup, (without classitis). It looks the same as the version with classitis.

```
<!DOCTYPE html PUBLIC "-//W3C//DTD XHTML 1.0 Strict//EN"
    "http://www.w3.org/TR/xhtml1/DTD/xhtml1-strict.dtd">

<html xmlns="http://www.w3.org/1999/xhtml" xml:lang="en" lang="en">
<head>
   <title>Classitis Example</title>
   <meta http-equiv="Content-Type"
     content="text/html;charset=utf-8" />
   <style type="text/css">
   /* elements */
   body { font-size: .9em; }
   h1 { font-size: 1.2em; }
   ul li { list-style-type: square; }
   div { float: left; }
   /* main styles */
   #main { width: 200px; margin-right: 15px;}
   #main h1 { text-decoration: underline; color: green; }
   #main p { color: #666; font-size: 1em; }
   #main ul li { color: #f60; }
   /* related styles */
   #main-related { width: 200px; }
   #main-related h1 { border-bottom: 1px dashed #f60; }
   #main-related p { color: maroon; font-size: .85em; }
   #main-related ul li { color: #666; font-size: .85em; }
   </style>
</head>
<body>
   <div id="main">
      <h1>My Header</h1>
      <p>My content goes here.</p>
      <ul>
        <li>Item one</li>
```

```
            <li>Item two</li>
            <li>Item three</li>
        </ul>
    </div>
    <div id="main-related">
        <h1>My Related Header</h1>
        <p>My content goes here.</p>
        <ul>
            <li>Item one</li>
            <li>Item two</li>
            <li>Item three</li>
        </ul>
    </div>
</body>
</html>
```

Superficially, this document looks exactly the same as the first. However, there is not a single class used: It has been reduced to a simple POSH document. Descendent selectors allow authors to set styles via context; this can be a powerful tool. This is not to say that classes should never be used; however, simplifying code in complex environments is never a bad thing. A POSH approach with simple selectors will get documents quite far and will be simpler to maintain.

Consider a situation where a designer might not be able to directly impact the markup because of business reasons or software architecture limitations, and this becomes even more powerful. Careful techniques involving hearty selectors and design changes can be pushed down into code that authors can't even touch!

Two Classes for the Price of One

Another robust technique worth noting is that the rules for markup allow multiple classes to be assigned to any given object. This is another powerful way to avoid using extra classes when they are not necessary (**FIGURE 2.9**).

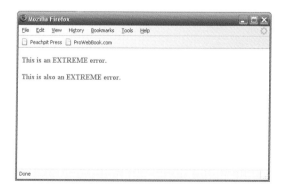

FIGURE 2.9 The result when multiple CSS classes combined.

Here's another style sheet example:

```
.error { color: red; }
.errorExtreme { font-weight: bold; }
.extaError { font-weight: bold; color: red; }
```

Note there are three classes defined: one making text red, the second making text bold, and the third combining both. Here is one usage of these classes in some XHTML code, where both sets of text are bold and red, but the author added an extra <span> to combine classes, and they also had to create the last selector, which does the same as the other two combined:

```
=<p class="error"><span class="errorExtreme">
This is an EXTREME error.</span></p>

<p class="extaError">This is also an EXTREME error.</p>
```

Now, consider the same style sheet without the last selector (which is not actually necessary):

```
.error { color: red; }
.errorExtreme { font-weight: bold; }
```

Finally, an author who exploits the features of standards-aware Web browsers can combine the classes using space-delimited lists inside the class attribute of elements, like this:

```
<p class="error errorExtreme">This is an EXTREME error.</p>
```

Again, the result is simply less code, and fewer classes. Advanced usage of CSS selectors takes Web standards-based techniques to the next level and can help style sheets scale without too much complexity.

TIP

The W3C CSS recommendations reference all manner of fantastic selectors that can be used to enhance the elegance and maintainability of CSS. While browser support is inconsistent, newer, more modern browsers such as Mozilla Firefox, Safari, Opera, and even Microsoft Internet Explorer 7 (and later) support most of the CSS 2 selectors module and in some cases some items from the CSS 3 module.

The CSS 2 selectors can be found at www.w3.org/TR/REC-CSS2/selector.html.

The CSS 3 selectors can be found at www. w3.org/TR/css3-selectors/.

THE HIERARCHY OF RULES

CSS selectors carry with them the notion of "specificity," which means how detailed and specific the rules are drives which rule takes precedence when conflicting rules show up. For instance, ID selectors are more specific than elements, and so forth. Specificity and other aspects of the "cascade" in CSS are described in the CSS recommendation at www.w3.org/TR/CSS21/cascade.html.

CSS File Content Structure

Some Web authors agonize over the structure of the CSS files' content. There are no absolute rules.

```
#singleLine { border: 1px solid red; padding: 12px; display: inline;
}
```

Some CSS authors prefer single-line rules, while others prefer rules that span multiple lines:

```
#multiLine {
    border: 1px solid red;
    padding: 12px;
    display: inline;
}
```

There aren't a lot of compelling reasons to use one over the other, except possibly for file size considerations where white space might be a factor. Whatever a team does, it's best to be consistent.

TIP

As part of their publishing procedure, some larger sites will employ a build process that strips out white space to help optimize the CSS files to a smaller size.

A basic guideline for what order or how to group selectors in a CSS file might be

❖ Define rules that are basic elements that don't depend on context.

❖ Define classes that are reused regardless of context.

❖ Define ID selectors roughly in their order, matching their usage in the markup.

❖ Define children of ID selectors based on rules set via context.

Another technique that is sometimes helpful, but takes the multiple-line setup to another level, is nesting CSS rules based on relationships, much like programming code.

```css
h1 {
    font-weight: bold;
    border-bottom: 1px solid blue;
}
#main {
    width: 600px;
    padding: 8px;
    float: left;

    #main h1 {
        font-weight: normal;
        border-bottom: 1px solid maroon;
    }
    #main p {
        margin: 0 0 12px;
    }
        #main p a {
            padding-right: 15px;
            background-image: url("out.gif");
        }
}
#siteinfo {
    position: absolute;
    bottom: 20px;
}
    #siteinfo p {
        margin: 0;
    }
```

Note how the indentations help provide context for the rules. This can get complex to manage as the rules get deep, but it can also help the maintenance and readability of the files. Rules that start as contextual might later be moved out and up to where they are more generalized, and it's important to watch the cascade and the level of specificity.

Consider the rule defined for <h1> elements without the #main ID that is bold, but with a blue bottom solid border, whereas the one in #main above is maroon and not bold. In time, or after a redesign, it might be determined that the <h1> elements should actually be all a normal font weight with a maroon bottom border. Rather than redeclare the rule, a maintenance activity would be to reorganize the style sheet:

```
h1 {
   font-weight: normal;
   border-bottom: 1px solid maroon;
}
#main {
   width: 600px;
   padding: 8px;
   float: left;
}
   /* note #main h1 is moved up and replaces the other rule */
   #main p {
      margin: 0 0 12px;
   }
```

WEB SERVERS AND CSS

If a CSS file does not seem to be applied to a document, and the page is displayed as plain text even though the files are properly linked, there may be a mime-type issue with how the Web server is returning the files. Some Web servers, usually older servers, will not be configured to correctly serve CSS files to Web browsers.

In particular, Mozilla-based browsers can have issues with CSS files that are not being sent with the correct content-type header on the HTTP response. This can happen particularly with browsers that are stricter in their interpretation of standards, so a site may look fine in one browser but not render with styles at all in another. Or, the file may work fine locally but blows up on the server.

CSS files must be served to a Web browser with the **text/css** content-type. With the popular Apache Web server (http://httpd.apache.org), this is a simple addition to the **.htaccess** configuration file, stored in the site root, as follows:

```
AddType text/css .css
```

Alternative Media CSS

One of the wonderful features of CSS is the ability to specify a specific media type for CSS files. Possible options include "all," "screen," "print," and "handheld."

For instance, a file might be labeled "screen" and the rules in the file are only applied to the document when viewed on a monitor screen:

```
<link rel="stylesheet" href="screen.css" type="text/css"
media="screen" />
```

The use of print CSS can be a powerful asset in any organization. It can actually reduce the workload where oftentimes a CMS or other software is employed to create duplicate or simple versions of documents that are easier to render on printed paper. This software may not be necessary if a print CSS file is attached. This is done the same way as the screen file:

```
<link rel="stylesheet" href="print.css" type="text/css"
media="print" />
```

In this case, when used with the `screen.css` file above, there are no styles applied from `screen.css` when the user clicks to print the file. However, the styles from `print.css` are applied, allowing authors the chance to apply very special formatting such as hiding menus and unnecessary design elements while giving emphasis to the content.

> **TIP**
>
> A classic article, written by Eric Meyer in the online resource A List Apart, discusses print CSS in particular detail (http://alistapart.com/stories/goingtoprint/).

A Print Style Sheet Example

Many organizations are effectively using print CSS files to create printed versions of their Web pages—which can be very nice, particularly for content articles where a printed version might be of real importance. In these cases, content is the critical factor, and the old paradigm of clicking print and getting something like what is shown on screen is really going by the wayside. What is on screen does not translate well to paper in most cases. An effective approach is to create a letter-head-type style emphasizing the content and hiding unnecessary menus and so forth.

An excellent example of the use of separate CSS style sheets for screen display and for print can be seen at the site for the Web design agency NavigationArts. The company's site was a collaborative CMS implementation, the front end of which was built using XHTML Strict and CSS by Web developer Michael Raichelson (http://michaelraichelson.com).

The content pages of the site (www.navigationarts.com/insight/web-standards) feature an inverted white logo graphic on an orange background (the company's signature color), and a basic three-column layout (**FIGURE 2.10**). Across the top is global navigation; the left side is main navigation; the middle content column

Figure 2.10 An example content page at navigationarts.com

features article content, details, and a graphic; and the right side features related tools. Under the hood, the code features both screen- and print-specific style sheets:

```
<link media="screen" rel="stylesheet" type="text/css"
   href=" /_res/css/main.css" />
<link media="print" rel="stylesheet" type="text/css"
   href=" /_res/css/print.css" />
```

First and foremost, it is important to recall that since the `main.css` file is set to screen, none of its rules will apply when the user clicks the Print button. So, the rules in `print.css` are coded from the ground up off a pure text display. Since the main graphic used on screen is actually inverted white against a background color, there's some magic going on behind the scenes in a `<div>` element hidden at the bottom of the document, which is exposed only when the printer CSS is applied:

```
<div class="ponly" id="print-logo">
   <img alt="" src=" /_res/img/navigation-arts.print.gif" />
</div>
```

This logo is used only for printed versions, and is grayscale for a good print representation. The screen CSS defines a class `ponly` which is applied to any object hidden on the screen, and therefore can be applied to many objects if necessary.

```
.ponly { display:none; }
```

The additional ID, `#print-logo`, is used to manipulate the position of the object in the `print.css` file during printing. Since this image is located at the bottom of the document, on-screen rendering or download times are not significantly impacted, as it is the last thing downloaded. Another set of objects radically manipulated when the page is sent to the printer is the footer (which also happens to be an `hCard` microformat, thank you), which on screen is at the bottom of the page, and when printed is actually moved to the top of the printed page. But how is all of this accomplished?

The print CSS starts by hiding all sorts of objects not required for printing:

```
#global-nav, #client-login,
#branding, #left-rail,#right-rail,
.geo, .include, .sonly, .honly, .license a,
#x, #x-insert, #x-image, #x-nav,
.readmore, .apply { display:none !important; }
```

Moving through the whole `print.css` file, there are even more elements, classes, and IDs that are hidden. This demonstrates how this technique is in fact an exercise in removing as much as possible. The above rules hide the global navigation as well as the branding, white-on-color logo, and the right and left columns. This essentially leaves the middle content and the footer, as well as the logo that is usually hidden at the bottom, at least on screen.

With this technique, there are a few more rules required for the printer CSS than with printing techniques that share the screen and print rules. The reason is that authors will need to set the fonts and colors for all type styles from scratch once again, since not a single rule from the `screen.css` file is applied to the print version. However, starting with a clean slate these days is typically more reliable for print CSS, since browser support is inconsistent and poorly documented.

Some more rules:

```
body {
    font-size:12px;
    color:#000;
    background-color:#fff;
    font-family:Arial,Helvetica,sans-serif;
    padding:120px 10px 20px;
    margin:0;
}
div.vcard {
    font-size:11px;
```

```
    position:absolute;
    top:25px;
    right:10px;
    text-align:right;
    width:400px;
}
div#print-logo {
    position:absolute;
    top:45px;
    left:10px;
}
```

The hidden print logo is not hidden in the print version, and both it and the footer are set to absolute and moved to the top of the document to establish a letterhead-like quality (**FIGURE 2.11**). Notice how the body has a padding-top of 120px, which leaves room for the absolutely positioned letterhead style print logo

FIGURE 2.11 The print CSS version of a content page at navigationarts.com.

and hCard data. The result is a well-formatted and easy-to-read printed page that emphasizes the content.

Using similar techniques can save time and effort on the server-side implementation of mixed-media and multiple-device publishing from a CMS or any other tool. CSS support for handhelds gets better ever day, and it will only allow for greater versatility as time goes by, lessening the burden and level of effort required to provide alternative forms of publishing of the same content.

Presentation Set Free

CSS is critical to a Web standards-based approach, since in a standards world—where HTML is virtually plain text—all presentation information is controlled from the CSS. This has numerous advantages, all the more so the larger the site, because all presentation information can be controlled from a manageable set of files.

It is true, however, that the larger and more complex the site, the more of a challenge managing effective CSS becomes, due to sheer volume. Having a clean base of markup and using effective linking strategies, combined with intelligent creation of selectors, will get a Web team halfway there already, providing them with a newfound sense of freedom and flexibility. Each environment will be different, of course, and it is important to make intelligent decisions on how to best manage the volume of design information that CSS needs to handle.

Once a base of markup and design is in place, adding interaction is another critical component to a modern Web site. Front-end markup impacts design, and both of these technologies interact with the scripting layer as well.

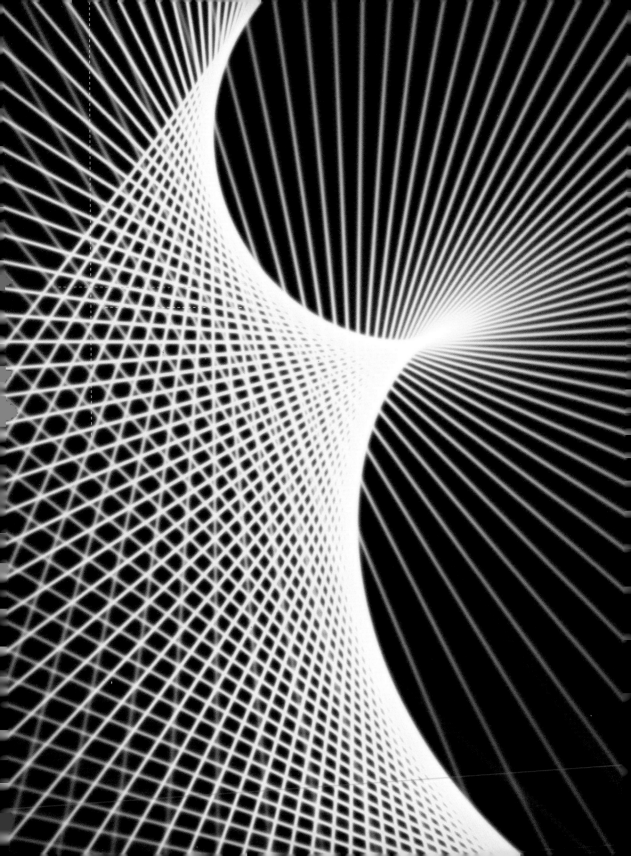

3

Integrating the Behavior Layer

Capturing, reacting to, and performing actions based on users' interactions with Web pages is the realm of the "behavior layer." While HTML and Web browsers have basic responses to "behaviors" such as clicking a link or submitting a form, today these responses can be enhanced radically through the use of scripts sitting on top of the markup. The scripts respond to logical decisions made by users, thereby creating a responsive user interface (UI) and controlling what and when (or even if) anything is actually sent to the server. Modern scripts can even control a UI by receiving data from the server and modifying an existing page without a full page refresh.

In a Web standards world, scripts and the behavior layer involve the careful application of JavaScript to enable both an event layer and the appropriate reactions to users' actions. JavaScript needs to be consistent, well organized, and respectful of the front-end presentation and structure layers.

In the past, JavaScript served a simple purpose: providing "stupid Web tricks" with varying degrees of usefulness. Today, with full Document Object Model (DOM) support, Asynchronous JavaScript and XML (Ajax), and richer experiences possible, JavaScript is getting more attention. It is moving beyond its past as a cut-and-paste language and is being adopted by large frameworks with very object-oriented structures and mature design patterns.

In some large organizations or complex environments, JavaScript is frequently applied as part of a front-end solution as well as the backend applications, yet it is frequently implemented by an altogether different team.

In most cases, except for more complex Rich Internet Applications (RIAs), modern scripts should be enhancements to existing pages and be laid over the top in a way that is not browser-specific and will allow the page to operate even if the user has scripts disabled or some other issue prevents them from executing.

While the percentage of users browsing the Web without scripts is small, one of the overarching tenets of modern best practices is that all types of users should have access to content, including users who have scripts disabled. This tenet also applies to the edge case where the site is developed for a specific browser and not built with open standards. Pages that rely on scripts for fundamental features and functionality, even items as mundane as links, go against this ideal and can cause problems and potentially irritate users who don't understand why something might not be working.

Modern Ajax Methods

In February 2005, Jesse James Garrett of Adaptive Path published an article discussing new techniques in Web scripting that had largely been operating under the radar. (His article is located at adaptivepath.com/publications/essays/archives/000385.php.)

Garrett's article, called "Ajax: A New Approach to Web Applications," defined Ajax (short for Asynchronous JavaScript and XML) as a new platform for Web technologies using JavaScript features to send XML communications from a Web page in the background, without interruption, to the server, without refreshing the browser window. There had been hacks and other workarounds for effects like this for years involving things such as hidden <iframe> elements.

While the core technologies he discussed had been around since the late 1990s, Garrett's article, combined with modern browser support, suddenly set off a virtual scripting revolution in Web development. When application developers realized JavaScript could function in ways desktop software could, with data interchange in the background, without users waiting for a form to be posted and responded to, JavaScript suddenly got tons of attention—and much more respect.

The term *Ajax* (also seen as *AJAX*) is defined in many different ways these days: from the strict background XML data interchange to a broad modern user experience featuring page updates, drag-and-drop, fades, animations, and other more desktop-software-like effects (an example of which is shown in **FIGURE 3.1**). In this sense, it describes the use of modern browsers with robust JavaScript support on faster and more advanced computers, combined with more prominent broadband access and traditional strict Ajax techniques.

Whatever the definition, it is clear that Ajax has brought specific attention to the techniques supported by JavaScript in modern browsers. Combined with Web standards-based approaches, it is quite a powerful "experience delivery" tool.

FIGURE 3.1 Apple's Web Gallery, a feature of its .Mac service, makes extensive use of Ajax. *(Image courtesy of Apple.)*

Web applications such as Google's Gmail (www.gmail.com, **FIGURE 3.2**) and Meebo's Web-based chat clients (wwwl.meebo.com, **FIGURE 3.3**) are helping to popularize Ajax-based techniques. They feature real-time, no-page-refresh applications that in many ways mimic desktop software behaviors. One example in Gmail is a background auto-save feature as you type the draft of your email message. Likewise, Meebo features a chat window where the conversation is updated in the screen without a refresh—it can also be dragged around the screen just as on the desktop. These basic, well-known features are powered by Ajax, and technically, under the hood by JavaScript.

Modern, Progressive, and Unobtrusive Scripting

Most experts today agree that modern JavaScript needs to move far beyond its early history of browser-specific techniques and inline code mixed within the HTML markup of the Web site.

Some ways modern scriptwriters have been doing this include

❖ Adopting a new progressive pattern and philosophy in which all scripts are "unobtrusive"

❖ Keeping the scripts' code separate from the content and presentation layers of the Web site, in external files where possible. If scripts were not separated, then the strict separation of content and presentation would lose its effectiveness. Unobtrusive scripts do not "intrude" into the other layers.

❖ Creating more mature, scalable, reusable, object-oriented code

❖ Using cross-browser feature sets rather than browser-specific proprietary ones

❖ In browsers visiting Web pages where the scripts do not work for some reason, making sure the Web pages still work and degrade gracefully

JavaScript has really entered a time and a state of organization, discipline, and responsibility. This is a far cry from the outmoded description given in Wikipedia: "a clumsy, hackish language unsuitable for application development" (http://wikipedia.org/wiki/Unobtrusive_JavaScript). Much of this bad reputation is due to its marketing history and the coders writing JavaScript, but that is changing. Doug Crockford, a frequent speaker on JavaScript, years ago wrote that JavaScript was "the world's most misunderstood programming language" (www.crockford.com/javascript/javascript.html).

JavaScript has earned the world's respect for sure.

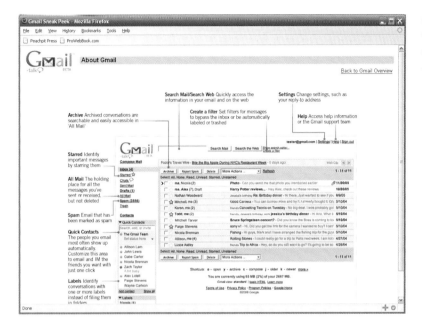

FIGURE 3.2 Google's Gmail service uses an enormous amount of Ajax and JavaScript.

FIGURE 3.3 Online chat service meebo.com also uses generous amounts of Ajax and JavaScript.

JavaScript Requirements: File and Function Inventory

Where the front end and the backend come together and interact with presentation and content—that's where the scripting layer comes in. And in that important place, it takes discipline to remove chaos, limit code bloat, and eliminate risk of inconsistent implementations. With more scripts comes a bigger need for Web teams to bring consistency and agree on internal standards and requirements. A more disciplined approach means creating site-wide requirements; an inventory of scripts, what they're for, how to get to them; and even rules for writing new scripts.

Many larger organizations with legacy code are faced with massive collections of scripts that are growing out of control. A common scenario is to see five different pop-up window scripts, a massive but flawed browser-detection script, and nowadays even several new Ajax scripts that do the same thing but are repeated and all downloaded to the end user. Additionally, there may be dozens of inline `document.write` statements or other functions that modify the UI with font sizes or colors. This is difficult to manage and violates the separation of the independent layers of a given design.

As with any software, an evaluation should be made of all the required functionality, a core set of functions created or agreed upon, and a standard way of interacting with UI elements created. Scripts should be stored in a central location and documented by a knowledgeable staff that is aware of what is available and what is needed.

A reference for a JavaScript function can be just like any other programming language. For instance, if there was a utility function to combine two strings together (not that someone would ever need such a thing), it might be documented as follows:

```
string myStringCombiner(string param1, string param2)
   Purpose: combines two strings, returns a new string
   Parameter  Description
   param1     Required. First string to concatenate to the second.
   param2     Required. Second string to concatenate to the first.
Notes: Function is available by including base-functions.js.
```

Bad Script, Bad

So what does modern, Web standards-respectful JavaScript code look like?

Arguably, a good way to show what modern code can look like would be to start with what *not* to do. Unfortunately, the bad code will look quite familiar.

The next few sections will start with the beginnings of a source document that includes some JavaScript and work through the code section by section, taking note of the serious problems that are demonstrated.

This document is fairly close to nonsense, of course—certainly not an example of good, modern scripting. With that in mind, a few years ago this would not have been an unusual sight (**FIGURE 3.4**):

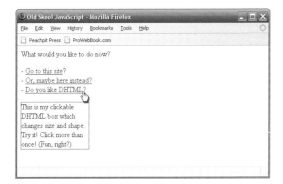

FIGURE 3.4 A meaningless JavaScript or "DHTML" screen.

```html
<html>
<head>
    <title>Old Skool JavaScript</title>
    <script language="JavaScript">
<!-- // cloaking device
b = navigator.appName
function callMe(){
    if (b.indexOf("Netscape") >= 0) { // detect Netscape
        alert("Sorry, this site is optimized" +
            " for Internet Explorer!")
    }
    else { alert("We welcome you:") }
}
```

As the page loads, it performs a poorly thought-out browser detection, alerts users of both Internet Explorer and Netscape (as near as it can determine), and then sets up the user for a series of actions. These are the first offenses (we'll number them as we go along):

1. The script features a very weak user-agent-based browser-detection script for questionable results.

2. The page appears to be targeted at Microsoft's IE browser and assumes that the only other browser coming to the site is going to be Netscape, which in

today's world is extremely unlikely. Today's scripts should never assume the audience is using a specific browser unless in a controlled environment.

3. The `language` attribute of the `<script>` tag is not required, and the `type` attribute is missing.

Moving further into the document:

```
function goThere(){
    window.open("http://cherny.com","myWindow",
        "height=500,width=500,scrollbars=yes")
}
function goHere(){
    window.open("http://www.google.com/","myWindow",
        "height=400,width=400,scrollbars=no")
}
```

Here we have two functions that do virtually the same thing, although this could be handled with a single, more robust function.

4. The script uses pop-up windows and has two functions to do this, when it could use one (whether or not this should be done in the first place).

More of the code:

```
function hookUp(){
    var x = document.all.tags("p")
    var el = x[1]
        el.style.cursor = "hand";
        el.style.width = "150px"
        el.style.height = "100px";
        el.style.borderColor = "red";
        el.style.borderWidth = "1px"
        el.style.borderStyle = "solid";
}
var on = false;
function update(){
    var x = document.all("myDHTML")
    if (!on) {
        x.style.width = "400px";
        x.style.height = "auto";
        x.style.borderColor = "green";
        on = true;
    }
    else {
        x.style.cursor = "hand";
        x.style.width = "150px"
        x.style.height = "100px";
```

```
            x.style.borderColor = "rcd";
            x.style.borderWidth = "1px"
            x.style.borderStyle = "solid";
            on = false;
        }
    }
    //-->
    </script>
</head>
```

The preceding section is full of problems:

5. The script uses Microsoft's proprietary `document.all` DOM technique, which will work only in IE. Modern scripts should avoid using proprietary techniques unless absolutely necessary.

    Separation of content from presentation places design into CSS; the above code violates this practice by placing presentation information into the JavaScript code. While scripts may need to make changes to page appearance, they should reference CSS classes, just like markup can. Design updates to the code above would be difficult at best and sabotage the code separation of CSS.

6. The script in several places modifies `.style` properties, violating the separation of layers. Sometimes this can be necessary, but certainly not here.

    Modern scripting also means that scripts can and should be linked from external files.

7. The full script is located in the `<head>` of the document, when it should be in an external file.

Now, the rest of the document body:

```
<body onload="alert('We like Internet Explorer!'); hookUp()">

What would you like to do now?
<p>
- <a href="javascript:goThere()"
  onclick="if (document.all){ alert('Do not leave my Web
site!')}">
  Go to this site</a>?
<br>
- <a href="#" onclick="goHere()">Or, maybe here instead?</a>
<br>
- <a href="#"
  onmouseover="document.all('myDHTML').style.visibility =
  'visible';">
```

```
    Do you like DHTML?</a>
<p onclick="update()"
  id="myDHTML"
  style="visibility:hidden;">
  This is my clickable DHTML box which changes size and shape.
  Try it! Click more than once!
  (Fun, right?)</p>

<script language="JavaScript">
<!--
callMe()
//-->
</script>

</body>
</html>
```

The first two links open pop-up windows. The last is a DHTML box that appears on mouseover to users of IE, and is clickable. When clicked, the box changes size and color. Quite pointless, but it will demonstrate a number of things for us.

From a modern, progressive standpoint, the above code is atrocious. Although many of its "offenses" were specified in context above, the rest of the problems are general:

8. The HTML features several inline event handlers, which mixes behavior-related code directly inside of the content and structure. Event handlers should be dynamically wired up when the page loads using the DOM.

9. The first link features the `javascript:` pseudo-protocol and no actual URI link. This type of link is nonstandard and can cause accessibility issues. No clicks should ever rely on the `javascript:` pseudo-protocol.

10. The second link features the `#` href attribute with an inline `onclick` handler and no actual URI that users without scripts can use. All links on a page should have a real-link URI. If it is a script-dependent issue, then the page objects should be added by the script.

11. The script also features inline logic, again using the `document.all` proprietary DOM method. All logic should be in external files.

Not to mention all the calls to `alert()` are just annoying to any user. There may even be more—frankly, it's hard to keep track of them all. Of course this document is nonsense, but a site may need to hook links up to some scripts and provide interactive widgets such as those on this page. Note also how poor markup decisions are involved directly in the poor scripting decisions. It is all interrelated.

Better Scripts

Today's best practices recommend a number of techniques to help improve the quality of JavaScript and how it interacts with the UI layer. As previously indicated, these techniques are often referred to as "unobtrusive" JavaScript. Some guidelines for unobtrusive JavaScript include

❖ Use W3C DOM techniques, as opposed to proprietary DOM methods, in order to target Web standards-supporting browsers.

❖ Avoid targeting scripts at specific browsers unless absolutely necessary.

❖ Use external files where possible, so as to avoid inline code in the XHTML.

❖ Avoid inline event handlers.

❖ Avoid `javascript:` pseudo-link protocol usage.

❖ Use object detection, as opposed to browser detection, if possible.

❖ Create references to presentation elements through classes and IDs or through distinctly separated, easy-to-modify code, if possible.

❖ Pages should work without scripts, if possible, and in older browsers.

❖ Dynamic elements, which are meaningless to users without scripts, should be added by the scripts.

Consider these guidelines in terms of the functionality that is required for your site. Modern browsers allow a pure separation of script from other layers, which can also improve the quality of the code. Additionally, scripts for links and other major functionality should never be tied to specific browsers unless there is a compelling reason, and there must be fallbacks in case users have scripts disabled or are using a different browser than expected. These days there are too many browsers to target specific vendors (except in extreme compatibility conditions). Using Web standards allows a single approach to maximize compatibility, because new browsing technologies will use those standards as their starting point.

Unobtrusive Improvements

There are several ways the badly scripted page above can be brought up to speed:

❖ Convert pseudo-links to actual links.

❖ Remove scripts to an external file.

❖ Convert invalid HTML to semantic and valid code.

❖ Add dynamic elements via scripts.

❖ Hook up event handlers dynamically.

❖ Remove browser detection, since there is no reason to have it.

❖ Remove proprietary techniques and replace them with DOM standards.

External Files and Dynamic Hookups

A big issue above is the inline `<script>` tags. In some cases they may be difficult to avoid, particularly in more complex environments where third-party code is being inserted, but where it can be done, such as with the scripts at the top of the example document above, scripts should be external files—for the same reasons that CSS files are better kept separate. Benefits include cleaner code, increased modularity, code sharing, and, when combined with other unobtrusive techniques, the ability to change the code in one location instead of having to plow through the content's entire markup. A compelling enough reason is that it helps enforce the purity of the separation of the documents layers.

A valid external <script> tag looks like this:

```
<script src="unobtrusive.js" type="text/javascript"></script>
```

Now, having moved the code outside of the document, what about all the references to that code? To obtain pure separation of content from behavior, all the inline event handlers need to go. Additionally, because the javascript: pseudo-protocol is nonstandard, those will be removed and replaced with their actual links (they are pop-ups; more on that in a bit). Also, the links that were in the javascript: function get pushed back down to the HTML for compatibility's sake. Finally, the "DHTML" aspects of the page, which are fairly meaningless if the user does not have JavaScript, are removed, to be added dynamically later.

With some cleaner, more "POSH" HTML as well, the code would look like this:

```
<body>
<p>What would you like to do now?</p>
<ul id="myUL">
    <li><a href="http://cherny.com">Go to this site</a>?</li>
    <li><a href="http://google.com">Or, maybe here instead</a>?</li>
</ul>
</body>
```

Notice that with all the event handlers removed, the code has achieved a separation of behavior from content and structure. So how is the code actually executed? In most cases, modern Web developers attach events and behaviors to a page on load, just not with a body onload attribute.

In unobtrusive.js, the scripts need to begin with this form:

```
window.onload = function(){
    // our code will go here, added in the next few sections
}
```

This simple item of code allows the same functionality as the body onload attribute. Not only will all the old code that was to execute on load be put here, but new calls to set up the other functionality that used to be inline will be put here as well. The modifications to the code will be further explained as the parts are improved one by one in the following sections.

No Proprietary Code

One of the biggest issues in older scripts (and in this example) is reliance on proprietary vendor techniques such as document.all, which has limited browser support beyond Internet Explorer. Web standards support open, nonproprietary technologies that work across browsers, and there are certainly alternatives defined by the W3C in its Document Object Model. Two of these alternatives are

❖ document.getElementById(id)

Returns an element when passed an id that is the ID attribute of the element; the ID needs to be unique in the document.

❖ element.getElementsByTagName(tag)

Returns a nodeList (JavaScript array) of the matching elements by tag.

There are several examples above where document.all can be seamlessly swapped out with document.getElementById. Replace the following:

```
var x = document.all("myDHTML")
```

with this:

```
var x = document.getElementById("myDHTML")
```

And replace this:

```
var x = document.all.tags("p")
```

with this:

```
var x = document.getElementsByTagName("p")
```

These two methods are key to W3C-based DOM scripting.

Pop-Up Windows

Most experts today recommend against opening links in external windows. There are a variety of opinions on the matter, but with modern browsers that support tabs, a huge volume of third-party add-ons that enable pop-up blocking, and a general desire to cater to users who find multiple windows confusing, pop-up windows are losing favor. Additionally, from a technical standpoint, the old browser-based (nonscripted) method of opening windows with the target="_blank" method is not valid: The target attribute is deprecated in XHTML transitional and removed altogether from XHTML strict.

However, the bottom line is that in many massive corporate environments these arguments are still difficult to win; management typically wants users who are leaving the corporate site to be directed to a new window in an attempt to keep the main site in the background. Compelling content might keep a user there, but that's another discussion. There are many techniques to get around pop-up windows, but creating them will be used here as an example of adding dynamic event handlers to elements on a page that need actions hooked up to them—and can degrade gracefully.

Adding Event Handlers and Scripting with Class

The first step in setting up proper event-handling was moving the links' addresses out of the JavaScript and into the href attribute to create real links as a part of the conversion to more "POSH" HTML above. JavaScript developers *should always use real links* when possible, because of usability and accessibility issues. Dynamic behaviors should be an enhancement to a page rather than a necessity. The conditions where dynamic behaviors might be considered a necessity is when there are alternatives, there is a controlled environment, or the functionality is not required.

One way of adding dynamic functionality to a page with an effective separation of structure and behavior is to assign a CSS class to elements that require scripting to be attached to them. Think of the elements with that specific class value as a defined type of object on a page, and methods, events, and behaviors are assigned to them with JavaScript. This "class" notion is in keeping with the object-oriented term *class*, which programmers use and which defines a type of object collection with properties and methods. The CSS class may or may not have presentation information referenced in the CSS. If there is no presentation information, it is safely ignored by the CSS, but can still be used by the JavaScript.

To use classes effectively, JavaScript authors often use a script function called "getElementsByClassName()" which, like getElementsByTagName(), returns a collection or array of elements. In this case, those returned have a given class

assigned to them. Searching through an entire document can be resource intensive, so these searches are often limited by a `tag` or ID.

Here is an example script that finds elements in a document with a class name,
limited to a specific tag:

```
/* LF = low fidelity: this thing is basic,
 *      folks, no spaces, a single class, etc.
 * there's plenty other good ones out there,
 *      this is for demo purposes only...
 */
function getElementsByClassNameLF(tagName,aClass){
   var z = [];
   if (!document.getElementsByTagName) return z;
   var x = document.getElementsByTagName(tagName);
   for (var i = 0; i < x.length; i++){
      if (x[i].className == aClass) z.push(x[i]);
   }
   return z;
}
```

An important feature to note is the check for `!document.getElementsByTag-`
`Name`, as this checks for support of an important object method which, if not
supported, will cause the script to give an error. Make sure the script is linked
from the document.

Now, classes and event handlers can be added to the two links without having the
code inline in the document.

First, the new links, with a class of "external":

```
<li><a href="http://cherny.com" class="external">
    Go to this site</a>?</li>
<li><a href="http://google.com" class="external">
    Or, maybe here instead</a>?</li>
```

Second, the new `window.onload` uses the `getElementsByClassNameLF()`:

```
window.onload = function(){
   // find a elements that have an 'external' class
   var linksExt = getElementsByClassNameLF("a",external");
   if (linksExt.length > 0){
      for (var i = 0; i < linksExt.length; i++){
         // add onclick handler to each!
         linksExt[i].onclick = function(){
            window.open(this.href,"ourExternals");
```

```
        return false;
      }
    }
  }
}
```

Adding classes to items in the document is just one way of adding functionality. Expert Web developers have the full range of W3C DOM methods and properties available to them, including walking the document tree and simply locating document IDs directly.

One last thing to note on the pop-ups: Notice how the `window.open` references `this.href`. Because `links[i].onclick` references the current item in the collection of returned links, `this.href` is a reference to that link's `href` attribute. This allows the links to stay in the document, and simply be used by the script via the event handler that is dynamically created.

NOTE

The Web Hypertext Application Technology Working Group (WHATWG) has included a powerful version of getElementsByClassName() in its Web Applications and HTML5 specifications, and this functionality is due to be included in Firefox 3. As with much of the WHATWG's specs, only time will tell if the W3C HTML Working Group includes this in its future work.

The W3C defines a number of ways to add event handlers to page objects. The bottom line is that inline event handlers are the method least recommended by modern scripting gurus: Don't use it unless there is a compelling reason. The W3C DOM defines a standard `addEventListener()` method. Unfortunately, Internet Explorer doesn't support this method, and so you should look online for compatibility functions that will help bridge the gaps in support. Just do a search on something like "attach JavaScript event listener."

NOTE

It is important to note that the example script here is for demonstration purposes only and does not have all the features of some functions by that name. Search online for other, more powerful examples that support multiple and combined classes; you'll find many useful results, including an excellent script from Robert Nyman and Jonathan Snook (www.robertnyman.com/2005/11/07/the-ultimate-getelementsbyclassname/).

> **TIP**
>
> A great place to start on cross-browser event handlers is Scott Andrew LaPera's now classic "addEvent()" and "removeEvent()" functions posted all the way back in 2001 (www.scottandrew.com/weblog/articles/cbs-events)

Dynamic Elements and innerHTML

The remaining step in improving the sample page is to add dynamic elements after the page has loaded. Unless the elements of the document can serve some purpose when scripts are disabled, it may be best to add the elements after the page has loaded.

The W3C DOM includes a whole series of functions for inserting content and markup into a document. These are highly effective; however, for expediency, Microsoft introduced a proprietary DOM extension called `innerHTML` that inserts snippets of code into a document. As fate would have it, this method is not only faster to code, but performs faster in the browser as well. The benefits were difficult to deny, so every other major browser vendor that supports W3C DOM standards-based code has implemented this feature. That makes it exceptionally safe and convenient to use. Although some purists balk at its use because it is considered nonstandard, for our purposes here it is too convenient *not* to use.

> **NOTE**
>
> Just like getElementsByClassName(), innerHTML is part of the WHATWG's specifications offered to the W3C HTML Working Group. As with all its recommendations, only time will tell if it is standardized.

In the case of our sample page, there is an object (a link in the original) that on mouseover shows a box that can be resized (for whatever reason), and the box changes its border color when clicked. This object will be inserted dynamically, as it is meaningless without scripts.

> **TIP**
>
> Because content is being inserted into the DOM of the document, this code needs to be placed **before** the code that was discussed above in the window. onload for the pop-up. This is because when DOM modifications happen, event handlers can be lost! There are ways around this; try searching online for "javascript event delegation" for some helpful links.

So here is some code that can insert the needed DHTML trigger to show the clickable box:

```
window.onload = function(){
// code below here is new
// check if the needed functions are available
it (!document.getElementsByTagName) return false;

// object that will be hidden and shown
var str = '<p class="' + LaF.classInit + '" id="' +
    LaF.classId + '">This is my clickable DHTML ' +
    'box which changes size and shape. Try it! ' +
    'Click more than once! (Fun, right?)</p>';

// add it to the body of the doc
document.getElementsByTagName("body")[0].innerHTML += str;

// add trigger to list that will show the object onmouseover
var ul = document.getElementById("myUL");
if (ul){
    ul.innerHTML += '<li><span class="' + LaF.classLi +
        '">Do you like DHTML?</span></li>';
    var myLi = getElementsByClassNameLF("span",LaF.classLi);
    if (myLi.length > 0) {
        myLi[0].onmouseover = function(){
        var sp = document.getElementById(LaF.classId)
            sp.className = LaF.classOff;
        }
    }
}
// add code to toggle the object when clicked
var box = document.getElementById(LaF.classId);
if (box){
    box.onclick = function(){
        box.className = (box.className == LaF.classOn) ?
            LaF.classOff : LaF.classOn;
    }
}
// code above here is new
/*
 * The modifications of the DOM above remove the Event Handlers
 * which we so carefully attach...sweet. so these need to happen
 * after any DOM mods. event delegation would resolve this.
 */
```

```
// find a elements that have an 'external' class
var linksExt = getElementsByClassNameLF("a","external");
if (linksExt.length > 0){
   for (var i = 0; i < linksExt.length; i++){
      // add onclick handler to each!
      linksExt[i].onclick = function(){
         window.open(this.href,"ourExternals");
         return false;
      }
   }
}
}
```

There is a lot of code here, and it is beyond the scope of the discussion to explain all of the nuances and techniques used in this JavaScript; however, there are a number of things worth pointing out:

❖ The code uses several functions introduced already, including `document.getElementsByTagName`, `document.getElementById`, and `getElementsByClassName`.

❖ A string variable is created that is the HTML for the box that's being hidden and shown. It's then appended with `innerHTML` to the body of the document.

❖ An item is added to the list to be the "Do you like DHTML?" trigger to show the box. A `<span>` element can be used instead of an `<a>` anchor element because there is no actual link (it's never going to take anyone anywhere).

❖ An event handler is added in the code to change the CSS class of the box when the user passes her or his cursor over the trigger `<span>`.

❖ Finally, the box that was added gets an `onclick` handler to also toggle its CSS class.

It is also worth noting that there is a little more JavaScript required for this, as well as some CSS. Notice how the script references the CSS classes via variables?

JavaScript Behavior with CSS and Presentation

In the purest sense, if the JavaScript is going to be pulled out of the markup, and the presentation information all lives in external files, shouldn't the CSS be pulled out of the JavaScript as well? That can happen only to an extent, and in this case there is a demonstration of the presentation aspects of the JavaScript code now being referenced by the classes in the CSS. The names of the class do appear in the JavaScript, just as they appear in the markup of an XHTML document. The classes and IDs are what bind everything together, in a manner of speaking. So in this case, the classes were pulled into a simple JavaScript object literal, which could be referenced and changed easily without plowing through any of the logic in the JavaScript.

```
// Look and Feel object to pull
//    superficial properties out of code,
//    especially classes
var LaF = {
   classExt : "external", // external link class from prior example
   classLi : "trigger",
   classInit : "set",
   classOn : "on",
   classOff : "off",
   classId : "myDHTML"
}
```

These are easily then referenced like this:

```
LaF.classLi // the class for the trigger to show the box
```

> **NOTE**
>
> For a more pure approach, a developer might code the JavaScript in a more object-oriented way. This might be to create a series of objects for each "thing," where each has its own CSS properties to be inserted into the document and add its own event handlers. This would separate and compartmentalize the code in the JavaScript even more from a maintenance and scope perspective.

For the most part, and in the purest sense, JavaScript should not directly call the .style property of any objects it is manipulating, so that the look and feel of those objects may still be controlled via CSS. A lot can be done by setting up different CSS classes, and those different CSS classes should be leveraged where possible, in order to maintain the purity of the separation of layers in Web standards-based code. As in any situation, there are exceptions, degrees, and nuances that may make it difficult to be 100% pure at all times; however, as with any Web standards-based best practice, there are ideals to aspire to and to weigh against business requirements.

A final note on the remaining CSS: A file is created and linked to the cleaned-up document that includes some rules making the trigger <span> look just like links and to distinguish the two states of our changing box.

```
a, span.trigger {
    text-decoration: underline;
    cursor: pointer;
    color: blue;
}
.off {
    cursor: pointer;
    width: 150px;
    height: 100px;
    border: 1px solid red;
}
.on {
    cursor: pointer;
    width: 400px;
    height: auto;
    border: 1px solid green;
}
.set {
    visibility: hidden;
}
```

This keeps the presentation aspects of the page in CSS, where they belong. The final document is essentially the same as the original, but without the browser detection and alerts, which served no constructive purpose (**FIGURE 3.5**).

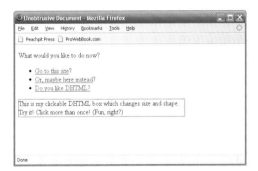

FIGURE 3.5   The improved, unobtrusive script page.

Say, for example, however, that the span.trigger class needed to be renamed to span.toggle for some reason. Then, using the JavaScript object literal, it is very easy to locate and make that change, rather than having to plow through the JavaScript logic:

```
// Look and Feel object to pull
//    superficial properties out of code,
//    especially classes
```

```
var LaF = {
    classExt : "external", // external link class from prior example
    classLi : "toggle",
    classInit : "set",
    classOn : "on",
    classOff : "off",
    classId : "myDHTML"
}
```

TIP

There is an enormous amount of new work being published online with regard to modern JavaScript design patterns and object-oriented techniques. Try searching online for "javascript object literals," "object oriented javascript," and "javascript closures" for some examples. Or, download a framework such as those mentioned in the next section and examine the source—it's all there for the taking!

Large Sites and Support for Multiple OnLoads

On larger sites, there are likely to be any number of things that need to be added to the page when it's loaded. This can lead to conflicts because there may need to be more than one onload JavaScript event handler:

```
window.onload = function(){
    // might be a couple of these?
}
```

There are several ways to deal with this. In a highly controlled environment, a team can aggregate all these calls into a series of setup functions:

```
function setup(){
    productSetup();
    salesSetup();
    uiSetup();
}
window.onload = setup;
```

Each team member who needs something executed on load would have his or her code added to the setup() function. This can be difficult to manage. The problem gets more complicated when some rogue developer tries to attach an onload event to the <body> element, causing conflicts and events not firing.

Another way would be to create a function that will aggregate load events, which programmer Simon Willison did and posted on his blog at http://simonwillison. net/2004/May/26/addLoadEvent/.

```
function addLoadEvent(func) {
   var oldonload = window.onload;
   if (typeof window.onload != 'function') {
      window.onload - func;
   } else {
      window.onload = function() {
         if (oldonload) {
            oldonload();
         }
         func();
      }
   }
}
```

Willison's code above allows multiple load events to be queued up in sequence and fire in order. To test this, all that is needed is a simple document that links to a JavaScript file that includes the addLoadEvent() function, with some additional code:

```
// global variable (typically, avoid this)
var x = "- Default value.";

// define first
function customFunction(){
   // add to the default value to the global var
   x += "\n- This is added to the string first.";
}

// call first
addLoadEvent(customFunction);
addLoadEvent(function() {
   // add to the default + first to the global var
   x += "\n- This is added to the string second.";
});
addLoadEvent(function(){
   // alert the string showing the calling order
   alert(x);
});
```

When the page loads, the browser shows the order in which the functions have been called (**FIGURE 3.6**).

Whatever page-loading strategy an organization picks should be consistent.

FIGURE 3.6 With the right scripting techniques, multiple onload events can be executed.

EXECUTE ON PAGE LOAD, OR EVENT ON DOM DOCUMENT LOAD

When a page has enough content and artwork combined with scripts, a traditional onload event handler delays the attaching of all scripts until the full document and all its assets, including graphics, have all loaded—which can introduce performance delays where it may appear to the user that nothing is happening, because the scripts have not fired yet.

A better idea is to attach all the dynamic behavior once the XHTML has loaded, because the document's full DOM is what is needed, not all the graphics. Some industrious developers have figured out ways to attach scripts once the DOM has loaded (just the XHTML, which is much quicker than loading the full page). Try searching online for "domcontentloaded" or "domloaded" for more information.

This can be a major performance win, and is discussed in Appendix C.

Custom Scripts vs. Frameworks

Depending on the experience of the team, resources, and requirements of a Web project, many different JavaScript options exist. Sometimes only basic scripts are needed and these can be found easily online and extended; however, the team should be exceptionally careful with these, because there are mountains of poorly written JavaScript code online. Additionally, grabbing large volumes of code from varied sources can be risky and result in

❖ Inconsistent quality and browser-compatibility issues

❖ "Frankenstein"-like sets of functions that use different techniques and styles or repeat core functions unnecessarily

❖ Maintenance problems

❖ Conflicts in variable and function names

Based on the requirements of a project, there are also "frameworks" and "libraries" of packaged code and modules, which include utility functions and objects that can be used to save time. Most are free and supported by communities, such as the Prototype framework (www.prototypejs.org) or the jQuery library (http://jquery.com). Some, such as Dojo (http://dojotoolkit.org), have sponsorships from a number of big companies, yet are still free to use.

A popular framework can be of value because it's very likely to have a higher level of quality due to the number of users who have contributed and who have been debugging. However, there are issues to consider:

❖ Does the framework include code and features you don't need? Is using a framework like using a sledgehammer on a thumbtack?

❖ Is downloading a large library of code to the browser on every page a worth-while expense, performance-wise?

❖ Is the development path of the framework active and evolving?

❖ Is there an active community that can help troubleshoot problems?

❖ Does the framework make any unexpected modifications to the core Java-Script objects that might conflict with other code?

❖ Does the framework adhere to best practices?

❖ Will the team be able to agree or set policy on a framework, and not have some members using one framework and others going off on their own? There is a cost associated with inconsistency.

Whatever decision is made, particularly in a diverse organization with a large Web presence, the choice should be weighed carefully and implemented in a controlled and consistent manner. The whole issue is essentially a build vs. buy (or, in this case, use someone else's) consideration, just like any other software components to be included in a project.

Example of jQuery Framework Code

For the purposes of this discussion, it makes sense to demonstrate the power available in using a JavaScript framework. It can save time, enforce a level of consistency across an organization, and eliminate browser-related bugs. It can also be a timesaver when performing common DOM operations against code.

First, let's look at an example of a fairly modern, unobtrusive page with some scripts attached (**FIGURE 3.7**). Here's the HTML:

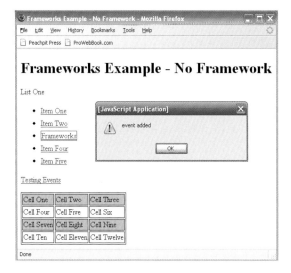

FIGURE 3.7 A JavaScript page without a framework.

```
<ul id="test-one">
    <li><a href="one.html">Item One</a></li>
    <li><a href="two.html">Item Two</a></li>
    <li><a href="frameworks.html">Frameworks</a></li>
    <li><a href="four.html">Item Four</a></li>
    <li><a href="five.html">Item Five</a></li>
</ul>

<p class="event-class">Testing Events</p>

<table id="test-two">
<tr>
    <td>Cell One</td>
    <td>Cell Two</td>
    <td>Cell Three</td>
</tr>
```

```
<tr>
   <td>Cell Four</td>
   <td>Cell Five</td>
   <td>Cell Six</td>
</tr>
<tr>
   <td>Cell Seven</td>
   <td>Cell Eight</td>
   <td>Cell Nine</td>
</tr>
<tr>
   <td>Cell Ten</td>
   <td>Cell Eleven</td>
   <td>Cell Twelve</td>
</tr>
</table>
```

Now let's add some scripts, including an onload handler, a dynamically added event handler, and some solid `getElementsByClassName()` action for good measure. The following script does a few small things:

❖ First, it finds links in a list and compares them against the current address to highlight the "current" page link.

❖ Second, it attaches a click event to a paragraph with a certain class attached.

❖ Third, it takes a specific table and zebra-stripes it; that is, it makes every other row a different color by adding a class to each one.

Looking over the code, it is nice and unobtrusive and fairly well structured for the demonstration purposes:

```
// get elements by class name (low fidelity)
function getElementsByClassNameLF(tagName,aClass){
   var z = [];
   if (!document.getElementsByTagName) return z;
   var x = document.getElementsByTagName(tagName);
   for (var i = 0; i < x.length; i++){
      if (x[i].className == aClass) z.push(x[i]);
   }
   return z;
}

// first/last child
function findLink(id) {
   var els = document.getElementById(id).getElementsByTagName("a");
```

```
    var i = 0;
    while (i < els.length){
       if (document.location.href.indexOf(els[i].href) != -1){
          els[i].className += " on";
       }
       i++;
    }
}

// zebra stripes (every other)
function makeStripes(els){
    for (var i=els.length-1; i>=0; i--){
       if (i % 2 == 0){
          els[i].className += " even";
       }
    }
}

window.onload = function(){
    var tab = document.getElementById("test-two");
    var x = tab.getElementsByTagName("tr");
    makeStripes(x);
    findLink("test-one");
    var ev = getElementsByClassNameLF("p","event-class");
       ev[0].onclick = function(){
          alert("event added");
       }
}
```

It would, however, take some time to put the code together and verify that it is all working as intended, as it includes loops and arrays and so forth.

Now, the same document's JavaScript code can be rewritten using the jQuery library framework (**FIGURE 3.8**), which has a pleasantly succinct syntax that's easy to pick up by coders and noncoders alike. One appeal of the jQuery framework is its reliance on CSS selectors to locate DOM nodes in the document, which typically requires a complex set of operations using the W3C DOM code. Note how much simpler the above code is, refactored using jQuery:

```
$(document).ready(function(){
    $('#test-two tr:even').addClass('even');

    $('#test-one a').each(function(){
       if (document.location.href.indexOf(this.href) != -1) {
```

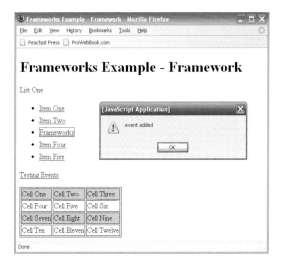

FIGURE 3.8 The same page as illustrated in Figure 3.7, now using the jQuery framework—looks the same on the front end, but the performance is significantly improved and the amount of code is significantly decreased.

```
        $(this).addClass('on');
    }
});

$('p.event-class').click(function(){
    alert('event added');
});
})
```

It doesn't take a JavaScript expert to notice how much more concise this code is, compared to the dozens of lines of code in the other version. It can take four long functions and distill them down to three easy statements.

What makes it so brief? The code uses the jQuery functions and syntax, which abstracts the heavy lifting. What's not seen above is there is also a 20KB file downloaded with that brief script, whereas in the first example, all that was shown was all that was required.

But the code to do the work is much simpler: Where in the original the getElementsByClassName() function involved getting a reference to an array, looping through all the items, and applying a click with a function reference, the jQuery version simply does this:

```
$('p.event-class').click(function(){
    alert('event added');
});
```

The power is in the exceptional $()$ function that takes all sorts of different selector references, such as #test-two tr:even, to retrieve every other row of a table. There is a reference online (http://docs.jquery.com) that shows all the different types of selectors that jQuery accepts. It supports CSS 1-3, XPath style selectors, and a number of custom ones.

Frameworks Make Ajax Easy

One benefit many are finding with JavaScript frameworks is that most of them make creation of Ajax code stunningly easy. For instance, using Ajax with jQuery is quite simple.

Imagine a simple HTML document that links to the jQuery library (**FIGURE 3.9**):

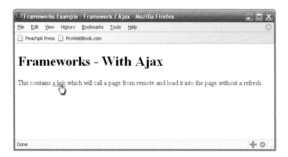

FIGURE 3.9 A sample document with a link that executes some Ajax using jQuery.

```
<h1>Frameworks - With Ajax</h1>

<p>
This contains
<a href="js-ajax-call.html">a link</a>
which will call a page from remote and load it into the page
without a refresh.
</p>
```

Now, link a simple script that unobtrusively adds a <div> element into which content can be loaded. The <div> is being added by the script because if the script did not run, the <div> would be meaningless.

```
$(document).ready(function(){
    $('body').append('<div id="ajax-div"></div>');
})
```

Then, wire up an onclick for the link in the paragraph. The actual link's href attribute will be used, so that if the script fails for some reason, the browser will still take and use the link value.

```
$(document).ready(function(){
    $('body').append('<div id="ajax-div"></div>');
    $('p a').click(function(e){
        var x = $(this).attr('href');
    });
})
```

Now, so far none of this is even technically Ajax, unless DOM manipulation and event handlers are added to the more broad definition. The actual Ajax in jQuery is the following line of code:

```
$('#ajax-div').load(x);
```

Which says, simply, load x into the <div> with the ID of #ajax-div (**FIGURE 3.10**). It doesn't get much easier than that. So, the final script, with an additional line of code that prevents the user, who just clicked the link, from being sent to the other page, is:

```
$(document).ready(function(){
    $('body').append('<div id="ajax-div"></div>');
    $('p a').click(function(e){
        var x = $(this).attr('href');
        $('#ajax-div').load(x);
        e.preventDefault();
    });
})
```

jQuery also includes methods that perform HTTP get and post operations, complete with error handlers and callback functions. Frameworks can be real timesavers.

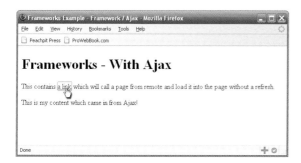

FIGURE 3.10 A framework can make Ajax easy.

Frameworks in a Nutshell

The bottom line is that the decision to use a framework should be a reasoned and thought-out decision, just like any other software choice. Frameworks are written by people, and despite the large numbers of testers and contributors, bugs do surface and they are difficult to troubleshoot due to the complex nature of their code bases. There are frequently workarounds, however, due to the vast number of ways the same tasks can be accomplished with these powerful tools. There are pros and cons, and sometimes the con of a large code base for a few simple effects is just not worth the extra bandwidth and downloads. Again, it is best to make a reasoned decision.

It's obvious that modern JavaScript programming has come a long way from the simple tricks and copy-paste scripts of the 1990s. Today's Web sites are being built with a keen attention to separation of content from presentation, and this separation is hobbled if the behavior layer of JavaScript is intermingled with the other front-end code. Scripts are becoming more mature, including Ajax and W3C DOM-based code as opposed to proprietary browser-specific code. Code can be isolated and reused in external files and even cleaned up using an independently tested and constantly evolving JavaScript framework.

In the end, however, a Web team should weigh the advantages of a scripting framework against its own site's and team's needs. This will determine the best approach—the one the team should stick with to avoid the inconsistencies of days past.

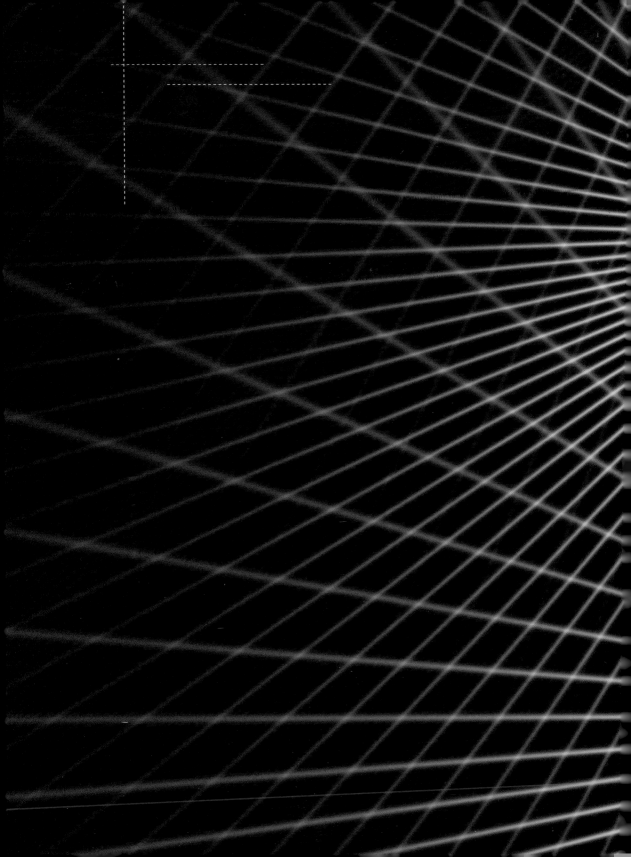

4

Developing Web Software Applications

Professional Web teams build Web sites not only to serve static content but also to serve dynamic applications and sites from Content Management Systems (CMS). These should employ user interface (UI)-layer code, further subdivided into markup, CSS, and JavaScript. The importance of this is magnified the larger the Web site or the longer the duration between major site overhauls. Why not reduce dependence on backend programmers or CMS experts, when the UI coders could largely manage UI changes themselves?

Add the challenge of integration with third parties and older and newer Web properties from across a Web enterprise, and you'll see there are endless aspects that can benefit from Web standards. In fact, anything within end-user interface has code that should be implemented using Web standards-based techniques.

Web Apps Stuck in the Past

Many Web application developers learned HTML in the 1990s and haven't updated their coding techniques to incorporate lessons learned since then. It can be an interesting experience to share new levels of separation and strict adherence to a standard or specification with an application developer who's grown tired of the tag soup of yesteryear. Modern standards-based approaches are much cleaner, more efficient and logical, and tend to appeal to software engineers' sense of "either it works or it doesn't"—often reviving their interest in front-end development.

By definition, standards-compliant Web sites strive for strict adherence wherever possible. When Web-based software intersects with or even produces UI layer code, the same levels of discipline should be expected. This benefits the site and the application in the long run by reducing the risks that come with a number of software modifications. Web standards-based approaches increase compatibility and accessibility, and reduce resources and efforts required to change the UI of the application or the static portions of a site alike.

The problem is that there is a huge amount of archaic, undisciplined, or just downright old-school code being implemented where Web software is concerned. We need to take a comprehensive look at custom-developed, in-house software and commercial product implementations to evaluate how and when sites' software can benefit from Web standards.

Software Quality and Inventory Analysis

In order to determine the nature of the situation, each and every piece of Web software employed in a project should be inventoried, cataloged, and evaluated for compliance (or noncompliance) with Web standards.

Web Application Development Problems

From a Web standards perspective, the trouble usually surfaces where the application developers need to create their UI layer—in the areas of maintenance, redesigns, subtle design tweaks, and of course accessibility and browser compatibility.

Typically, a Web programmer is either dropping code into templates provided by a design team or attempting to match a look and feel demonstrated in static representations of their application. There are also software packages that generate UI code with different levels of customization available. And, of course, application programmers writing their own front-end code will achieve varying degrees of standards compliance—some are quite successful and adept; others are not.

A multifaceted problem, of course, but the point is that application frameworks, education materials, generated code, and tools are seriously lacking in best-practices demonstrations. Many developers rely on some form of integrated development environment (IDE), code libraries, or copied code that may or may not follow any sort of best practices.

The results are backend code that produces ugly markup with inline presentation, table-based layouts, extra unnecessary markup, and front-end scripts that conflict, are browser specific, or don't take into account other front-end scripts. Design changes become a real problem—and they don't need to be.

The UI layer is either generated by human effort or it's generated by software (with little effort) and blindly accepted by humans.

But how much effort? Since today's application engineers, server platforms, and tools don't typically create standards-based front-end code by default, the quality is all over the board. It takes a certain amount of effort to achieve standards-compliance on the front end of applications and content management. By establishing a set of best practices for the UI code in server-side software applications, we have something against which software can be evaluated for improvement.

It's important to acknowledge that there is a real tradeoff between solving a problem that will eliminate issues later and simply trying to get the product out the door. Striving for Web standards-based UIs will, in the long run, reduce risk by pulling apart the layers of application logic, presentation, and UI. However, sometimes it takes time to get there.

Evaluation Criteria

For each document within an application, a series of questions or evaluation criteria should be considered:

❖ Where does the UI layer come from?

❖ How is the front-end code structured?

❖ Does it use valid HTML or XHTML?

❖ Is there a DOCTYPE declaration and is the document rendered in standards or quirks mode?

❖ How are presentation aspects declared?

❖ Do the application developers understand the UI code?

❖ Do the UI programmers understand the backend code?

❖ How many staff members understand how the UI and the backend are integrated?

❖ How is markup generated?

❖ Does the software reference any current presentation code, such as CSS files? If so, which files? Are those files changing in a redesign?

❖ How tied to the backend business logic, if at all, is the front-end code?

❖ Is there any way to abstract the UI code from application code?

❖ If the application generates front-end code, is there any way to control how?

❖ If users have the ability to generate content or code, is there a way to lock down what they can do?

❖ What is the level of effort involved in UI layer modifications?

❖ What is the risk to the application of UI layer modifications?

❖ What are the potential hazards or drawbacks of not redesigning the application?

❖ What are the limitations of how third-party software may need to be customized?

Clearly, there is an enormous amount of information to be collected, evaluated, and weighed.

Can Applications Be Updated?

In the end, aspects of some software may be beyond help. There may simply be no way to bring them up to date with the latest Web standards front-end code, either due to architectural issues or unacceptable risk. In these cases, the efforts become an exercise in compromise. Either there needs to be a long-term plan to resolve the issues or both the users and the business will just have to suffer through painful update processes.

This is essentially a tradeoff between short-term effort and risk, and long-term effort and risk. Some partial solutions include either an implementation of some styles (even extracts from or specific CSS files) or a superficial re-creation of the look and feel for a given application. In the long run, though, the organization suffers because it will become more difficult to apply changes to applications that become special cases and need to be evaluated every time a change is made. The critical turning point varies by organization.

Guidelines, Rules, and Web Standards

An organization's Web applications can benefit from establishing standards, coding guidelines, and interaction points and references for the way the UI code should be written and styled.

Rules To Code By

These are coding-quality and consistency standards much like those frequently placed on application developers; however, they now extend to their front-end code, which may be a new thing.

❖ Any UI code should be built following basic Web standards-based best practices involving the use of POSH, CSS, and unobtrusive JavaScript (as described in Chapters 1, 2, and 3 respectively).

❖ Browser independence, accessibility, and graceful degradation are key.

❖ Programs should reference UI CSS classes and IDs by pulling them from deep within application logic to reachable points in the code, so that making changes to the presentation information poses minimal risk to the application. These CSS classes and IDs might be superficial properties of object classes, stored in configuration files, or application-level variables, so they can easily be changed later.

❖ Avoid inline presentation styles or attributes at all costs.

❖ Collaborate on JavaScript applications with front-end coders to share scripts as much as possible and avoid conflicts.

❖ Distill the applications to the most simple and semantic markup possible.

❖ Create basic, standard CSS rules for forms so that when new ones are added, they can have CSS applied without effort.

By following these guidelines and adopting clean, separated, Web standards-based code, you will ensure that applications and business-critical software won't need significant or risky modifications when a redesign is required.

Unfortunately, these sorts of guidelines can only go so far with software packages, tool kits, and code generated by IDEs or WYSIWYG editors. These tools let authors go only so far to remove inline presentation settings, push the settings into CSS classes, and so on. It may take some effort to examine alternative settings or experiment with one feature over another to get the tools to do what needs to be done. However, there are often simple steps to decouple application logic from backend code.

Better Forms with Modern Markup

Most Web-based applications include some variety of forms. It is not uncommon for Web authors to use an HTML table to obtain a nice layout for these forms.

While there is nothing inherently wrong with this practice, tables are for tabular data. Here there is no tabular data and no reason for the table. There are also presentational attributes such as bgcolor, align, and width, and no accessibility gains from any modern Web standards-based approaches. Additionally, often this form will include some server-side code to populate the values of the form (more on that later).

For example, here is a table being used to display a very simple data form (**FIGURE 4.1**):

FIGURE 4.1 Forms are typically coded using HTML tables and presentational markup.

```
<p>Please complete the following form:</p>
<p><b>User Information</b></p>
<form action="submit.php" method="post">
<table width="300" border="0">
<tr>
   <td bgcolor="#cccccc" width="30%" align="right">First Name:</td>
   <td><input type="text" name="txtFName" size="30" /></td>
</tr>
<tr>
   <td bgcolor="#cccccc" align="right">Last Name:</td>
   <td><input type="text" name="txtLName" size="30" /></td>
</tr>
<tr>
   <td bgcolor="#cccccc" align="right">Title:</td>
   <td><input type="text" name="txtTitle" size="30" /></td>
</tr>
<tr>
   <td colspan="2"><input type="submit" value="Go" /></td>
</tr>
</table>
</form>
```

Consider a newer version of code for essentially the same form (**FIGURE 4.2**):

```
<p>Please complete the following form:</p>

<form action="submit.php" method="post">
<div id="formBlock">
   <fieldset>
   <legend>User Information</legend>
   <p>
      <label for="txtFName">First Name:</label>
      <input type="text" id="txtFName" tabindex="1" />
   </p>
   <p>
      <label for="txtLName">Last Name:</label>
      <input type="text" id="txtLName" tabindex="2" />
   </p>
   <p>
      <label for="txtFName">Title:</label>
      <input type="text" id="txtTitle" tabindex="3" />
   </p>
   <p><input type="submit" value="Go" tabindex="4" /></p>
   </fieldset>
</div>
</form>
```

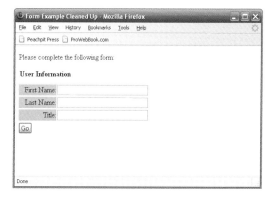

FIGURE 4.2 Modern markup makes it very easy to code simple forms.

The above can be paired with the following CSS, which could be applied to every form on a site to make them all follow the same setup. While this might seem like extra code, setting up a consistent way that forms are to be marked and styled, external to the program, is a huge benefit.

```css
h1 {
   margin: 0;
   font-weight: normal;
   font-size: 15px;
}
#formBlock {
   width: 300px;
}
#formBlock p {
   margin: 0 0 3px;
}
p {
   width: 100%;
}
label {
   background-color: #ccc;
   display: block;
   float: left;
   width: 28%;
   text-align: right;
   margin-right: 2px;
   padding: 2px 0;
}
input {
   float: left;
   width: 65%;
   margin-bottom: 4px;
   margin-top: 1px;
   padding: 1px;
}
input[type=submit] {
   width: 10%;
}
fieldset {
   border: none;
   padding: 0;
   margin: 0;
}
legend {
   font-weight: bold;
   margin-bottom: 12px;
}
```

Looking at the new XHTML standards-based approach reveals several fundamental enhancements over forms created without a semantic approach:

❖ There is no longer a meaningless HTML table required for the markup of the form.

❖ The form now features `<label>` elements that associate the text label with the actual form control—a great accessibility and, in general, user-centric feature supported by most browsers.

❖ A tabindex is applied, to facilitate a tabbing order and increased keyboard accessibility.

❖ The form is grouped into a `<fieldset>` and labeled with a `<legend>`, which groups and explains the form for greater accessibility.

❖ Because it is a much cleaner piece of code, the form itself, which is bound to be tweaked by the application developers, is much easier to read and modify.

Server-Side Frameworks and Template Tools

Several Web scripting technologies have been around for some time, including PHP (PHP: Hypertext Preprocessor), Classic ASP (Active Server Pages), and Adobe (formerly Macromedia) ColdFusion, to name a few popular ones. These language platforms for server-side tasks have models that put front-end alongside backend code in the same files. On one line, authors will see programming logic inside technologies delimiters (examples include <%...%> and the like), and then the following line will have standard HTML. Additionally, the server-side code will use `print` statements to output HTML, oftentimes with inline presentation information.

There are also frameworks and coding techniques—such as the ColdFusion Fusebox (fusebox.org) framework and the PHP Smarty templating system (http://smarty.php.net)—that modularize these layers, attempting to pull the logic and front end apart, creating template files that include front-end code while the backend code is in different sets of files. In reality, the results are often mixed, because the bottom line is that the server-side code still must output a UI.

The question in the end is this: What is the quality of the markup for the UI even with it separated from business logic? All the application software tiers in the world will not help if the basic HTML code violates best practices or resides in files that the UI developers can't control or wade through.

Simple Steps to Better Server-Side Scripts

All frameworks or templating systems aside, some simple steps can be taken to limit the potential damage even with a barebones PHP or similar environment. In the most basic sense, any application data output or UI code being generated would be subject to the same rules that pertain to UI code that has nothing to do with databases. The only difference is that such code is simply generated, as opposed to coded by hand.

It should be noted that the challenges involved in producing clean separation of server-side business logic and presentation layers are not unique to PHP, as most server-side languages depend on good programming practices and discipline. PHP, "Classic ASP," and ColdFusion in particular share the characteristics of the application logic frequently being embedded into the same files as the front end.

```php
<?php
// Printing results out
echo "<table border=\"1\" width=\"400\">";
while ($row = mysql_fetch_assoc($result)) {
    echo "<tr valign=\"top\">";
    echo "<td bgcolor=\"#ffffcc\"><b>$row['username']</b></td>";
    echo "<td>$row['firstname']</td>";
    echo "<td>$row['lastname']</td>";
    echo "<td><font color=\"grey\">$row['notes']</font></td>";
    echo "</tr>";
}
echo "</table>";
?>
```

The preceding code does a simple thing in PHP: It iterates through rows in a data set returned from a database query. Most scripting languages like this have similar techniques for outputting database results with looping structures. Obviously this is a small and simple example, but it could be buried inside other looping structures or complex business logic.

There are drawbacks to the above PHP (and to other similar server-side code):

❖ Inline presentation elements are buried inside of the looping iteration.

❖ Design changes require changes to the application. A programmer may need to be involved, instead of having it be a CSS change external to the application.

❖ Any time there needs to be a change to the way the table looks, a programmer must locate the presentation code and make the modification directly inline inside the application logic.

❖ The presentation attributes are escaped because of the quoted attributes in HTML, making the code difficult to manage.

❖ The presentation aspects must be applied manually to every table on the site.

While simple, this example demonstrates intermingling of code with presentation attributes. Imagine that the results were in nested tables just to create borders and menus, and there were different presentation attributes per column… the code would begin to get quite hairy. A cleaner alternative is:

```
<style type="text/css">
#results {
   border: 1px solid #000;
   width: 400px;
}
#results td {
   border: 1px inset #000;
   vertical-align: top;
}
td.username {
   background-color: #ffc;
}
td.notes {
   color: gray;
}
</style>
<?php
echo "<table id=\"results\">";
while ($row = mysql_fetch_assoc($result)) {
   echo "<tr>";
   echo "<td class=\"username\">$row['username']</td>";
   echo "<td>$row['firstname']</td>";
   echo "<td>$row['lastname']</td>";
   echo "<td class=\"notes\">$row['notes']</td>";
   echo "</tr>";
}
echo "</table>";
?>
```

While this shows only the CSS in a `<style>` block for convenience, it demonstrates that to change the look of the table and the alignment of the table cell content or font settings, not a single line of PHP would need to be touched. A rudimentary example, to be sure, but the point is clear: The more complex the business logic, the more benefit to the application logic in not having inline presentation information.

> **NOTE**
>
> In the table above, the ideal solution would also include a row with `<th>` element table headers to label the columns. This is an added accessibility benefit, as well as more semantic. If the design does not call for the headers to be displayed, they can be hidden with some creative CSS, while still making them available to assistive technologies.

The Problem

The benefit of technologies such as PHP or even Classic ASP is that the Web programmer has full control over the UI code being produced—an advantage that shouldn't be undervalued. Upkeep and maintenance of an application's user interface can get difficult in a team environment, where it is possible that the UI code was not written by the programmer. In these cases, communication and simple iterations of review are critical. Obviously, these are business procedures as opposed to a coding technique, but these critical processes often do not happen.

The problem is, in today's world there are many newer products and technologies gaining wide acceptance, which make reviews and UI development involvement in the backend phases harder than ever. For complex business applications, scripting languages like those discussed so far have fallen out of favor in some circles because the framework itself doesn't impose layered application architectures. The onus is on the programmers to follow structured design patterns that enforce good programming practices. Older tools such as PHP and ColdFusion were often more accessible to UI designers or developers than some of the newer technologies.

The fundamental problem remains, or has even gotten worse, in most new server-side coding environments. It can apply whether it is inline server-side scripting such as PHP or Classic ASP, or now ASP.NET, which has a layered approach that attempts to separate business logic and backend code. It can also come up where XSLT is being used to generate XHTML or HTML from XML.

So, what is this fundamental problem? While the software engineers were building with more mature and tiered backend to front-end environments such as Java, ASP.NET, or XML/XSLT, the front-end designers and developers don't know the front-end portions of these software environments—*and frequently never will.*

Typically the front-end portions of these software platforms just output the same bad legacy nonstandard code for the front end that they always have. The challenge is in pushing Web standards into the front end of these applications.

Beware Server-Generated Code

Some more modern application environments have features designed to help remove the "burden" of generating HTML or other UI code from the application developers' plate. The concept is that HTML (or XHTML) can be easily abstracted and then dynamically generated by commands passed into the programming language of the tool kit. These are usually properties assigned to data sets being returned from database queries, or other similar structures that control the dynamic output.

The problem with this is that both the design and the ultimate code that is outputted are largely at the mercy of the writers of the software framework that abstracts and generates the code. Success also depends on the level of effort put in by the programmer to exploit whatever UI features are available. Different frameworks have different levels of quality. Authors will need to "view-source" and actually observe how the markup code is structured when it is output as opposed to just how it looks, because the markup is dynamically generated.

Nothing can replace the human element in most cases. It just takes that extra step of seeing what the code is doing and figuring out how to mold it. Sometimes there are things that can be done; sometimes there aren't. Having made it this far into this book, it should be obvious that getting the front end standards-compliant can be a significant benefit.

Microsoft ASP.NET Framework

One framework that has gained massive adoption, particularly in large commercial enterprises, is Microsoft's critically acclaimed ASP.NET framework (the successor to "Classic" ASP). The .NET foundation classes, objects, and APIs are powerful.

ASP.NET enforces, by its model, layers of code that abstract database and program logic to a degree from "front end" files with the ASPX extension. These files are HTML and custom ASP.NET tags, which will be discussed later. In theory, UI coders learn these tags to control the front end with hooks for the programmers to use. This is certainly a possibility, but in reality is rarely done. The Web team would need to make a conscious decision to educate the UI team and collaborate on these efforts, and the UI team would have to be willing to learn. It could happen.

Typically, ASP.NET Web applications are created in an IDE called Microsoft Visual Studio.NET. This IDE has a WYSIWYG window that complements the programming view and allows programmers to rapidly drag form objects onto pages and set properties, including presentation attributes, without writing a line of code. These settings generate HTML.

Not That We're Picking on ASP.NET

In fact, quite the contrary. The following examples demonstrate the power and versatility of ASP.NET and similar application platforms in the hands of someone who knows how to nudge the software to produce Web standards-based code. Many such frameworks exist and most offer ways to tweak the front-end output, but it takes that extra effort to get it there and locate the features that help generate high-quality front-end code.

Platform to platform, the concepts are very much the same. The point is, a little extra effort, taking the time to understand what is being output other than "does it look right superficially," allows users, your business, and everyone to win. Application developers get pretty wound up in making their software work and often don't take those last steps. Of course, exceptions exist, but this section isn't targeted at those individuals.

From a Web standards standpoint, there are several issues that can be of concern with Visual Studio.NET, particularly versions earlier than 2005, and ASP.NET's server-generated code:

❖ Most ASP.NET examples, which everyone learns from, feature bad code.

❖ Visual Studio.NET 2003 and earlier was notorious for (when a programmer entered this design mode) rewriting and reformatting the HTML of the page in question, even if it was created and carefully crafted in another application or plain text editor by a UI coder.

❖ Form inputs and data controls can be ASP.NET "tags," which frequently have presentation attributes applied to them. The code output is often not valid XHTML or HTML code, although in version 2005 this situation improved greatly. These tag attributes output a massive amount of inline presentational attributes if the author does not make the extra effort to control the output.

❖ In versions 2003 and earlier, when an author uses the built-in tools to create a page, it creates HTML pages in quirks mode, because the DOCTYPE declaration applied to the document does not include a URI.

❖ ASP.NET features "adaptive rendering," which means the server makes decisions about what type of UI layer code to send to the Web browser based on server-side settings that "guess" the level of support a browser has for certain technologies.

❖ ASP.NET's server-side code makes great use of ID attributes on the controls
embedded in the page code. Frequently, depending on the context, these IDs
are dynamically renamed based on their location in the document, so CSS
and JavaScript authors may have difficulty referencing page objects by their
IDs even though that is the open, internationally recognized, standards-based
way of doing things. In some cases a CSS class might be more appropriate, or
trying to apply the required ID to a parent element and referencing the object
by context. Ideally, front-end designers and backend programmers will collaborate on setting UI IDs in the best way to leverage the strengths of both front-
end code and backend code—but this is not always the case.

It is interesting to note, however, that even these concerns can be mitigated with
some extra effort, time, and attention to the front-end aspects of the code.

TIP

One way to cope with "adaptive rendering" is to set the ClientTarget settings to
"Uplevel," so ASP.NET will stop assuming the only browser with any advanced
features is Internet Explorer and will send advanced code to everyone. However,
this can open up trouble with regard to some features, particularly ASP.NET 1.1
JavaScript features, which might only be supported by IE because Microsoft
wrote browser-specific code in some places. Be aware, and carefully test before
deploying ASP.NET solutions. Further, these features changed slightly in ASP.NET
2.0—another reason to test early and often.

BIG IMPROVEMENTS IN ASP.NET 2.0

In both ASP.NET 2.0 and Visual Studio.NET 2005, Microsoft made strong
commitments to make the generated code both more standards-compliant
and more accessible. Another improvement is that the new version of the IDE
rewrites much less code when in design view.

The controls and form code generated automatically by Visual Studio.NET
and the ASP.NET framework are generally XHTML Transitional-compliant by
the strict nature of the specification. However, the programmer must still go
to the extra effort of avoiding inline presentation attributes and making code
more accessible. In some cases there are better controls to use than others,
offering more flexibility in the code being output. The options to do this
improved in ASP.NET 2.0.

ASP.NET Data Output

Like other languages, ASP.NET features database output; however, one way
Microsoft implements this is through its server-side tags. These tags all have
presentation-related attributes that allow the programmer to control the XHTML
presentation aspects of the output. Here is a typical sample of controls using
an ASP.NET feature called a DataGrid control to output a table of items from a
database. This code is embedded in an ASPX file surrounded by the rest of the
document's (X)HTML (**FIGURE 4.3**).

FIGURE 4.3 An ASP.
NET DataGrid control
displaying data.

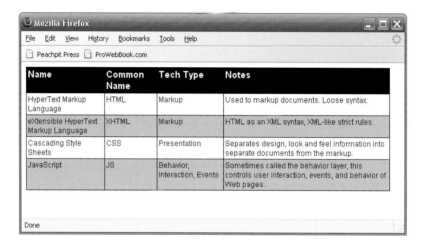

```
<asp:DataGrid ID="catalog" runat="server" AutoGenerateColumns="false"
   CellPadding="2" Width="600" BorderColor="black">
   <ItemStyle Font-Names="Arial" Font-Size="12px"
      ForeColor="#800000" VerticalAlign="top" />
   <AlternatingItemStyle Font-Names="Arial" Font-Size="12px"
      ForeColor="#400000" BackColor="#cccccc" />
   <HeaderStyle Font-Bold="true" Font-Names="Arial" Font-Size="15px"
      ForeColor="white" BackColor="black" VerticalAlign="top" />
   <Columns>
      <asp:BoundColumn DataField="Name" HeaderText="Name" />
      <asp:BoundColumn DataField="abbr" HeaderText="Common Name" />
      <asp:BoundColumn DataField="typeof" HeaderText="Tech Type" />
      <asp:BoundColumn DataField="notes" HeaderText="Notes" />
   </Columns>
</asp:DataGrid>
```

This describes a data output table including alternating row colors. The attributes
that describe the look and feel of the table are just some of the options that are

available; the options are in fact extensive. The source of the data coming back is in another layer of code, an ASP.NET feature for separating data and presentation, which is, in theory a great idea. Here is the code the above sample generates:

```
<table cellspacing="0" cellpadding="2" rules="all" border="1"
id="catalog" style="border-color:Black;width:600px;border-collapse:
collapse;">
    <tr valign="top" style="color:White;background-color:Black;
font-family:Arial;font-size:15px;font-weight:bold;">
    <td>Name</td><td>Common Name</td><td>Tech Type</td><td>Notes
</td>
    </tr><tr valign="top" style="color:Maroon;font-family:Arial;
font-size:12px;">
    <td>HyperText Markup Language</td><td>HTML</td><td>Markup
</td><td>Used to markup documents. Loose syntax.</td>
    </tr><tr valign="top" style="color:#400000;background-
color:#CCCCCC;font-family:Arial;font-size:12px;">
    <td>eXtensible HyperText Markup Language</td><td>XHTML
</td><td>Markup</td><td>HTML as an XML syntax, XML-like strict
rules.</td>
    </tr><tr valign="top" style="color:Maroon;font-family:Arial;
font-size:12px;">
    <td>Cascading Style Sheets</td><td>CSS</td><td>Presentation
</td><td>Separates design, look and feel information into separate
documents from the markup.</td>
    </tr><tr valign="top" style="color:#400000;background-
color:#CCCCCC;font-family:Arial;font-size:12px;">
    <td>JavaScript</td><td>JS</td><td>Behavior, Interaction, Events
</td><td>Sometimes called the behavior layer, this controls user
interaction, events, and behavior of Web pages.</td>
    </tr>
</table>
```

The table is simple, with alternating colors and font family settings, and nicely uses CSS as opposed to <font> tags. However, this is a common sample of the code used in tutorials in describing DataGrid use. The CSS gets repeated inline within the generated code due to the use of the ASP.NET tagging attributes such as ForeColor, BackColor, and others. Additionally, the top row of content, which is intended to be a header row, is simply contained in <td> elements and is set as bold.

It is a shame, because ASP.NET does in fact feature the ability to assign CSS classes for most of these values, and in ASP.NET 2.0 there are features to generate <th> elements for headers. The CssClass attribute is available for most tags and there are others that allow classes to be assigned to tags in many scenarios. Note the UseAccessibleHeader attribute of the <DataGrid> element used below. It's too bad that programmers have to go out of their way to intentionally make the code accessible, but that is the nature of the beast—and it's fortunate the features are there in ASP.NET 2.0.

Here are the small adjustments that can be made to the ASP.NET code to improve the quality of the output:

```
<asp:DataGrid ID="catalog" runat="server" AutoGenerateColumns="false"
    CssClass="grid-class" UseAccessibleHeader="true">
    <ItemStyle CssClass="item" />
    <AlternatingItemStyle CssClass="item-alt" />
    <HeaderStyle CssClass="item-header" />
    <Columns>
        <asp:BoundColumn DataField="Name" HeaderText="Name" />
        <asp:BoundColumn DataField="abbr" HeaderText="Common Name" />
        <asp:BoundColumn DataField="typeof" HeaderText="Tech Type" />
        <asp:BoundColumn DataField="notes" HeaderText="Notes" />
    </Columns>
</asp:DataGrid>
```

Pair the above code with CSS such as

```
.grid-class {
    border: 1px solid black;
    width: 600px;
    border-collapse:collapse;
}
.grid-class td {
    vertical-align: top;
    padding: 2px;
    border: 1px solid black;
}
.item {
    font: 12px arial, sans-serif;
    color: #800;
}
th {
    font: bold 15px arial, sans-serif;
    background-color: black;
    color: white;
    vertical-align: top;
    text-align: left;
    padding: 2px;
}
```

```
.item-alt {
   font: normal 12px arial, sans-serif;
   background-color: #ccc;
}
```

In this case, the HTML table looks identical with a better, more Web standards approach to the same code. Here is the new XHTML output (**FIGURE 4.4**):

```
<table class="grid-class" cellspacing="0" rules="all" border="1"
id="catalog" style="border-collapse:collapse;">
   <tr class="item-header">
      <th scope="col">Name</th><th scope="col">Common Name</th>
<th scope="col">Tech Type</th><th scope="col">Notes</th>
   </tr><tr class="item">
      <td>HyperText Markup Language</td><td>HTML</td><td>Markup
</td><td>Used to markup documents. Loose syntax.</td>
   </tr><tr class="item-alt">
      <td>eXtensible HyperText Markup Language</td><td>XHTML
</td><td>Markup</td><td>HTML as an XML syntax, XML-like strict
rules.</td>
   </tr><tr class="item">
      <td>Cascading Style Sheets</td><td>CSS</td><td>Presentation
</td><td>Separates design, look and feel information into separate
documents from the markup.</td>
   </tr><tr class="item-alt">
      <td>JavaScript</td><td>JS</td><td>Behavior, Interaction,
Events</td><td>Sometimes called the behavior layer, this controls
user interaction, events, and behavior of Web pages.</td>
   </tr>
</table>
```

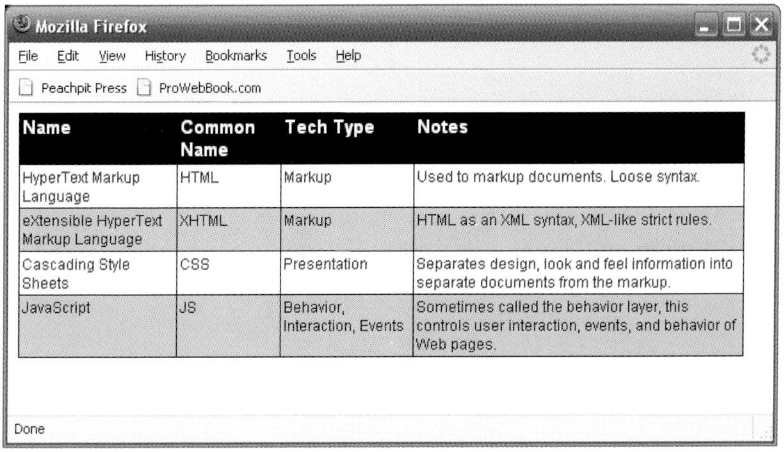

Name	Common Name	Tech Type	Notes
HyperText Markup Language	HTML	Markup	Used to markup documents. Loose syntax.
eXtensible HyperText Markup Language	XHTML	Markup	HTML as an XML syntax, XML-like strict rules.
Cascading Style Sheets	CSS	Presentation	Separates design, look and feel information into separate documents from the markup.
JavaScript	JS	Behavior, Interaction, Events	Sometimes called the behavior layer, this controls user interaction, events, and behavior of Web pages.

FIGURE 4.4 The same ASP.NET **<DataGrid>**, with standards-based enhancements, looks the same.

Note the addition of the <th> tags (complete with a scope attribute), CSS classes on most elements including the alternating rows of color, and lack of (most) inline presentation. While the code is not perfect, it is a great improvement, with a small technique to improve the output. This sort of improvement requires front-end coders with knowledge of the backend, or backend programmers who know the front end.

There are a dozen or more options for tags to output ASP.NET database code. Sometimes, another tag altogether might be a better option because there is more control over what UI code is being produced. For instance, a Repeater control is a great choice for simple data output, as it defines an output loop with small templates of code an author can specifically set as she or he sees fit:

```
<asp:Repeater id="catalog" runat="server">
<HeaderTemplate>
<table class="grid-class">
<tr>
    <th>Name</th>
    <th>Common Name</th>
    <th>Tech Type</th>
    <th>Notes</th>
</tr>
</HeaderTemplate>

<ItemTemplate>
<tr class="item">
    <td><%#Container.DataItem("name")%> </td>
    <td><%#Container.DataItem("abbr")%> </td>
    <td><%#Container.DataItem("typeof")%> </td>
    <td><%#Container.DataItem("notes")%> </td>
</tr>
</ItemTemplate>

<AlternatingItemTemplate>
<tr class="item-alt">
    <td><%#Container.DataItem("name")%> </td>
    <td><%#Container.DataItem("abbr")%> </td>
    <td><%#Container.DataItem("typeof")%> </td>
    <td><%#Container.DataItem("notes")%> </td>
</tr>
</AlternatingItemTemplate>

<FooterTemplate>
</table>
```

```
</FooterTemplate>
</asp:Repeater>
```

The above code generates an HTML table as follows, and, paired with the same CSS as in the first example, is fairly clean, and free of even more unnecessary inline presentation attributes. While it is a little more code in terms of the Repeater tags, it does give more control of the output (**Figure 4.5**).

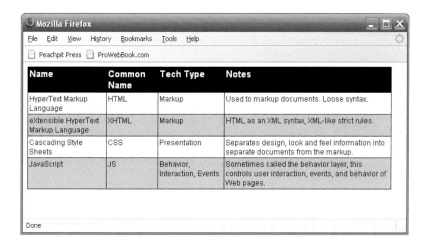

FIGURE 4.5 Using an ASP.NET Repeater control to render the same table with leaner code, while still looking the same.

```
<table class="grid-class">
<tr>
    <th>Name</th>
    <th>Common Name</th>
    <th>Tech Type</th>
    <th>Notes</th>
</tr>
<tr class="item">
    <td>HyperText Markup Language </td>
    <td>HTML </td>
    <td>Markup </td>
    <td>Used to markup documents. Loose syntax. </td>
</tr>
<tr class="item-alt">
    <td>eXtensible HyperText Markup Language </td>
    <td>XHTML </td>
    <td>Markup </td>
    <td>HTML as an XML syntax, XML-like strict rules. </td>
</tr>
```

```
<tr class="item">
  <td>Cascading Style Sheets </td>
  <td>CSS </td>
  <td>Presentation </td>
  <td>Separates design, look and feel information
     into separate documents from the markup. </td>
</tr>
<tr class="item-alt">
  <td>JavaScript </td>
  <td>JS </td>
  <td>Behavior, Interaction, Events </td>
  <td>Sometimes called the behavior layer, this controls
     user interaction, events, and behavior of Web pages. </td>
</tr>
</table>
```

This is a clean example of HTML code generated from ASP.NET server-side logic, showing that reasoned application of the features does provide some control of the output.

Looking over the tag-based code, it is obvious why Microsoft's pulling the application logic into other files and using these front-end ASPX files with tags is not a bad concept. Some front-end teams could certainly manipulate and modify this code without having to learn C# or Visual Basic.NET.

ASP.NET HTML Controls, Web Controls, and More

There are some other areas where ASP.NET commonly generates UI code for the programmers. Instead of sticking to simple HTML tags, ASP.NET has features that output HTML tags and provide server-side access to the document in ways quite similar to the DOM, although with their own proprietary syntax. Examine the following screen and code (**FIGURE 4.6**):

```
<script runat="server">
void Clicker(Object sender, EventArgs e)
{
   Response.Redirect("http://www.cherny.com");
}
void Page_Load()
{
   if (!IsPostBack)
   {
     // Web Controls
     myLink.Text = "Pro Web Book Dot Com";
     myLink.NavigateUrl = "http://www.prowebbook.com";
```

```
      myLink.CssClass = "webControl";

      // HTML Anchor Controls
      myOtherLink.InnerText = "NavigationArts";
      myOtherLink.HRef = "http://www.navigationarts.com";
      myOtherLink.Attributes.Add("class","htmlControl");

      // Label Control
      myLabel.Text = "Hey Look! This span is meaningless!";

      // Literal Control
      myLiteral.Text = " (A Bad Link!)";

      // Paragraph HTML Control
      myPara.InnerHtml = "Pro Web Book " +
              "Links <strong>Rock!</strong>";

      // Paragraph HTML Control 2
      myPara2.Visible = false;
   }
}
</script>
<form id="form1" runat="server">
<ul>
   <li><asp:HyperLink runat="server" id="myLink" /></li>
   <li><a runat="server" id="myOtherLink" /></li>
   <li><asp:LinkButton Text="Click This"
        OnClick="Clicker" runat="server" /></li>
</ul>
<p><asp:Label id="myLabel" runat="server" /></p>
<p id="myPara" runat="server" />
<p id="myPara2" runat="server">This will be hidden.</p>
</form>
```

FIGURE 4.6 Various ASP.NET server controls for outputting dynamic content.

There is a lot to look at here, to illustrate a number of different points:

- ❖ The whole thing must be a `<form>` element with `runat=server` in order to use the `<asp:LinkButton />` control. This control should be avoided if possible, as will be seen in a moment when the resulting XHTML is examined.

- ❖ Note the first ASP.NET server tag in the unordered list is in the form of `<asp:HyperLink />`. This is a Web Server Control that generates an HTML link and provides program access to all the attributes and text of the tag, as demonstrated in the `<script>` block above where the myLink references are located.

- ❖ Note the second link has no `href` attribute and is also programmatically controlled from the `<script>` block above. This is a server-side HTML control (note the `runat=server` attribute) that also allows programmatic access to the item's attributes. This grants more control over the output but fewer server-side features.

Adding an `ID` and the code `runat=server` to just about any HTML tag provides access to the tags, which is exceptionally powerful because programmers can control the tag's visibility, content, and attributes with a few lines of code, located at the programming layer.

Both link controls do virtually the same thing, and while the Web controls provide added features over and above the HTML controls, the Web control is less predictable and features presentation attributes frequently used by programmers after the quick fix. When using Web controls, programmers should try to stick to the `CssClass` attributes, avoid presentation attributes, and use HTML controls for greater predictability in the code output, unless it is necessary for the specific case.

Keep watching the paragraphs at the end of the document:

```
<p><asp:Label id="myLabel" runat="server" /></p>
<p id="myPara" runat="server" />
<p id="myPara2" runat="server">This will be hidden.</p>
```

These are all executed server-side as well.

The `<script>` is the server-side code that is not sent to the browser, and frequently this code is in a separate file altogether. It programmatically generates the following XHTML (aside from some other .NET code that is meaningless to this discussion):

```
<script type="text/javascript">
<!--
var theForm = document.forms['form1'];
if (!theForm) {
  theForm = document.form1;
}
function __doPostBack(eventTarget, eventArgument) {
  if (!theForm.onsubmit || (theForm.onsubmit() != false)) {
    theForm.__EVENTTARGET.value = eventTarget;
    theForm.__EVENTARGUMENT.value = eventArgument;
    theForm.submit();
  }
}
// -->
</script>
<ul>
  <li><a id="myLink" class="webControl" href="http://www.prowebbook.
com">Pro Web Book Dot Com</a></li>
  <li><a href="http://www.navigationarts.com" id="myOtherLink"
class="htmlControl">NavigationArts</a></li>
  <li><a href="javascript:__doPostBack('ctl00','')">Click This</a>
</li>
</ul>
<p><span id="myLabel">Hey Look! This span is meaningless!</span>
</p>
<p id="myPara">Pro Web Book Links <strong>Rock!</strong></p>
```

Some more observations about the code output:

❖ Note that there are several ways to output a simple link in ASP.NET: the first two as described above with Server and HTML controls and another that creates the third link, the `<asp:LinkButton />` control.

❖ The third link code generated above demonstrates why it is best to avoid using the `<asp:LinkButton />` control under most circumstances, as it produces an `href` attribute with a JavaScript link, which breaks every rule in this book.

❖ The `<asp:Label />` control used in the first paragraph above outputs a `<span>` for no reason. The label control is considered nice because programmers can assign presentation aspects to it, but it is possible to use the `<asp:Literal />` control instead, which outputs the lovely message "(A Bad Link!)" above. It is often claimed that one downside to using this control is that there are no presentation aspects for it—which is exactly why using it is a great idea.

❖ Programmers can also control the text of tags with HTML controls for paragraphs, as demonstrated by the paragraph above with the ID of myPara.

❖ Note that programmers can also hide and show HTML controls: The last paragraph in the server-side code is set to visible = false and not sent to the browser.

HTML controls offer ASP.NET code a lot of power, but for various reasons ASP. NET tutorials downplay their use. From a Web standards perspective, however, these are very powerful tools and often preferable to Web server controls.

ASP.NET REQUIRED READING FOR WEB STANDARDS

When developing ASP.NET code, it is not too difficult to come closer to a degree of professional Web standards. It is an exercise in making informed and intelligent decisions about the code style.

Microsoft has posted on its MSDN (Microsoft Developers Network) Web site an article to help authors convert to using ASP.NET's Web standards and accessibility features. This article should be required reading for all ASP.NET technologists; unfortunately, it is buried on the site and the techniques are not used in most of the ASP.NET examples online. The article can be found here:

http://msdn2.microsoft.com/en-us/library/aa479043.aspx

Finally, Microsoft has released some open-source code that builds on the extensible nature of ASP.NET, which allows authors to change the XHTML output from a number of the ASP.NET tags built into ASP.NET. The code is called the "ASP.NET 2.0 CSS Friendly Control Adapters" and can be found here:

www.asp.net/cssadapters/

With a little extra effort, the server-side code generated by ASP.NET can come fairly close to generating valid and accessible code.

Server-Side Collaboration with UI Designers

The bottom line is that programmers, developers, and designers should collaborate as closely as possible when programming server-side applications, to make sure the UI markup follows Web standards-based best practices. This often means picking the right tool on the server. Keep the UI out of the application and use classes and clean code; this keeps the design in the hands of the UI team, reducing risk and the potential need to involve a programmer just for a UI change. When applications are complex or based on older code bases, compromises may be necessary, but ultimate goals, standards, and guidelines should be set toward the goal of bringing consistency in the long run.

Content Management

When a Web site needs to be updated by nontechnical users, gets larger, or includes content that needs to be reused, cataloged, searched, or shared, the typical solution is content management software. Content management software is one of the most common Web applications that any Web development team will encounter. This is because it is a common solution to business users' request for more control over a site.

Unfortunately, content management applications often insist on producing their own markup or require a fair amount of effort to shoehorn into a Web standards-based world. Fortunately, this is often not as hard as it seems initially, at least with a decent content application. Honestly, the hard part is often determining where to look for the right pieces of code that actually generate output.

There are countless content management systems (CMS) of varying degrees of flexibility and Web standards compliance. The flexibility, from a standards perspective, depends on the nuances of the software's capabilities as well as the implementation, which is the responsibility of the Web team.

Baseline Content Management

The better CMS solutions allow a team to generate the UI code they want—as opposed to what the tool wants. There are a number of ways Web standards can assist with a content management solution:

❖ Abstracting content's presentation away from the content store

❖ Employing fewer CMS templates through effective use of CSS

❖ Reusing content, because its markup will not be presentation-specific

❖ Simplifying content authors' jobs, through fewer presentation aspects being required of them

❖ Expanding the ability of redesigns with less CMS team involvement

Content Management and Clean Content

The simple process of storing content in a central content repository, with clean markup, is in and of itself a good way to facilitate content reuse, because the markup will be simple and can be styled with CSS on different portions of pages based on context. Beyond that, here are some common best practices and scenarios involved in professional content management and design with CSS:

❖ Design with CSS based on context. For example, an article description can be rendered as an <h1> level header set in a large maroon font on the article page, but a smaller black font on the archive page, because the CSS can control that difference.

❖ Store content in as plain a format as possible. Use as few CSS classes as you can, and minimal if any presentation-specific element attributes.

❖ Stick to semantic markup alone, leaving the content marked up in a meaningful and portable format that can be styled and reused at will. Recall that expert CSS coders can apply different styles based on contextual position in the site template via an ID or class.

❖ Teach content authors only basic HTML structure tags. Ideally, content authors will need to learn few if any CSS classes. They just need to know that the first-level header in the content area is an <h1>. Or, that making a plain bulleted list will result in little icons for bullets, and the header in the related content region on the right is dark blue. Design can all be applied via CSS and not stored in the CMS content repository. Content authors can concentrate on content, not design.

❖ Context on a given page is a useful tool, but context within a site can be equally important. A common design scenario these days involves different sections of a site having different color themes extended from the primary brand. Content itself, stored in a database, does not need to know these things, and should be portable between site sections. CSS can be driven from a <body> tag class or ID set by site section, which can toggle different color themes down through all semantic tags for that portion of the site.

Content Management Output and Modules

Content management tools can pose a challenge when it comes to figuring out how to control the output and produce standards-based code. The hard part is often determining where to start and whether the output *can* be controlled. Typically, a CMS outputs pages formatted with code sourced from one of several areas:

❖ Built-in modules that produce output based on proprietary features or out-of-the-box functionality

❖ Page-level templates used to display different types of pages

❖ Browser-based word processor-type editors (used by content authors)

The most challenging portions of a CMS application in terms of outputting valid standards-based code are often the built-in features over which a team has little to no control. The features to watch out for include what someone claimed to be the great thing about a tool since supposedly the tool can be installed and you have a Web site out of the box.

Risky portions can include

❖ Administrative modules embedded on public pages

❖ Traffic-tracking code or built-in scripts

❖ Advertising modules

❖ Anything that generates menus

❖ Special controls that might produce lists of content (like a News or product archive)

❖ Search results

> **TIP**
>
> Anything "out of the box" is suspect unless the tool has already been brought up to modern standards.

A powerful tool will let a Web team have access to the code that produces this output or insert custom modules that can replace or extend built-in functionality. Ideally, there are built-in templates or snippets of code that can be updated. Be especially wary of tools that claim to allow customization of the look and feel through some sort of control panel, unless it actually exposes code that can be modified.

Content Management Templates

Most CMS tools associate pages with templates, each of which is a reusable layout. Authors pick the correct template for the section or type of page. The more templates, the more the content authors need to keep track of—and the more confusing site maintenance becomes. Intelligent use of CSS and Web standards can actually mean fewer templates.

Templates are typically driven by the grid of the page, and this typically means different markup. In the Web standards and CSS world, this isn't necessarily the case.

Imagine a three-column layout such as what follows here (**FIGURE 4.7**):

```
<!DOCTYPE html PUBLIC "-//W3C//DTD XHTML 1.0 Strict//EN"
    "http://www.w3.org/TR/xhtml1/DTD/xhtml1-strict.dtd">

<html xmlns="http://www.w3.org/1999/xhtml" xml:lang="en" lang="en">
<head>
    <title>Template One</title>
    <link rel="stylesheet" type="text/css" href="style.css" />
</head>

<body class="typeA">

<div id="wrapper">
    <ul id="nav">
        <li><a href="...">Navigation 1</a></li>
        <li><a href="...">Navigation 2</a></li>
        <li><a href="...">Navigation 3</a></li>
        <li><a href="...">Navigation 4</a></li>
    </ul>
    <div id="content">
        <h1>Content Area</h1>
        <p>Lorem ipsum dolor sit amet, consectetuer adipiscing
            elit. Nam sit amet nulla. Ut ut urna ac lectus</p>
        <p>Ut ut urna ac lectus tincidunt sollicitudin. Sed rutrum
            interdum lorem. Integer aliquam pellentesque
            neque.</p>
        <p>Curabitur a neque a libero gravida dignissim. Sed
            eget tellus.</p>
    </div>
```

FIGURE 4.7 A three-column CMS template.

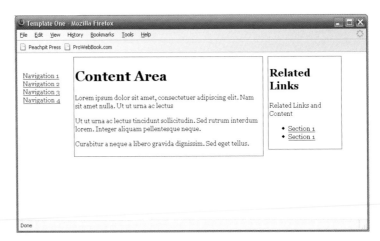

```
<div id="related">
   <h2>Related Links</h2>
   <p>Related Links and Content</p>
   <ul>
      <li><a href="">Section 1</a></li>
      <li><a href="">Section 1</a></li>
   </ul>
</div>
</div>

</body>
</html>
```

The above document sample has three `<div>` elements with IDs: nav, content, and related (or #nav, #content, and #related, in CSS selector terms). These can be easily styled with CSS to be three columns. The content inside of the #content and #related `<div>` elements might be created by a content author and is here represented by "Lorem ipsum" and the "Related Links and Content" text respectively. Furthermore, the related column link might even be generated dynamically server-side, based on content relationships, and there may be cases where this column is not needed.

Note the class on the `<body>` element. A content author might need to select this template in order to queue up a page with the appropriate number of columns. Program logic can tweak the `<body>` class of the document to restructure the page into navigation and a single column of content so multiple templates do not need to be created in the CMS tool, and so a content author does not need to select a different template (**FIGURE 4.8**).

FIGURE 4.8 With little change to the CSS, the same CMS template can do two columns.

```
<!DOCTYPE html PUBLIC "-//W3C//DTD XHTML 1.0 Strict//EN"
   "http://www.w3.org/TR/xhtml1/DTD/xhtml1-strict.dtd">

<html xmlns="http://www.w3.org/1999/xhtml" xml:lang="en" lang="en">
<head>
    <title>Template Two</title>
    <link rel="stylesheet" type="text/css" href="style.css" />
</head>

<body class="typeB">

<div id="wrapper">
    <ul id="nav">
        <li><a href="...">Navigation  1</a></li>
        <li><a href="...">Navigation  2</a></li>
        <li><a href="...">Navigation  3</a></li>
        <li><a href="...">Navigation  4</a></li>
    </ul>
    <div id="content">
        <h1>Content Area</h1>
        <p>Lorem ipsum dolor sit amet, consectetuer adipiscing
           elit. Nam sit amet nulla. Ut ut urna ac lectus</p>
        <p>Ut ut urna ac lectus tincidunt sollicitudin. Sed rutrum
           interdum lorem. Integer aliquam pellentesque
           neque.</p>
        <p>Curabitur a neque a libero gravida dignissim. Sed
           eget tellus.</p>
    </div>
    <div id="related">
    </div>
</div>

</body>
</html>
```

The #related <div> is collapsed and no content is output. At the CMS level,
changing the <body> class to typeB switches the page layout without changes to
the markup and means one less template than might otherwise be required. This
also preserves the separation of markup from presentation. Here is the style sheet
required:

```
body { font: normal .9em Georgia; }
body.typeB #related { display:none; }
body.typeB #content { width: 600px; }
```

```
#nav { list-style-type: none; width: 100px; float: left;
   margin: 30px 0 0 5px; padding: 0; }
#content { width: 400px; float: left; margin-left: 10px;
   border: 1px solid red; padding: 3px; }
#related { width: 150px; float: left;
   border: 1px solid red; margin-left: 10px;
   padding: 3px; }
```

Content management tools are just another software mechanism to deliver a Web site. They are a fact of life in larger organizations, and most are full-featured development platforms that can be leveraged to allow standards-based output, which can only help make a site more accessible or compliant. Whether the tool features raw output or content being transformed from XML with XSLT (eXtensible Stylesheet Language Transformations), the output should be clean and thought through. As a complement, effective use of Web standards can also reduce the number of CMS templates and make it easier to author content.

WYSIWYG for Content Authors

When working in Web content environments, most nontechnical content authors use some form of lower-end WYSIWYG software tool to help facilitate content entry. These tools can range from browser-based editors to tools like Adobe Contribute for simple site maintenance. They are not development platforms such as Adobe Dreamweaver or Microsoft Expression Web, and have far fewer features. Just like any other software, these tools have configuration options and varying degrees of Web standards compliance.

As a general rule, the strongest editor setup for content authors is one where as many formatting features as possible are disabled, because the formatting features rely on code that a Web team won't be able to control. Effective support for CSS is the key.

Browser-Based Editing

Browser-based editors have been around for a while. Microsoft first introduced an ActiveX-based editing component in Internet Explorer 4. Since then, native Java-Script support has been added and editors are usually script-based, Java-based, Flash-based, or ActiveX-based. Script-based components for browser-based editing are showing up with support in most modern Web browsers, including Safari and Opera. For widest compatibility, one of these should be chosen.

Unfortunately, out of the box these browser-based editors are not very robust. Internet Explorer outputs `<font>` tags and Mozilla generates inline styles. They render exactly what the browser can render, but the editor features must largely be built from the few hooks that are available in the browser's DOM. That being the case, it is exceptionally hard work to churn out a custom editor, although they are getting better every day. You can find a modern editor to create valid code and support CSS.

Editor Configuration

Web developers should take steps to prevent these browser-based editors from jeopardizing all the hard work that has gone into defining styles and coding standards for their sites. They may have to go so far as to integrate new user steps, or even new software.

Considerations include

❖ Perform reviews of the WYSIWYG editor's code output under a variety of situations. It's not unusual for these editors to generate invalid code; however, the marketplace is maturing, and many can output valid HTML or even XHTML with configuration changes.

❖ Some editor tools include a source-code view. This may need to be disabled or enabled depending on the skill levels of the authors. Some tools include a permission model, which can enable the source code view for some users and not for others.

❖ Features that control presentation should be limited. Disable features that control font face, font colors, and background colors. These should be controlled only from CSS.

❖ The editor should be able to apply CSS classes. A good editor will support association of a CSS file with the editor. Some will require developers to configure which items appear in the CSS class menus. The best will support context and only allow application of some classes based upon the CSS rules, such as not allowing a rule p.error to be applied to a <span>.

❖ Support for CSS class application should include some facility to apply CSS to specific elements. That is, it should be just as easy to apply a class to a <ul> as an <li> nested inside via a selection process of some form. A common way to enable this is a simple click to select DOM tree in the status bar (body > div > ul > li > a).

❖ CSS files that are associated with an editor may need to be an extract of the main CSS files because the rules may be too complex to be interpreted, and full context rules, such as <p> elements inside of #content as opposed to #related, might not be supported or possible. Depending on the editing context, multiple CSS files may be another solution.

❖ The editor should support basic XHTML semantic tags such as the built-in headers (1–6), paragraph formatting, at least two types of lists, blockquote, preformatted text, and addresses.

❖ A good editor will also strip garbage and invalid tags from content pasted from the clipboard, or have multiple options for cleaning pasted content. Often, content copied from word processors or Web pages will retain its formatting information when pasted into WYSIWYG editors. This information, when introduced into valid code, often invalidates it, and can modify styles that should be applied only from outside the content via the CSS.

❖ You may want to tell content authors that if their editing application won't strip invalid tags from incoming content, they should strip the formatting by pasting that content into a plain text editor prior to pasting into the WYSIWYG editor.

❖ Ideally, locate a browser-based editor that can support as many browsers as possible and achieve the above feature sets. It is not uncommon to find WYSIWYG editors configured only for IE; however, today editors are available for Windows and Mac OSX in just about every browser.

Following the above rules and evaluation criteria can mean the difference between creating a reliable, standards-complaint site and having a content editor program destroy a lot of hard work. The quality and performance of any editor program you've already got in production should be evaluated against these standards and modified to produce code that is as close to valid as possible.

Third Parties

Larger Web sites often need to propagate a certain look and feel to third-party sites or business applications hosted elsewhere, such as an Investor Relations site or perhaps a job board. These sites can be branded to look like the main site, and users are intended to not know that they have navigated to another site altogether.

Web standards-based approaches are ideal for such scenarios because not only can the artwork and scripts be hosted on the main corporate servers, but so can all the CSS files, or at least the CSS that controls the main look, feel, and corporate brand standards. In these cases, a company can have third parties link to some or all of the CSS files, and tweak them as necessary over time, with the changes showing up without hosting the third-party applications.

In such cases, you will probably need to provide the third parties with documentation of the correct style classes and image headers for certain design touches.

You should also supply sample code, with example templates that represent how the pages and designs should be built.

Just like any organization or software platform, however, third parties are going to have varying degrees of ability to accommodate a Web standards approach. For example, their platform may not be compatible with a corporate style sheet. In these cases, compromise may be necessary. Again, this may mean simple extracts of CSS files or creating different markup templates for the exceptions. In the long run, however, a transition plan should be considered and discussed with third-party vendors who can't keep up with the rest of the industry.

How To Approach Web Apps

A Web standards-based approach means a strict separation of content from presentation, so it follows that it also means the separation of business logic from presentation. Web teams building Web-based applications and software can benefit greatly from building their user interfaces with modern approaches that reference CSS as opposed to inline presentational attributes.

Less inline presentation means less to risk to business logic when design changes are pushed into software. Additionally, in a potentially complicated software environment it can mean that the expert front-end developers can help make these UI changes without having to update backend code or even involve backend programmers.

A challenge going forward is to know where to start to update Web applications and exploit the features of the technologies that are available. New features of Web standards-based techniques can be a powerful ally for a Web team both in Web applications built from the ground up and in commercial off-the-shelf content management tools.

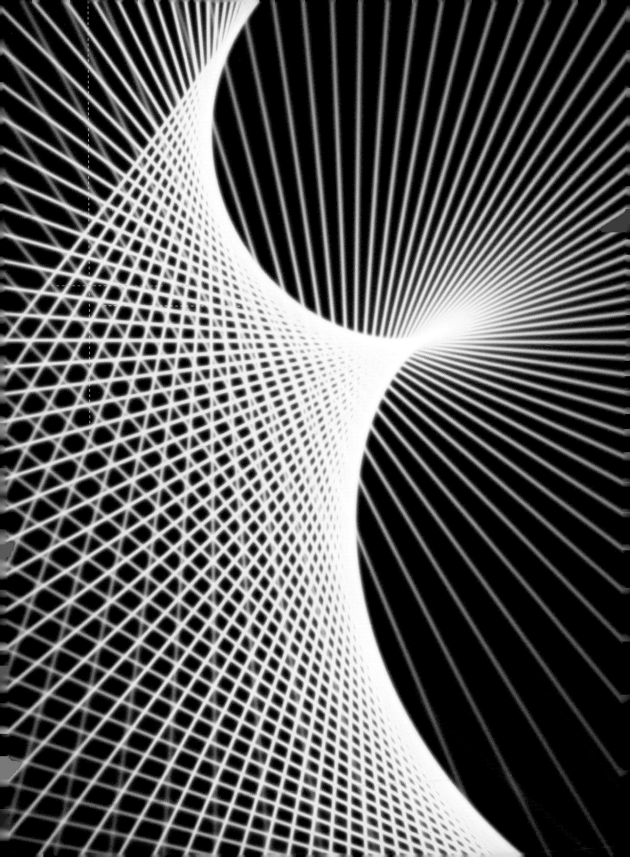

5

The Circle of Standards

If you're working for a multi-person organization, you're probably used to following rules: submitting timesheets, requesting time off, or following a project process are just a few.

But what about rules that guide the work you do? If you're a designer, you may be accustomed to following a style guide. Developers might have a set of coding practices they're asked to abide by. Do you have any rules—or standards—like this that you're asked to follow? If so—and be honest!—how often do you follow them?

Based on my own experience, I'd bet that you don't follow them as often as you should. Or, if you do follow your standards, you probably feel that others don't. Does this sound familiar?

From large corporations to small consultancies, a lack of standards and standards-compliance impedes Web development progress. Why is this? And what can be done to solve this problem?

Organizational Inertia

Let's assume that you already have some sort of standards—design or technical—in place. If you asked people why they don't follow the documented standards, what would they tell you (**FIGURE 5.1**)?

While it may seem that the people are negative, it's important for a manager to deduce the deeper problems (**FIGURE 5.2**).

FIGURE 5.1 What does it all mean?

FIGURE 5.2 The meaning behind the messages.

What's standing in the way of success is timely updates, regular communication, and constant reinforcement, so what you need is a strategy for maintaining the standards, communicating them appropriately, and ensuring their correct use.

And what if you don't have any standards? You may have more inertia to overcome than an organization that has something in place, but the same process will help you get in gear.

You may be skeptical, but I know from experience that change is possible. I saw it happen at AOL, where I worked on standards for five years. Its situation a few years ago may not be unlike yours today. AOL had some standards documented but they weren't complete, nor were they regularly updated. There was some management support for them, but that support was inconsistent. And there was little communication about the standards, which meant that only a fraction of the people were even aware of them.

All of that changed, thanks to the Circle of Standards.

Introducing the Circle

Instituting standards and getting people to embrace them is all about change. As any business student will tell you, effectively instituting change is all about managing organizational behavior. And what's the best way to manage change in organizational behavior? The answer is *process*.

The Circle of Standards (**FIGURE 5.3**) is a three-stage cycle that enables the successful adoption and continued implementation of standards by addressing their management, training and communication, and continual review—all of the problem points identified above.

FIGURE 5.3 The Circle of Standards.

The Quality Review Process

Standards Creation and Documentation

Training and Communication

The Standards Manager

To get things started, the standards process itself must have a champion within an organization. At the outset it's not always possible for the champion to devote full time to this role, but as standards become more and more important to the organization, it becomes increasingly important to the organization's management team to put someone in charge of standards—a standards manager.

Depending on the size and reporting structure of an organization, it's possible to have one person fulfill this role; however, I usually suggest a team of at least two people, even in the smallest organizations, for greater morale, workload balancing, and redundancy.

Putting together a standards-management team is especially necessary when managing standards for multiple disciplines (such as design and development). Having more than one person addressing standards allows each individual to focus on the standards that are most closely related to their area of expertise.

Here are a couple of sample organization charts for standards-management teams (**FIGURE 5.4**):

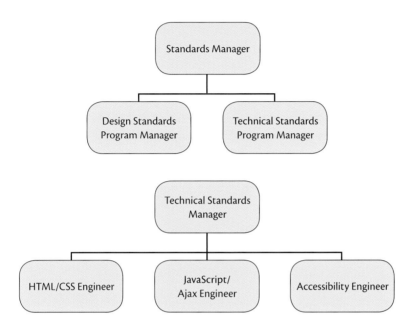

Figure 5.4 Typical standards-management teams.

Standards Creation and Documentation

The first and most important phase of this process is, of course, the creation and documentation of standards. The success of the training and review phases depends on this.

Merriam-Webster's online dictionary defines *standard* as "established by authority, custom, or general consent"; so some standards will be dictated (like branding), some will document current practices (like page layouts or choice of DOCTYPE), and the rest will be determined by interested parties who sit down to resolve issues (like whether to indent code with tabs or spaces).

Standards are best set by the appropriate party or decision process and then thoroughly documented by someone who pays excellent attention to detail.

If you want a complete set of standards, look at your organization from various perspectives, seeking to document the organization's needs from every angle, such as user experience and design (including user interface design, interaction design, and visual design); technical implementation (including front-end, middle-tier, and back-end coding); and potentially others including content (language style, imagery, and photography) and marketing.

To help an entire organization to at least start from the same baseline of standards, it's helpful to give everyone the same basic goals and rules. **TABLE 5.1** provides a brief checklist of suggested content for both design and technical portions of a project.

TABLE 5.1 A Standards-Based Content Checklist

For a design style guide	For front-end technical standards
Browser support matrix	Browser support matrix
Accessibility policy	Accessibility policy
Optimization guidelines	Optimization guidelines
Creative vision statement	Coding rules (syntax and style) for each language, including HTML, CSS, and JavaScript
Branding, including logo usage rules	Naming conventions and semantic model
Grids, page layouts, and dimensions	Standardized code snippets for common UI elements
Persistent page objects (like header, navigation, and footer)	Information on shared code libraries and APIs
Color palette and typography	Best-practice coding techniques
Content layouts and standard image sizes	
Interactive elements (links, forms, menus, wizards, dialog boxes, etc.)	
Multimedia design information	
Advertising considerations	

Note that the first three standards are shared between design and technical scenarios.

Getting started with creating and documenting standards can be easy or hard—all depending on where your organization stands currently with respect to standards. Here are a few scenarios:

The Full Glass Scenario

Everyone in your organization is pretty much on the same page (**FIGURE 5.5**). Overall, there is clear creative direction and good code consistency. What are you waiting for? Just do it! Start documenting the institutional knowledge. Peer reviews of the documentation can catch most problems, and a final review by a creative director or technical manager can garner the necessary management signoff. Post the information online and/or print it out, and your standards are official.

FIGURE 5.5 Glass Full.

The Glass Half Full Scenario

Most people in your organization care about standards and want to be on the same page, but things are a mess and no one knows where to start (**FIGURE 5.6**). Outsourcing would be beneficial in this case. Find a consultant who has experience in creating guidelines and standards documentation; he or she will ask the right questions to help your organization determine what standards are needed. If you have the budget, the consultant could also create your initial documentation, so you start with solid groundwork.

FIGURE 5.6 Glass Half Full.

The Empty Glass Scenario

Only a few people in your organization care about standards (**FIGURE 5.7**). There's a lack of creative vision or code consistency, and leadership isn't doing anything to help. In this case, pull together the most talented, engaged people you can find and start doing whatever you can. Evangelize your work to peers; demonstrate the benefits to management. As more and more people buy in to even small portions of your work, you'll find that they'll start to expect more. With that support, you can grow into one of the other two scenarios!

FIGURE 5.7 Glass Empty.

A NOTE ABOUT OUTSOURCING

Even in cases where documenting standards in-house could be done very rapidly, sometimes it can still be easier to outsource the production of a standards resource. I don't say this as a former standards consultant—I say this as a standards manager. While the consultant is busy writing documentation, you can work to prepare the organization for what's coming by building and training a team of evangelists. On the other hand, if there's no budget for a consultant, you can engender support for the standards by divvying up smaller tasks, such as creating figures, code samples, and downloadable templates, among a group of designers or developers to lessen your workload.

As important as the standards themselves is the process by which your organization plans to keep them updated. Standards need to be updated on a regular basis—for example, as rebranding or redesign efforts take place or as new interaction models or technologies are implemented.

To figure out how to manage standards updates, think about the rate of change and the size of your organization.

In a large organization, change typically takes time, so quarterly updates may be all you need. In a smaller organization that is changing rapidly, you may need to manage monthly or biweekly updates. Plan for both best- and worst-case scenarios, and you'll be prepared for whatever happens.

Training and Communication

As the standards start to take shape, be in constant communication with your audience about what's taking place: Send periodic newsletters, cross-communicate among disciplines, meet with managers, conduct Q&A sessions, and report upwards.

During the early stages, you may be able to experiment a bit with formats and frequency, but try to establish a pattern of communication that can be maintained for the long term. Eventually, you'll have people trained to expect updates!

Planning for training programs can also begin as the content outline for the standards is finalized. There are three kinds of training curricula that need to be planned:

❖ **Staff training**—Level-setting intensive introductory training, required for all staff as soon as possible following the completion of the standards. The goal is to rapidly get everyone who has some functional relationship with the standards up to speed with what's in them. Functional relationships include people managers, project managers, and product managers, so make sure the content is customized for their needs as well the needs of the design and technical staff.

❖ **Individual training**—For newcomers to the project/team/organization, offered when the need arises. This may end up being the same curriculum as in staff training, but may be presented in a different format (such as computer-based training or video) to accommodate small groups of people.

❖ **Routine training**—Periodic refresher classes or updated training modules. While the content of these courses won't be determined at the outset, planning now will help set expectations for the future (and avoid unwelcome surprises). Devise a tentative plan that addresses frequency, expected content, delivery format, and recommended participation levels. Make sure that people managers are aware of your schedule so they can plan for their teams' participation.

As with the standards themselves, outsourcing the development of training programs can speed up the creation of coursework and presentation materials; it's also an excellent path when a large organization has few qualified trainers in-house. A training consultant can also coach individuals within the organization to prepare for future training efforts.

If the size of the organization doesn't warrant bringing in consultants, or if the budget isn't available to make this possible, finding individuals in-house to help develop and deliver the training program is key. You want to find people who can rapidly learn and apply the standards and who have strong presentation and/or written communication skills.

In both communications and training, be honest about the process by which the standards were created and open about processes for updating and adding new standards. Transparency into the process of how standards are made will demystify them and make it easier for people to use them.

A FINAL NOTE

Finally, keep in mind that communication isn't a one-way street; always ask for feedback! Anyone participating in training should be given some sort of survey at the end, and online communications should include some easy means for asking questions.

The Quality Review Process

Once the standards have been created and everyone has been educated about them, people should not simply return to their work and assume all is well.

Every project needs to be reviewed at specific milestones to ensure that the standards are being adhered to as well as to keep an eye out for new standards that need to be documented.

Designers may be familiar with the design review process, which usually involves a review by the person who owns the creative direction of the product. Other aspects of the design review process vary from organization to organization. In some but not all companies, peer and/or managerial reviews must be conducted before the creative director will review a design.

On the technical side, developers may be accustomed to documenting their development plans in a technical design document (TDD), which undergoes peer and/or managerial review before work commences. In smaller organizations or on smaller projects, the TDD may be skipped. A peer code review is probably more common, to help developers find and resolve bugs.

Design and code reviews make for a good start, but aren't enough to ensure adherence to the standards. Why not? Unless your creative director crafts all of the design standards and is thus intimately familiar with them, details are bound to be missed. Peer code reviews are useful in cases where everyone's a control freak, but friends will sometimes go easy on one another and not call out inconsistencies. You need a separate standards-compliance review as shown in **FIGURE 5.8**, conducted by the standards manager, to ensure total compliance.

FIGURE 5.8 Ideal user interface or visual design quality review process.

In the quality review process as shown in **FIGURE 5.9**, peer reviews help individuals prepare for standards-compliance reviews, and standards-compliance reviews are required before creative or launch approval can be given.

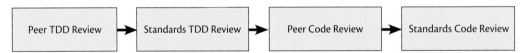

FIGURE 5.9 Ideal development quality review process.

For those already operating with some sort of review process, an additional standards-compliance review may sound like extra work that will slow operations. But if standards-compliance reviews are conducted regularly or on demand, the overall time required is negligible. More importantly, in some cases, they can garner huge gains, because the standards-compliance review may find potential issues that can be fixed before any time is wasted waiting on the approval end.

These review processes work well when designers and developers are implementing based on existing standards, but what happens when something new, for which there is no standard, needs to be implemented? One of two things can happen:

❖ The standard can be driven by the project team, closely monitored by the standards manager, who will need to keep up with the project team on every decision or execution point to ensure that a true standard can be derived from the project work.

❖ The project team can hand off the standards-related work to the standards manager, who then produces both the standard and the deliverable(s) needed for the project.

Which way is better? I'm of two minds about this: I think the first scenario works better for design projects and standards, and the second scenario works better for development projects and standards. However, I've seen both work equally well for each discipline, given the right level of involvement and communication. If you devise a plan to handle both scenarios, you'll be able to decide which will work better for any given project.

Setting the Wheel in Motion

Now that you've learned about the Circle of Standards, how do you put it into practice? First, find willing, strategic allies who can help you gather information and from whom you can learn about aspects of the organization you're not familiar with.

If your organization has an operations manager or team, contact them and let them in on what you're trying to do. Seek out people in operations, as they tend to be kindred spirits when it comes to instituting standards and modifying processes to accommodate those standards.

Next, get organized! Inventory what standards you have, if any, and start a list of what's missing. Review current training materials to determine where they fall short on evangelizing the standards. Iterate through your product development life cycle (PDLC) to determine where reviews are or ought to be happening and where standards could come into play.

Figure out who you need to sell on this methodology and how best to enlist their support. Document your findings in a slideshow deck or manifesto, practice your pitch, and set up a meeting to engage your targets. If you get some pushback or even an outright dismissal, *don't give up*. Persistence is crucial in standards evangelism. Take a step back, restrategize, and try again.

All the while, keep working on crafting your standards and evangelizing them. Grassroots work is just as important and effective as setting top-down policies.

Keeping Up Momentum

Sometimes being a standards manager can seem like thankless work—relentlessly pursuing stodgy executives, dealing with complaints from cranky designers and developers—what's the point? The point is to ensure that your organization produces consistent, high-quality work, which it wouldn't be able to do without you. Make sure the organization takes time to celebrate every success—every product launch, every new standard, and every standards conversion. By recognizing the projects and teams that implement the standards, people will come to realize that standards are the key to success.

To keep up momentum, maintain a rotation of volunteers who work with the standards manager. If you have representatives from different teams or disciplines working with you, give them a break from time to time—not to discourage or punish them, but as a reprieve from working an extra job! Finding additional volunteers helps build support for the standards by including more people, and giving people a short break from "imposing" the standards ensures they come back to the effort energized and ready to do more.

If you're able to have a whole standards team, make sure there's variety in each person's work. Simply reviewing others' work and writing documentation isn't enough to keep someone engaged, so offer them the chance to participate in design or development work, to keep their skills up to date. Have them expand their skill sets by giving talks or conducting training sessions. And always make sure your team is having fun.

Conclusion

Standards evangelism is exciting work, but it's also difficult work when you don't have a plan for making standards a reality. Process management might seem boring, but it's a very useful tool in successfully changing organizational behavior. The combination of the two—believe me—makes for dynamic, rewarding work.

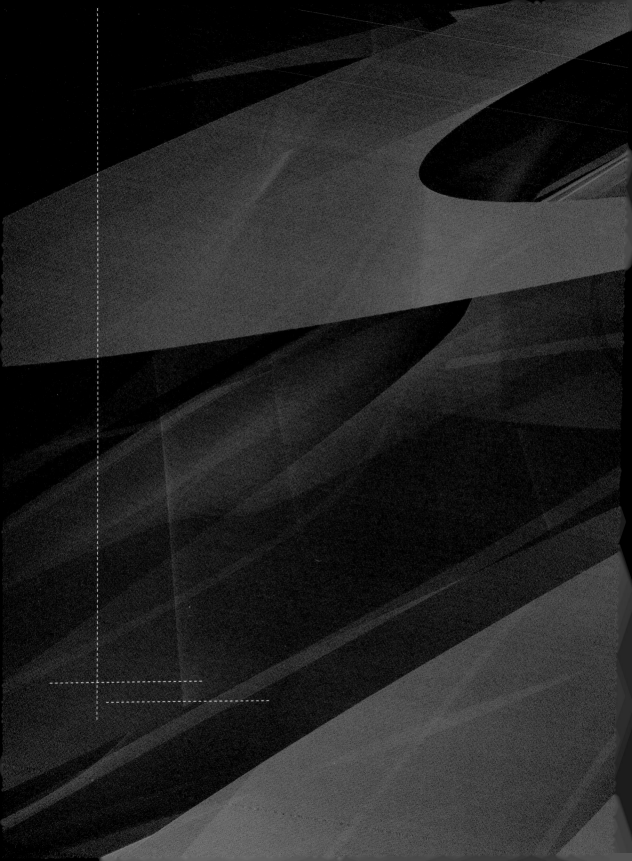

Part 2

Case Studies

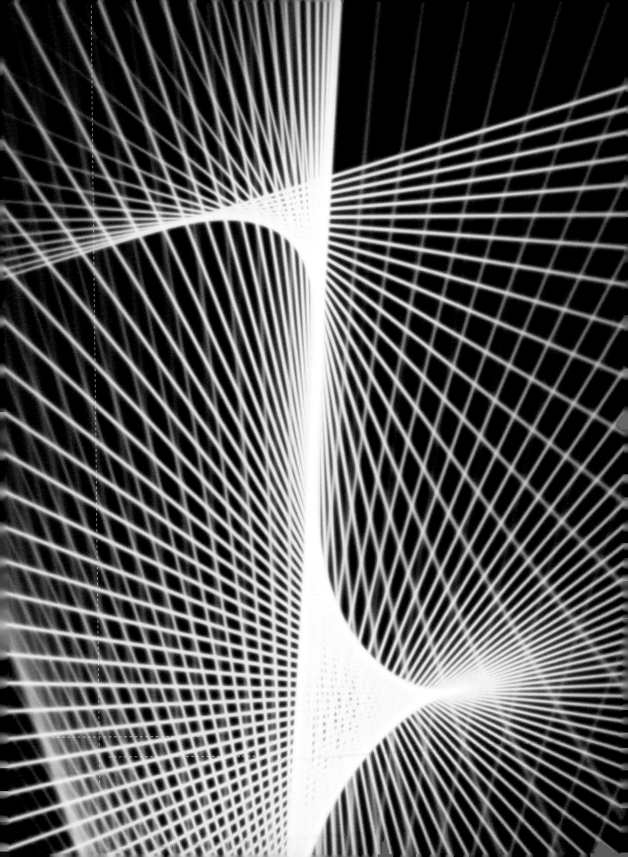

Practice Doesn't Make Perfect

The concept that practice leads to perfection is flawed. There is no perfect practice—merely perfect academic exercises such as school assignments that can be done for instructors or proof of concepts created as examples for clients.

Technology, scope, client relationships and implementations could always be done better when viewed in hindsight.

This doesn't mean we shouldn't try for perfection.

Only by going through real-world development with clients and attempting—successfully or not—to launch internal projects (often with punishing deadlines) do we hone our skills, learn our lessons, and, importantly, become strong enough and flexible enough to apply those lessons "the next time." That's striving for excellence, also known as professionalism.

Although learning specific skills and techniques and standards is critical to our becoming better developers, there are key areas that can be imparted only by working on actual Web development projects: communication, adaptation, and persistence.

Communication

The Internet is about communication. The list of technologies that facilitate human contact goes on and on: instant messaging, email, VoIP when the telephone gets dated. Those meetings your colleagues describe as too long and pointless could instead be about finding consensus, focused on agreeing on the best solutions, if everyone has already discussed the problems before they reached the meeting room.

Adaptation

Beginning Web developers test—and sometimes break—the rules for good development as they learn what works and what doesn't. Of course it's important to pick up what's right and wrong, black and white, but it's equally important to be able to see the grey, ambiguous area and know that the "best" solution isn't always, well, the best.

For example, sometimes loading a page up with the appropriate DOCTYPE-, Section 508-compliant tags hinders Google too much for it to deliver a fast experience for its users, and you have to ditch the DOCTYPE tags. Even the best techniques and technologies can be thrown out of the window as long as you know how that will affect your audience. Adaptation is about knowing when to break the rules for the right reasons.

Persistence

Life happens. Vendors overstate their competencies. Clients change the scope of their projects. Web developers get sick or, worse, go on honeymoons.

A professional takes on the project or part of the project he or she has been given and doesn't let go. *Circumstances* change, but a true professional makes sure a project doesn't get out of hand, persisting with the help of communication and adaptation. It's not easy—but then, nothing of value ever is.

Trials and Tribulations

The following case studies showcase how developers tackled their projects. They used the skills and Web standards to the best of their abilities to create some of the most highly profiled sites on the Web. Thankfully, their mistakes and failures can be shared to allow us to better make the next generation of sites.

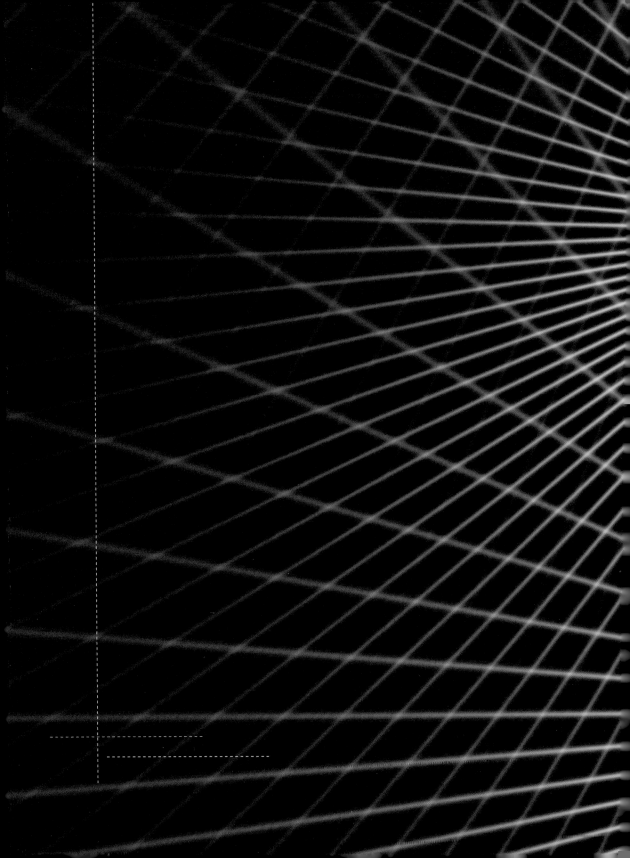

6

EverythingTori.com

Long after releasing her first single in 1980, singer-songwriter Tori Amos continues going strong. It isn't often a singer stays in the public eye for over two decades, continually selling out concerts. The audience is bound to see a change in the musician and her music when a career lasts that long, and that certainly applies to Amos.

For an artist, a Web site must reflect the artist's persona and art. The release of her album *American Doll Posse* put Amos' focus on the strong woman. The posse contains five different characters that together create a complete woman and her role today. The album and tour involve four other singers who each represent a "part" of Amos—accompanying Amos.

So what did this mean for the Web site? Amos' management wanted to create, own, and manage a site separate from the record label's site, ToriAmos.com. The idea was to make it the authoritative site providing information about Amos' career and not just her latest work. They used the domain ToriAmosCom.com and posted a placeholder on the Web site—and they hired Philip Fierlinger to create harmony between Tori's music and her Web site (**Figure 6.1**).

Fierlinger landed the project because of someone he knew who had worked with Tori Amos. During initial discussions with Tori Amos' team, Fierlinger found them eager to build the site, but he discovered fan sites already doing a great job providing regularly updated and high-quality content. Fierlinger delved deeper to find the motivation for building the site, while considering his concerns that the management team would have limited access to content for logistical and legal reasons. He nearly talked himself out of a job during this discovery phase.

Backstage

A passionate designer, Fierlinger wouldn't design a Web site without meaningful and compelling reasons. He wanted to provide fans a place where they could get content and have an experience that they couldn't find on any other site. He continued to review the official record label site and fan sites, and discovered these sites were missing the components of good design from the audience's perspective, such as usability and a well-thought-out information architecture.

He began the project by exploring Tori Amos-related Web sites to see what was out there and where the gaps were. As soon as the project received direction, Fierlinger proceeded with the project using the standard Web design process, from building the wireframes and getting feedback on the initial comps to building the site's structure and taking advantage of the power of CSS.

Digging into the World of Tori Amos

The record label's site looked slick, but had Flash usability issues and content based on what the record labels believed important, not what the fans wanted. On the other hand, fan sites like The Dent (www.thedent.com) contained obsessively detailed and relevant content, and provided a stunning experience. But while the content more than satisfied fans' thirst for Tori Amos-related information, its design lacked the quality demanded by the management team. Here In My Head (www.hereinmyhead.com), another fan site, succeeded in the area of design and contained up-to-date content.

FIGURE 6.1 The official Tori Amos site, EverythingTori.com, after launch.

After completing his research, Fierlinger believed he could build a site that complemented fan sites and the label site while offering higher design standards and unique content. Although he wouldn't control or maintain the content, he believed he could encourage the application of good content practices by building the site with the right content management system (CMS), including a blog that listed events, and providing RSS feeds.

Furthermore, he gave the team suggestions and ideas for content, even some that didn't make it past the concept stages. One idea proposed that band members, Tori, fans, and other artists record their impressions and stories on audio and video resembling DVD commentaries. Another involved creating e-cards with interactive music that played audio and animation, like little digital vignettes. Neither idea made the cut because of the time and effort involved, and because providing the fundamentals had a higher priority.

Putting the Design Process to Work

The project took five months, from July through November 2004. Fierlinger used the following basic Web design process:

❖ Gather requirements

❖ Develop concepts

❖ Create information architecture

❖ Design comps

❖ Provide time and budget estimates

❖ Receive feedback, iterate, and resolve the overall design direction

❖ Design and build

❖ Iterate, iterate, iterate

Applying Web standards best practices also played an important part in the project, says Fierlinger, because Web standards provided better usability and accessibility, helped with search engine optimization, encouraged smart and flexible engineering as well as visual design flexibility, and afforded him the opportunity to stretch his design skills. At the time of the project, many designers hadn't adopted Web standards.

Building the Wireframes

Not surprisingly, as in so many Web projects, creating content for the site was a slow and difficult process. Fierlinger, knowing that this process is usually underestimated, started requesting content early on in the project. The client submitted

CDs with photos and short audio clips with interviews; the client wanted the full record catalog, tour history, press clippings, and links to Tori Amos' charity as content along with an online store. Based on this information, Fierlinger drafted a high-level information architecture that defined the main parts of the site:

* ❖ Music

* ❖ Tours

* ❖ Photos

* ❖ Videos

* ❖ Press

* ❖ FAQ

* ❖ News and blog

* ❖ Footer utilities: Email a friend, subscribe, contact, site credits

Fierlinger put together the initial wireframes linking the frames to create a clickable prototype, as shown in **Figure 6.2**. Instead of pen and paper, he used Flash

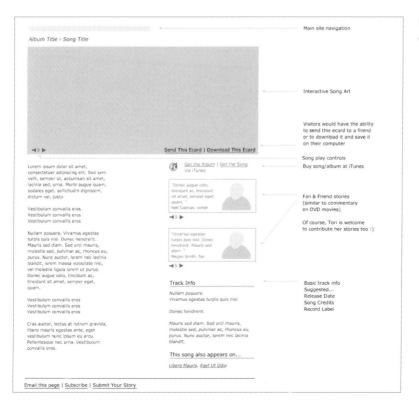

Figure 6.2 The clickable prototype.

for the wireframes and screenflows, because the application simplifies the process of sketching ideas and wiring them together to see how things flow and to find the gaps.

Based on this architecture, Fierlinger created the full-blown wireframes shown in **FIGURE 6.3**, and discussed them with the client over the phone. He documented changes through several iterations. The wireframes included everything the client wanted to do and the time and cost estimates for the project using a spreadsheet outlining milestones, tasks, costs, and timeframes. The designer started by designing the wireframes with a grand vision and then stripped it based on the client's feedback.

As expected, the client wanted a lower time and cost estimate. So the designer returned to the designing board and redacted the sitemap with red slashes to offer two additional approaches, as **FIGURE 6.4** shows. The client received a choice of a full-blown version, a scaled-back version, and a basic version. The client chose the scaled-back version.

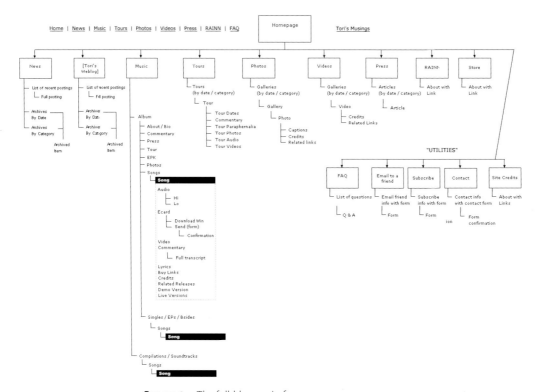

FIGURE 6.3 The full-blown wireframe.

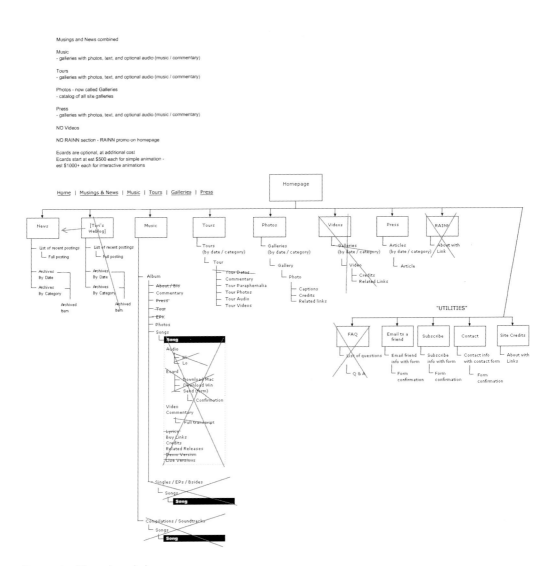

FIGURE 6.4 The redacted plans.

After making that decision, the designer switched from holding phone discussions to conversing with the client via videocasts, which helped him explain and clarify ideas as they developed.

After agreeing with the wireframes and sitemap, Fierlinger reviewed thousands of Web site screenshots that he had collected over the years for inspiration and reference. He flagged those that had elements he thought would work for the project. Using those elements and adding typography and photos of Tori Amos, he mixed the assets. He shared his favorites with the clients so they could pick the aspects and elements of the designs they liked. These set the tone for the design direction shown in **FIGURES 6.5** and **6.6.**

FIGURE 6.5 The first of two prototypes for the site's look and feel.

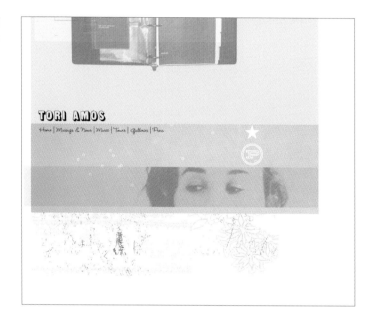

FIGURE 6.6 This second prototype provided another option for the design direction decision.

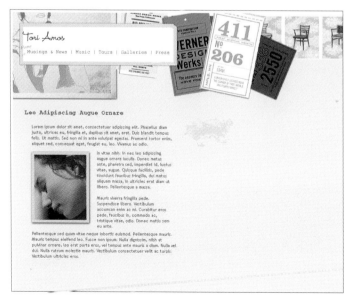

The client loved both collages, especially the typography shown in **FIGURE 6.7** and the texture and scrapbook feel from **FIGURE 6.8**. Based on that feedback, Fierlinger combined the elements of the wireframes to create detailed comps, as shown in **FIGURES 6.9**, **6.10**, and **6.11**. The design process continued iteratively, with Fierlinger posting the latest designs on the staging site for the client's review and updating the designs based on client input.

FIGURE 6.7 Client preferred the typography shown in this prototype.

FIGURE 6.8 Client chose the scrapbook look and feel from this prototype.

FIGURE 6.9 First comp based on the client's input.

FIGURE 6.10 Detailed comp of the Music section.

FIGURE 6.11 Initial detailed comp of the Galleries section.

Designing the Site

During the design phase, the designer searched for a CMS for the site. While he could've built the whole site from scratch in Dreamweaver, he opted not to go in that direction, as this approach would make it difficult for the client to update the content. He investigated blog engines and open-source CMS solutions. He considered Movable Type, but shied away due to concerns about the application's complexity and its limited PHP support.

The PHP-based ExpressionEngine had potential, with its design flexibility and powerful features. He decided to use it, though first he had to learn how to use it himself. Conceptually, ExpressionEngine worked like other blog engines, but in practice it more closely resembled a big CMS system or Dreamweaver due to its use of object-oriented templates and subtemplates. The object-oriented and modular application used a different approach for site modeling and content creation. Adopting ExpressionEngine required changing the way of thinking about and building a Web site that runs on a CMS.

FIGURE 6.12 shows ExpressionEngine's control panel, which gives only a small taste of the application's power. It lets designers hack things in interesting ways, and blend in custom PHP code as needed. In a typical project, Fierlinger generally avoided adding much customized PHP. However, for this project, the gallery structure needed heavy-duty PHP. The nature of the content required a gallery format, so the designer needed to figure out the best way to design and build the gallery.

It would've been simple to build the gallery as a basic blog sequence in which users accessed entries sequentially with a preview and links to the next and previous entries. However, the designer wanted to offer more by setting up the gallery

FIGURE 6.12 Expression-Engine did the grunt work in managing the site behind the scenes.

to appear as a set of pages containing a manageable number of thumbnail pre-views. He had customized a CMS for a photography site, so he adopted that same approach, which gave him the ability to generate an entire site design and layout as a gallery structure. **FIGURE 6.13** shows the front page of the Galleries section.

FIGURE 6.13 The home page of the photo gallery contains thumbnails of several separate albums, each of which contains collections of photos.

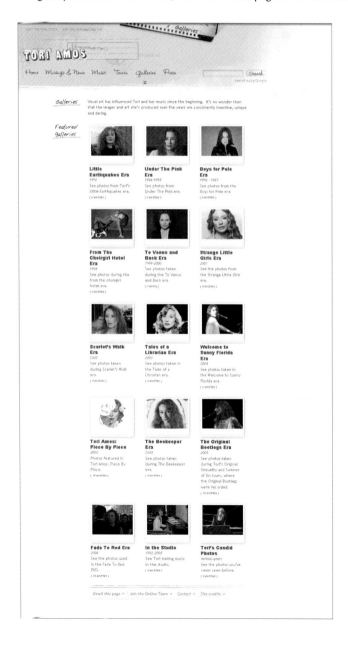

The most challenging part of designing the gallery was getting the thumbnail subsets to paginate, or automatically break up by pages. The gallery displayed up to nine thumbnails per page. If the gallery has more than nine images, then the CMS he designed created a new page for the next set of nine thumbnails. He applied the concept, not the code, from his photography site CMS, and built the gallery in ExpressionEngine with customized PHP. The gallery turned out well (see **FIGURES 6.14** and **6.15**) because of the mind-bending amount of work he invested in building it.

FIGURE 6.14 The Fade To Red Era gallery.

FIGURE 6.15 Second page of the Fade to Red Era gallery.

With the CMS decided, the project moved forward using the following build process:

❖ Design the layouts in Photoshop.

❖ Use Dreamweaver for designing the HTML and CSS structure.

❖ Carve the design file for background images.

❖ Build the initial templates so they work on the local machine to test and ensure all code works before migrating.

❖ Migrate everything into ExpressionEngine.

❖ Add dynamic elements in ExpressionEngine—the biggest job.

❖ Tweak the design, HTML, and CSS in ExpressionEngine.

In working on the design approach, Fierlinger wanted to ensure the layouts were scalable. This scalability would allow the site to accommodate content, large and small, so the content could grow along with the site. To build a flexible structure for scalable layout, he used grid patterns with CSS, which play well together, since CSS provides the freedom to work with an underlying grid pattern without the restrictions that come with hard, formal, and obvious boundaries.

The flexible and scalable structure led Fierlinger to use backgrounds to loosen up the grid, to extend and overlap the edges, and to create a highly textured scrapbook feel. Though he designed the site with content scalability in mind, nothing will scale elegantly in situations where the copy, being either too short or too long for a given space, doesn't synchronize with the design.

Behind the CSS Scenes

Since ExpressionEngine relied on PHP, the site loaded CSS using PHP with @ import to separate the code from style. This allowed the site to import section-specific styles for each area of the site. In spite of these advantages, the site contained many <div> tags, leading to a case of "Divitis," a common Web site ailment. The main role of <div> is to group the page into sections, such as the navigation, header, footer, and body. For EverythingTori.com, no other solution accomplished what the site needed. Though having many <div> elements and classes adds as much weight to a page as tables do, CSS still has advantages over tables. For instance, those using screen readers experience fewer problems with CSS than with tables. After all, it was 2004—a time when CSS wasn't widely adopted by designers and supporting browsers.

The site's subtle background images led to unforeseen issues cropping up in the design. For example, the home page's "Musings & News" height is shorter than the background image, so the design crops it to the height of the block. Fortunately, it works naturally for the site with its use of textures and randomness to give it a scrapbook look and feel.

But the designer worried more about making the background images seamless while overlapping or tiled vertically or horizontally. Beyond that, it was better for the design to look random.

In dealing with browser issues, Fierlinger relied on "build, test, build, test, repeat" until the design behaved the way it should. He aimed to ensure the site worked with Internet Explorer 5.5 and FireFox 1.5 (remember, this was 2004). When he couldn't find a solution for a situation, he resorted to the magic bullet: the underscore hack. The underscore hack isn't valid CSS, but it did the trick:

```
hr {
    height:3px;
    _height:4px;
}
```

The three-pixel positioning looked right in every browser except Internet Explorer; four pixels worked better for IE. The underscore acts like a comment, and most browsers ignore anything with an underscore in the CSS. Internet Explorer is an exception, however, so it dutifully obeys the style following the underscore. (To make it work, the underscored attribute must come after the original attribute so IE obeys the "last command" it receives.)

While some purist designers believe that using the hack is a sin, Fierlinger believed the hack was, at least, more elegant than other hacks. So what if the site didn't validate? The site would survive, and serve its purpose.

Another interesting aspect of the site comes in the sharing of the same HTML structure while giving each section a distinctive look through the different background textures. The texture frames the page and the custom imagery to define each section. Each section also features different search field and button styles. The underlying HTML all comes from the same template, demonstrating the beauty and ease of using CSS to separate structure and presentation. **FIGURE 6.16** shows an overview.

Most sites feature a `<div>` to frame the header, usually something like #header. In the case of the Tori site, using a header `<div>` would have restricted the background textures to a limited space. To get the textures to extend and flow into the overall page, Fierlinger used #body to define the background imagery. Notice that the page includes a drop shadow, adding dimension and depth and enhancing its tactile feel. He added a #page-shadow `<div>` with a margin-left of 780px

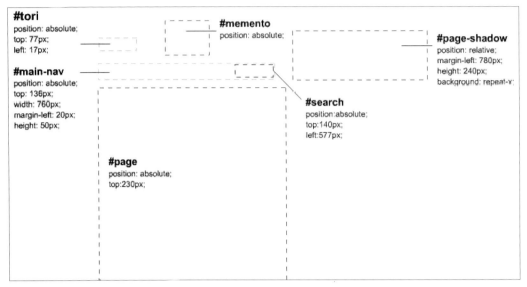

#tori
position: absolute;
top: 77px;
left: 17px;

#memento
position: absolute;

#page-shadow
position: relative;
margin-left: 780px;
height: 240px;
background: repeat-x;

#main-nav
position: absolute;
top: 136px;
width: 760px;
margin-left: 20px;
height: 50px;

#search
position:absolute;
top:140px;
left:577px;

#page
position: absolute;
top:230px;

FIGURE 6.16 High-level overview of the different sections along with their `<divs>`.

to extend the shadow to the full page width, to accommodate varying browser widths. Thus, starting from the minimum page width of 780px, the background image extends to the right infinitely with the use of `repeat-x`. In some cases, Fierlinger added a background image in the #page `<div>` to frame the page content. The following CSS contains sitewide styles as well as styles specific to sections:

```
#page-shadow {
   top:0;
   height:200px;
   margin-left:850px;
   }
#memento {
   position:absolute;
   top:0px;
   left:320px;
   }
#tori {
   position:absolute;
   top:77px;
   left:17px;
   }
```

```
#main-nav {
   position:absolute;
   top:136px;
   width:760px;
   margin-left:20px;
   height:50px;
   border:0px solid green;
   }
#main-nav a {
   display:block;
   height:30px;
   margin-right:20px;
   text-decoration:none;
   float:left;
}
#nav-home {
   width:46px;
   background: url("../img/nav/home.gif") no-repeat 0 -30px;
   }
#main-nav a:hover#nav-home {
   background-position: 0 0;
}
#nav-musings {
   width:126px;
   background: url("../img/nav/musings.gif") no-repeat 0 -30px;
   }
#main-nav a:hover#nav-musings {
   background-position: 0 0;
}
#nav-music {
   width:48px;
   background: url("../img/nav/music.gif") no-repeat 0 -30px;
   }
#main-nav a:hover#nav-music {
   background-position: 0 0;
}
#nav-tours {
   width:48px;
   background: url("../img/nav/tours.gif") no-repeat 0 -30px;
   }
#main-nav a:hover#nav-tours {
   background-position: 0 0;
}
```

```
#nav-galleries {
   width:65px;
   background: url("../img/nav/galleries.gif") no-repeat 0 -30px;
   }
#main-nav a:hover#nav-galleries {
   background-position: 0 0;
}
#nav-press {
   width:46px;
   background: url("../img/nav/press.gif") no-repeat 0 -30px;
   }
#main-nav a:hover#nav-press {
   background-position: 0 0;
}
#search {
   position:absolute;
   top:140px;
   left:577px;
   border:0px solid yellow;
}
#search-box {
   width:124px;
   font-size:.9em;
   border:none;
   padding:6px 8px 6px 4px;
   border:0px solid black;
   float:left;
   }
#search-button {
   border:0px;
   width:66px;
   height:25px;
}
#search p {
   border:0px solid white;
   text-align:right;
   color:#999;
   font-style:italic;
   padding:0;
   margin:0;
   }
#search a:hover {
   color:#666;
   }
```

The following code comes from the Tours section's CSS to show how its header differs from other sections:

```
body {
   background: #F3F7F7 url(../img/tours/bkgd.jpg) no-repeat;
}
#page-shadow {
   margin-left:850px;
   background:url(../img/tours/page-shadow.gif) repeat-x 0 0;
}

#mic-chord {
   position:absolute;
   top:0px;
   left:320px;
}

#nav-tours {
   width:48px;
   padding-bottom:20px;
   background: url(../img/tours/tours-current.gif) no-repeat 0 0;
   }
#main-nav a:hover#nav-tours {
   background-position: 0 0;
}
#search-box {
   background:url(../img/tours/search-box.gif) no-repeat 0 0;
   _background-attachment:fixed; /* underscore hack for IE
positioning */
   _width:120px; /* underscore hack for IE positioning */
}

#search-button {
   _height:28px; /* underscore hack for IE positioning */
   background:url(../img/tours/search-button.gif) no-repeat 0 0;
}
#tours {
   display:block;
   float:left;
   width:181px;
   height:51px;
   }
#intro {
   width:46em;
```

```
      float:left;
      padding-left:10px;
      padding-bottom:30px;
      }

.featured {
   display:inline;
   float:left;
   width:170px;
   padding-right:20px;
   margin-bottom:20px;
   }
.featured img {
   width:170px;
   height:108px;
}
.featured a img {
   padding: 0 2px 2px 0;
   margin-bottom:5px;
   background:url(../img/drop-shadow.gif) no-repeat 100% 100%;
   }
.featured a:hover {
   text-decoration:none;
}

.featured a:hover .title {
   text-decoration:underline;
}
.featured .title {
   font: 1.25em "Arial Black";
   }
.featured h3 {
   font-size:.9em;
   font-style:italic;
   font-weight:normal;
   padding:0;
   margin:0;
}
.duct-tape {
   position:absolute;
   padding-left:70px;
   margin-top:-8px;
   z-index:2;
   }
```

```
img.duct-tape {
   width:40px;
   height:15px;
   border:none;
   }
```

Here's the HTML for the headers on the home page:

```
<title>Everything Tori | Home</title>

<style type="text/css">
@import url("http://everythingtori.com/go?css=core/general-css");
@import url("http://everythingtori.com/go?css=home/home-css");
</style>
<script type="text/JavaScript">
<!--
function MM_openBrWindow(theURL,winName,features) { //v2.0
   window.open(theURL,winName,features);
}
//-->
</script>
</head>
<body>

<div id="page-shadow"> </div>
<img src="img/home/tori.gif" alt="Tori Amos" id="tori" />
<img src="img/home/memento.gif"  id="memento" alt="" />

<div id="sitewide-store-link"><a href="http://www.thetoristore.com/"
target="_blank" title="Link opens in a new window.">visit the Tori
Store</a></div>
<div id="sitewide-mail-link"><a href="Javascript:MM_openBrWindow('/
mailing.html','mailing','width=400,height=450')" title="Link opens in a
new window">Join the Tori mailing list</a></div>
<div id="main-nav">
   <a href="http://everythingtori.com/go/home/" id="nav-home"
   class="hide-text">Home</a>
   <a href="http://everythingtori.com/go/musings/" id="nav-musings"
   class="hide-text">Musings &amp; News</a>
   <a href="http://everythingtori.com/go/music/" id="nav-music"
   class="hide-text">Music</a>
   <a href="http://everythingtori.com/go/tours/" id="nav-tours"
   class="hide-text">Tours</a>
   <a href="http://everythingtori.com/go/galleries/" id="nav-
   galleries" class="hide-text">Galleries</a>
```

```
      <a href="http://everythingtori.com/go/press/" id="nav-press"
      class="hide-text">Press</a>
  </div>
  <div id="search">
  <form method="get" action="http://www.google.com/search">
        <input type="text" name="q" maxlength="255" value=""
        id="search-box" />
        <input type="image" src="img/x.gif" value="submit" alt="Search
        (using Google)" title="search using Google" id="search-button"
        />
  <p>search using Google</p>
        <input type="hidden" name="domains" value="everythingtori.com"
        />
        <input type="hidden" name="sitesearch" value="everythingtori.
        com" />
  </form>
  </div>
```

Compare the home page HTML to the Tours section's header HTML:

```
<title>Everything Tori | Tours</title>

<style type="text/css">
@import url("http://everythingtori.com/go?css=core/general-css");
@import url("http://everythingtori.com/go?css=tours/tours-css");
</style>
<script type="text/JavaScript">
<!--
function MM_openBrWindow(theURL,winName,features) { //v2.0
   window.open(theURL,winName,features);
}
//-->
</script>
</head>
<body>

<div id="page-shadow"> </div>
<img src="img/tours/tori.gif" alt="Tori Amos" id="tori" />
<img src="img/tours/memento.gif"  id="memento" alt="" />

<div id="sitewide-store-link"><a href="http://www.thetoristore.com/"
target="_blank" title="Link opens in a new window.">visit the Tori
Store</a></div>
```

```
<div id="sitewide-mail-link"><a href="Javascript:MM_openBrWindow('/
mailing.html',mailing,width=400,height=450')" title="Link opens in a
new window">Join the Tori mailing list</a></div>
<div id="main-nav">
    <a href="http://everythingtori.com/go/home/" id="nav-home"
    class="hide-text">Home</a>
    <a href="http://everythingtori.com/go/musings/" id="nav-musings"
    class="hide-text">Musings &amp; News</a>
    <a href="http://everythingtori.com/go/music/" id="nav-music"
    class="hide-text">Music</a>
    <a href="http://everythingtori.com/go/tours/" id="nav-tours"
    class="hide-text">Tours</a>
    <a href="http://everythingtori.com/go/galleries/"
    id="nav-galleries" class="hide-text">Galleries</a>
    <a href="http://everythingtori.com/go/press/" id="nav-press"
    class="hide-text">Press</a>
</div>
<div id="search">
<form method="get" action="http://www.google.com/search">
    <input type="text" name="q" maxlength="255" value=""
    id="search-box" />
    <input type="image" src="img/x.gif" value="submit" alt="Search
    (using Google)" title="search using Google" id="search-button"
    />
<p>search using Google</p>
    <input type="hidden" name="domains" value="everythingtori.com"
    />
    <input type="hidden" name="sitesearch" value="everythingtori.
    com" />
</form>
</div>
```

Adding #memento gave each section a defining symbolic image, which seamlessly integrated the background texture and the page shadow. Other standard header elements include the #tori logo, the #main-nav, and #search. The search input field #search-box and the #search-button use background graphics to blend smoothly with the overall page texture. To achieve that effect, the search button used a fully transparent x.gif so that it can use the same HTML template sitewide, and then the CSS defined the custom background image for the button and the input field.

Launching the Site

Many Web design projects tend to have project-management and designer/client communications challenges. Fierlinger worked closely with Chelsea Laird from The Bridge Entertainment Group, Tori Amos' management company, during construction of the site. Chelsea handled the content loading, along with the day-to-day client coordination. As the project neared completion, the project involved many content and design changes. The team coordinated and managed all of the work online, including uploading the changes directly to the site. Communications relied heavily on email exchanges and daily instant-messaging conversations.

The team selected the go-live date to coincide with the launch of a new book and album. As with most design projects, something entered late in the game—suddenly, the client wanted a new section of the site dedicated to the book project. The team rushed to put together a blog section for the book and launch the site. Adding the new section was easy because all of the elements for the framework were in place.

Upon site launch, fans raved about the new site, to the great relief of the design team. Only one major issue occurred after launch. The site contained full-length, high-quality MP3 files for every track from every album and single Tori Amos released. It was a great idea, but the challenge came in preventing the ability to illegally download the tracks. Fierlinger monitored the Web site's traffic and the forums for people discussing the site. More importantly, he wanted to watch for the possibility of someone copying all the MP3 files.

Within a couple of weeks after launch, someone figured out how to do it, and mentioned it in one of the forums. As a result, the client edited all of the tracks down to 30-second samples.

The designer continued supporting the site until the management team got into the swing of updating and editing content, and they took control of it.

The site has been successful for over three years now. Fierlinger kept an eye on the site by subscribing to its RSS feed and receiving user feedback through emails. He concluded that the site continued to perform well and was doing exactly as expected. The client has successfully added new pages or sections, and frequently updated the content. Furthermore, the home page changed nicely to reflect the newest project. Thanks to the planning for growth and evolution, the original structure has adapted well to continuous changes.

Meet the Designer, Philip Fierlinger

Philip Fierlinger's parents ran an animation studio out of the family's home, surrounding him with the whole design and production process. He took an interest into computers as a child and learned BASIC by playing around with Beagle Brothers, the first "open source" code he ever used. Eventually, he expanded his knowledge to include databases, and created a contact database for his mom. He studied industrial design in college, completing his final semester in an internship with a top-secret startup called General Magic in Silicon Valley. Though he received an internship offer from Sony in New Jersey, he couldn't pass up the opportunity to work with the original Macintosh team on a new handheld computer platform.

How did you get started in Web design?

In 1994, I started Turntable with my brother, Peter. We believed we could create interactive designs and do development better than many of the companies we knew. With no money and nothing to lose, we applied their powerful ideas and passion to build a prototype of an interactive online music store. This came at a time when Mosaic [one of the earliest Web browsers] didn't exist; people considered CD-ROMs an expensive and unattainable technology; and 14.4 BPS modems were state-of-the-art technology, only known to über geeks. The store focused on the ability to browse an online music catalog, to listen to samples, to watch music videos, and to buy music online. This idea was almost 10 years ahead of its time.

We pitched our prototype to several major record labels. They were baffled and perplexed. They had no idea what to do with us. Although they were impressed, they were unconvinced that what they saw was relevant to their business. I emailed Ian Rogers, a kid in Indiana who did a fan site for the Beastie Boys. I told Rogers about an idea for a Beastie Boys CD-ROM that connected to and integrated with his fan site. It turned out the Beastie Boys hired Rogers, who pitched my idea to the band. Within a few weeks, I went to L.A. to do a QuickTime VR [experimental technology then still in development at Apple] shoot of the Beastie Boys' studio. Those of us involved in this project were among the first to use QuickTime VR. We also worked out a deal with Microsoft to include Internet Explorer 1.0 on the CD because of the difficulties in dealing with Netscape. This tie-in was one of the first browser bundle deals.

The Beastie Boys project established our company as a leading digital design and development company. We had no trouble landing projects from biggies like Apple, Palm, and Macromedia. We continued to take on projects for underground bands we loved, including Dr. Octagon, the Invisible Skratch, Piklz, Money Mark, and Mo'Wax.

Thanks to our relationship with Macromedia, we developed the first Shockwave audio player soon after Shockwave came out. Later, I started working on Flash 4, when Flash came with programming capabilities. Unexpectedly, we stayed busy during the dot-com days by designing and developing sites for many crazy startups.

By 2001, I moved to New Zealand with my wife and son, where I went to work for the country's top Web agency, Shift (shift.co.nz). The company gave me the incredible opportunity to work with a team of young designers doing some of the best design work in the world. With Shift, I put my Flash skills to work in building powerful cultural Web sites—a stark and refreshing change from the dot-com and rock-star Web sites.

During my time with Shift, I learned heaps about designing for large-scale online publishing, giving me the skills to design for scalability and performance and develop flexible templates using dynamic grid systems. Obviously, this experience with Shift prepared me for the Tori Amos project.

While I worked on the Tori Amos site, I worked on a redesign for NewZealand.com at Shift. The redesigned site won a Webby Award for best tourism site and a nomination for best home page design, and another Webby the following year. I moonlighted on projects for U.S. clients while still working full-time for Shift in New Zealand. I worked with U.S. clients, including DreamWorks, Comcast, Warner Brothers, and Capitol, and many others from New Zealand—the geographical separation didn't cause any issues.

Not one to shy away from new things and innovation, I helped form Xero.com, a startup based in New Zealand, which created an online accounting system. As lead interaction designer, I enjoyed the challenge of turning the boring and painful world of accounting into a sexy, simple, and fun experience. It was an appreciated chance to focus on a product and continuously refine it, rather than switching between projects and clients.

How did you take an interest in Web standards?

I started moving away from designing and building static sites into creating dynamic, data-driven sites. In the process, the limitations of defining visual design in HTML became painfully obvious. Building database-driven sites frees up the content into an abstract object that you can manipulate independently of the code and the visual presentation. If you use HTML for both structure and style, then you are very limited in what you can do with your content. Any changes you want to make require editing code across every page and template in your site. Everything is hard-coded. Changes are painful and extremely prone to errors. Plus, your design options are very restricted.

Ideally you want to write and edit your code in one place and have it referenced in many places across your entire site. CSS is designed to do exactly that: You can make one simple change in one class and it instantly changes your design wherever you use that class reference within your entire site. That makes building sites very efficient. It also gives you a lot of design flexibility and freedom.

Of course, massive credit is due to Jeffrey Zeldman for his crusade to make people aware of CSS and Web standards, plus David Shea for putting together the CSS Zen Garden, making the path to better design and development quite obvious.

For these reasons, I applied Web standards to EverythingTori.com.

What are the more common issues you run into with CSS? How do you deal with them?

Browser issues and general quirks make working with CSS tedious. It's amazing how quickly you can get 90% of your design built in CSS. Finishing that last 10%, getting things pixel perfect, can be excruciating. The problems become exponential when you're targeting a wider range of browsers, especially older ones. Therefore, I try to limit the number of target browsers and keep it to the most current. Of course, IE is always the biggest nightmare, and there's generally no avoiding it.

Also, it's very annoying that tables handle many layout and grid structures exactly how you want, much easier and more predictably than using CSS floats, but they often don't play well with CSS and they have their own drawbacks. Being able to use the table attributes of CSS would be great, if browsers supported it properly. CSS still isn't ideally suited as a complete publishing solution. It was never really designed to handle grid layouts with multi-column flow, so the solutions people use are all hacks. It would be wonderful if CSS 3 became mainstream, but it seems like that day, sadly, is still far off.

Who or what influenced you?

My biggest influence is my wife Hadley (www.shescrafty.com). It's extremely hard to pass the wife test, and it's a great feeling when it happens. Over the years, I've collected screenshots of any Web site that catches my eye. I wish I'd been doing it my whole career, because there are some sites that are long gone that I wish I could refer to. I often peruse my collection for ideas and inspiration. Here's a short list of some of the sites and designers that always grab my attention and give me ideas:

❖ grant.robinson.name—online home of one of the best designers and Flash developers I have ever had the pleasure to work with

❖ Shift.co.nz

❖ 37Signals.com

❖ Google.com

❖ Flickr.com

❖ Odopod.com

❖ CSSZenGarden.com

❖ CactusLab.com

❖ l3che.com

❖ cape-acrona.com

❖ ths.nu

❖ AestheticApparatus.com

❖ Ourcommon.com

❖ Wrecked.nu—the original Wrecked.nu had incredible textures and interactions.

❖ Urban Outfitters—for years I collected their print promos at their stores; their emails can be really excellent.

❖ Iso50.com

❖ SecondStory.com

❖ Gutterlife.com

❖ 24-7media.de

❖ Miikasaksi.com—his original site Smallprint.net had a huge influence on me.

❖ Dooce.com—she used to do constantly changing, beautiful headers for her old site.

End Song

These sites undoubtedly influenced Fierlinger's works, as some of their elements appeared on his designs. And as an innovative designer, his work most likely influenced many other designers. Concerning the Tori Amos project, Fierlinger said he was happy with the project and its results. He had fun designing and building it, since it gave him the opportunity to design something visually expressive with a solid and smart structure. Furthermore, he had creative freedom and the client listened to his ideas and direction. In turn, the client provided him with great guidance, feedback, and support for managing the content.

Looking back at a project, most designers, including Fierlinger, cringe at all the glaring imperfections taunting them. They dwell on the things they didn't have time to fix, or discover that the client mucked things. For EverythingTori.com, Fierlinger was completely satisfied with, well, everything. He didn't see anything he wished he could've done differently. The fast-changing world of Web design and development can quickly outdate a Web site, but not with EverythingTori. com. He can look back on this project with complete satisfaction.

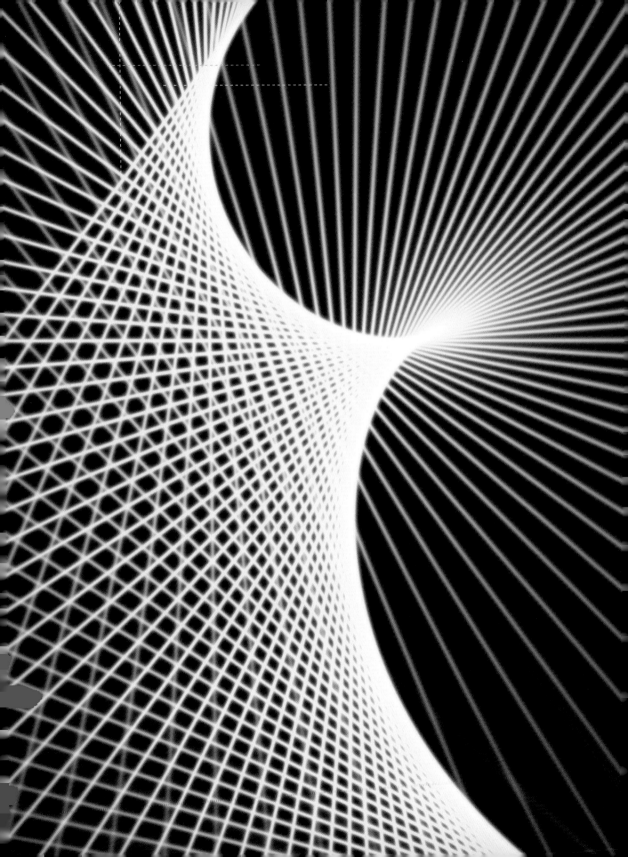

7

AOL.com

AOL has a long and conflicted history with the Web. AOL started its "life" as an Internet Service Provider (ISP), and all the content viewed by our members—before the Web was born—was experienced in a series of proprietary screens we called "forms." As a company, it took a while for us to "get" the Web and understand the value of moving our content out of the AOL client and onto the open Web. The company's main portal, AOL.com, had already been around for years (see FIGURE 7.1), more of a marketing site than a content portal.

This first-person perspective is provided by Kevin Lawver, a 12-year veteran of AOL's Web development teams.

FIGURE 7.1 AOL's home page circa 2000.

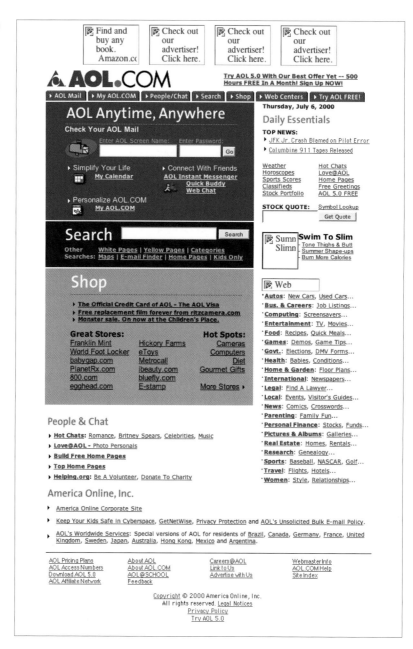

FIGURE 7.1 AOL's home page circa 2000.

In 2005, Jon Miller, AOL's then-CEO, started a project to change all of that. He wanted AOL to open up, to get *all* of our content onto the Web and outside of the traditional desktop client. The first step to this was to open up the company's home page. As with most high-profile projects with a lot of executive involvement, the timeline was short, the list of requirements long, and the expectations high.

A small group of folks did the development work on AOL.com, integrated all the different Web services, wrote all the code, and worked with our internal experts in design, optimization, and accessibility to make it work in as many browsers as possible, as quickly as possible, and available to as many people as possible.

This chapter shares, directly and indirectly, some of the processes, techniques, and lessons they learned while building and maintaining one of the largest and most highly trafficked sites on the Web.

Setting Your Team Up for Success and Avoiding Failure

Launching a complete redesign of your company's site, knowing that you're facing dozens of integration points and an army of stakeholders, all under a tight deadline that the *entire company knows about,* is daunting. That AOL.com launched on time (or at all) was due more to the efforts of the team setting themselves up for success at the very beginning of the project than to any other factor.

The key to speeding things up during the process of defining the requirements and design for AOL.com was getting the developers involved in the process early. We'll discuss what went wrong with the project, and how the development team compensated and handled those setbacks by "cheating ahead" and being flexible.

What Went Wrong

No project is perfect, and AOL.com had its fair share of problems from the start. The AOL.com redesign was the cornerstone of AOL's move from being primarily a dial-up ISP, built around yearly client releases, to a Web company built around Web products supported by advertising and premium services. This was a bold move by the company's CEO, Jon Miller. He wanted to make a statement to the company, AOL's users, and the market that AOL was changing, and AOL.com was the main vehicle for that change. That kind of visibility to all parts of the company and to upper management meant that almost every product decision went through several layers of management in order to come back to the team as an actual requirement. This created "swirl," which is deadly if you're looking at a hard end date.

Another important part of this project, as with most large development efforts, was communication. Because of all the groups involved both in the requirements phase and in integration, there were copious opportunities for communication to break down, for things to get missed, and for unforeseen problems to cause major delays.

A third issue was dealing with a development process that didn't fit the project and caused more problems than it solved.

To wrap up this section, we're going to talk about attitude, and how to think of development as a craft. During the interviews conducted for this book, it became clear that a common thread ran through all them: These folks all treated their profession as a craft. We'll define what it means to be a craftsperson and how that can help you deal with even the most problematic projects.

We'll start by letting the main players introduce themselves and explain their roles on the team.

Let's start with you, Michael—what do you do?

Michael Richman: I'm the technical lead and architect on AOL.com backend and front-end and client-side.

And for people reading the book who don't know what an architect does...?

Michael: I help to shape the decisions on the best way to implement each of the requirements that come to us, balancing all of the stakeholders' concerns. So, my goal is always to make every constituency happy. That includes product, project management, portal, the performance team, the accessibility team, the QA team, the development team, and ops. So, basically, in every step of the way I want to meet the requirements either perfectly or better than they envisioned it. I want to do it in a way that makes it easy to test.

I want to try to repass the requirements and anticipate what extra requests are going to come down the pike in the future to kind of get ready for those. So when we design the solution and design the implementation of a requirement or set of requirements, we want to do it in a way that's flexible enough so when they inevitably come in with a different spin on it, we actually have already done that.

And then, also, we've learned over the past few years to keep in mind the accessibility and the performance teams' requirements as well, which was definitely a learned behavior.

And Kevin, what about you?

Kevin Luman: I'm the technology manager for AOL.com, which always involves me being the first line of, I don't want to say, defense…

If it is, it is.

Kevin: [laughs] Or point of contact, you could say, between all of these groups. It doesn't mean they don't go to Michael or any other individual contributor. But I see one of my main goals as trying to filter out as much as I can so that when they come to the team, at least the request comes with as much meat as possible, as well-formed as possible, so they can continue doing what it is that they love, which is writing software.

When I worked in Search, we used to call that the "umbrella." Is that how you still see it?

Kevin: Yeah—my job is to keep the rain off.

Michael: I like to think of Kevin more as a momma bird…We have a dev team of tiny chicklets sitting in a nest squawking with their beaks open waiting for the manna to fall from heaven. Oh no, I've mixed my metaphors.

Kevin: I think it's probably appropriate, especially in this place and this product where it really is a never-ending onslaught of just random requesters for a feature or just they want information. It could be other technologists looking for data.

Michael would never be able to do his job if he was having to do nothing but field these requests on top of all the other requests that really are related to a particular release we're working on at that point in time…so I'm trying to do a lot of advance work too.

It's not only protecting but sheltering the team from a lot of these requests. But it's actually working to refine them, as well as trying to do some advance work.

We'll continue the interview in the following sections to illustrate exactly how Kevin and Michael led the team through the different challenges they came upon (and continue to—the team is still together and still working on AOL.com, so a lot of these lessons are from more than just the one redesign we're discussing in this chapter).

Rowing Through the Swirl

The number of stakeholders in AOL.com was daunting. Every decision was up for debate at several levels of management, from directors all the way up to the CEO of the company. This created a lot of uncertainty, misinformation, and a constantly moving target. This made it very difficult for design and development to move forward on anything other than the most preliminary of explorations.

How would you guys define **swirl?**

Kevin: For me, the experience is generally comes from a lack of defined leadership in that it creates a vacuum, and swirl is kind of an appropriate metaphor in that people just kind of move around and there's no real goal or aim. They tend to debate and go to these meetings upon meetings on just something. And it's somewhat aimless. I think an example right now that I'm working with is the Mexico and Puerto Rico portal. They want to start it but they're not quite sure how. It's not in the official channels even. It's not on the Plan of Record [a list of priorities for a particular business unit within AOL].

And they're asking me about the level of effort. Well, hey you guys, first let's step back, because they're starting to swirl. And if you let it continue on that path, the worst possible scenario is people actually start doing work on this thing that's not quite defined. And who knows if it has executive sign-off to even launch if it got code ready.

I see two types of swirl: Vertical, which is where a product manager makes a decision, people start moving on it, their boss remakes the decision, it goes up, like hail where it starts as a raindrop but it keeps getting kicked up and down the management chain until it becomes this gigantic ball of ice and crushes your car.

And then there's horizontal swirl, where it's just peers, and you can't decide on what the priorities are, and therefore you get into a stalemate and end up not accomplishing anything. I think AOL.com had both because everything had to go way up the management chain. And even when it went up all the way, it sometimes came down totally different.

Kevin: It comes down filtered or reinterpreted. I see a lot of it, and it looks like it arises from an offhand comment that an executive makes that is interpreted as a mandate.

Michael: I would only add that swirl is largely marked by a series of unproductive and circling meetings.

Kevin: And I would add, part of my job if I'm doing it correctly is that Michael's not, and the rest of the team are not, in those meetings. Hopefully I'm successful, for the most part.

That leads right into my next question: How do you stop swirl and get someone to make a decision? And how do you make progress while it's going on, because you still have a hard date at the end?

Kevin: The biggest thing is finding out what are the decisions to be made, and defining that. And from my experience, what we try to do is just tell them: "Stop. And step back. What are the goals you are after?" And then, if they don't know, tell them: "Well then, why don't you take a couple of days, write a PRD [Product Requirements Document] or an email, or document in some way what it is you're after, and come back."

Michael: The other aspects of it I think are effective are having a really strong facilitator on meetings, and a very strong position when you're representing the dev team and saying: "We can do this, whatever you want to do once you define it, but here are the impacts." And it's one of the things that we do, if there's swirl going on, we say: "We need to know by this date, or the date slips day for day."

And that's the kind of thing that's really effective, because the dates are really important to upper management, usually. So as soon as you put it in very real terms and put your stake in the ground, you have to say: "Hey, you can't do work until what you are supposed to do is clearly defined."

So that's one mistake. The other way around for the mitigated is to say: "You have until next Monday, or next month," or whatever it is, give them a specific date, say: "This is when we need to know the final requirement, if we are to keep the schedule. If you don't care about the schedule, then you can take as much time as you want, we're not going to work on anything."

Kevin: Generally, we say we're going to continue proceeding upon the current path, or whatever path, but generally it's current path, and like Michael was saying, at such and such point, it's too late. Without impact. Like, this is the point we can't absorb it anymore. Or, beyond this, if it's not in their work too far in development, we'll have to scapegoat.

Communication Is Everything

As soon as requirements came up, Kevin and Michael started doing research. They did their best to uncover integration points and potential problems, and communicate those back to the team. The larger a project team is and the more groups it involves, the more important communication becomes. A good project manager is essential to getting the right information to the right people, but developers often lack communication skills or inclination to communicate problems and issues back to the team. It's not a sign of weakness to have issues; it's a fact of life in every development project. Being able to communicate effectively is a key skill that developers need to cultivate: communicating just the facts, without emotion, while explaining the likely consequences and possible solutions.

You've mentioned setting deadlines and measuring the impacts. How do you develop this skill of laying out those facts and communicating them up in a way that will drive people to do the right thing?

Michael: I think a lot of that has to do with our track record as a team. I mean, you can do that if have a strong position and a strong way of delivering it. We have a really good working relationship with Product and Project Management, and we have also a good history on delivering things on time, and have been fairly accurate on our estimates. So, maybe that's somewhat of a credibility issue. But I think you can do it also if you are just confident in your delivery, frankly.

And it doesn't have to be antagonistic. I'm not painting an adversarial picture, it's more…collaborative.

What I've always tried to do is to be as transparent as possible. To build trust. So I figure, if they know everything I'm doing, there's not that question of, "Well, is that padding, are they overestimating a feature because they don't really want to do it?" Right?

Michael: Yeah, kind of like our reviews…

Kevin: …in the standard document I do for LOEs (Level of Effort), right? Where it's a very formal, tabular format; I repeat their product request. We go through it, we put the hours there, how many developers can work on it; and then all of our assumptions. So they see what we're thinking, what we were thinking when we came up with this.

And I think that leads to that sort of transparency, credibility, and you build that. You know, you won't have it at [first], but the more open and transparent you are with your internal processes, especially in dev, I think kind of nips in the bud any of those distrusts.

Right. You've both touched on it: Trust is key. And, you didn't use these words, but "constructive" and "collaborative…" You don't just say "Oh, this is a stupid idea."

Kevin: Yeah, you say "Here are the issues that we have, technically, with this idea; and here's what we've seen work with other products." It usually comes up with regard to a feature that maybe, you know technically as a developer, is just crazy, as far as a request goes. But you don't want to say: "Hey, that's a crazy obscene request," you know? Just tell them the facts: "That's going to be weeks of development."

But I always say, that's only half. Because I've seen that happen before with other managers and leads, where it's just shoot down, shoot down. And Michael is very good at this...you want to do it in a constructive way, and you can do that in telling them a cost. Because that's really what they want to hear and what, more than anything you could say, will kind of hit them with the reality of it, is just the time it will take, and the cost.

But you don't want to leave them hanging there, right, with their product up in the air?

Kevin: Right, you need to think about, can that feature, if tweaked another way, can they get half of what they want? Can they get 95% of what they want, if they'd just drop maybe one particular piece?

Michael: Right. Mostly you have think that the product-owners don't really know where they benefit from the collaborative relationship with dev.

Kevin: It builds trust.

Michael: Yeah. The other thing—the only negative effect of being kind of reactionary to crazy requirements is that you don't want a product to be gun-shy, and that's what you get with that. You want them to think pie-in-the-sky, because for all you know, they're going to think of a really neat feature that is actually easy to implement, whereas if you have this kind of knock-heads relationship where they're somewhat timid about bringing requirements, or they perceive it as complicated or difficult to implement, they might just not bring it, and you definitely don't want that.

Kevin: And that's what I say: If it's an us-versus-them, an adversarial relationship, and not a team...you've lost before you've started. If that's how you're coming in as a dev team approaching your product, whether you're a contractor or internal—you've lost before you've started. It's not that they're your customer, it's that they're your peer, your equal, and we're all trying to create this one product, and we all have come at it with a different aspect.

Battling the Waterfall: Getting Involved Early

When the project started, AOL still operated in the "waterfall" method of development. Each group involved in a project did its bit pretty much in isolation:

❖ Business owners created requirements and produced a Product Requirements Document (PRD).

❖ Designers produced user interface and visual designs, and went through a lengthy review process through several layers of management, and then produced a Design Requirements Document (DRD).

❖ Development didn't usually start development until at least the PRD was complete and signed off on. Once the PRD was signed off, the development lead produced a Technical Requirements Document (TRD) and a System Design Document (SDD).

This model is great if you want to produce a *lot* of documentation, are working on huge projects with lots of integration, and have both a long development cycle and a known end date far in the future; and it was developed while AOL was producing client software that had maybe two releases a year. It's not so great if you have to produce a final product very quickly, or for things that move quickly, like most Web applications. Most teams at AOL are switching to the more agile and collaborative Scrum model of development but AOL.com is a good example of a team working around a cumbersome process to get things done the right way, and to get them done more quickly than working within the usual system would have allowed.

During the requirements-gathering phase, while the PRD was still being created, Kevin Luman and Michael Richman would find requirements that felt very close to final and start working on them. This might be as small a thing as looking for services within the company that provide that feature, or building infrastructure to feed the user interface. That "cheating ahead" allowed them to make progress while the rest of the organization made up its collective mind, and get some time back for the inevitable last-minute changes and additional requirements.

David Artz and Kevin Lawver were involved in the design process from the beginning, weighing in on both potential performance problems and technical feasibility. They worked with designers and executives to lay out the pros and cons of each and give guidance where needed. Their success proves the point that it's essential to have the developers get involved early on. We'll talk more about this in detail in the next section.

*So the big question—and I think the one that developers are most concerned
with—is: How do you insert yourself into the process early on while still
being collaborative and constructive and not coming off as intruding on the
process?*

Kevin: A lot of it, again, comes back to that trust factor in a team. If you have that
trust, you are invited. And if you don't, then I would reach out and tell them,
"Hey, we are really interested in what is going on in design. Could we come to
one of the meetings?" Just ask. Let them know, it's not the whole team, but we
would like to get some insight.

I think we are still using the waterfall and it has actually been pretty productive. The way we do it is that a lot of it is in parallel, just kind of staggered, like
in a staggered, parallel well. Take the co-brands (advertising features on AOL.
com): I have done a lot of work without even Michael there, working with
them in the PRD and even like the DRD requirements and just sanity checks.
Then bringing Michael in when it is a little more baked. That's how I have seen
what's been going on.

Michael: I think that's right. Interestingly, we are probably not as involved as the
Scrum process has the whole team involved and everybody involved. But it
hasn't really presented too much of a problem for us.

Recently we actually had a Scrum-like brainstorming session for requirements
and it was really productive. I think everybody thought so—product, QA,
development, everybody. Several ideas from that made it into the next set of
requirements.

So I don't know that we as a team really know the full benefits of the more
Scrum-like process because we haven't done it so much. But, like I said, we
haven't really run into many problems with the process probably because we
are a tight team. Maybe we don't know what we are missing, what potentially
great things could have come out of the last year and a half or two years if we
had been doing that process. But to the extent that we have had the involvement, it has been working fine.

Kevin: But I wonder too, and having not done Scrum I don't know. Like Michael
mentioned, we could be missing out. The process right now—the sort of
waterfall-ish process we use, the parallel waterfall, has been working well. We
have been getting tons of releases out on time.

I don't know if AOL.com as a product would lend itself to Scrum very well,
given that a lot of it is date driven. From upper management and—sometimes

not necessarily so much from upper management but because of contracts that are due. Especially with co-brands—you will get a contract that has to be done by this timeline. And they really need that projection, especially with sales, because marketing and sales sell ahead and they need to know, "OK, what are the new spots going to be? And when are they going to be delivered?"

Maybe Scrum can be worked in that. I don't know.

It can. So to go back, it sounds like the "how" is you just have to build that trust relationship. You have to start by being open and transparent and putting your cards on the table first, before anyone else will.

Michael: Yeah, it's funny how we keep going back to that—much more than I had anticipated.

That's come up more and more for me recently. All development problems and everywhere that a project goes wrong is very rarely technology. It's almost always people. And it all comes back to trust. If development doesn't trust design and vice versa, then you don't have that collaboration because collaboration is built on trust. If design thinks that we are going to use that against them or not implement what they deliver and we think that they are going to give us crap that is not implementable, well, that is exactly what you're going to get.

It's the same relationship on either side of the development. You've got product. If you don't trust product you're not going to believe that what they want is actually what they want. If QA doesn't trust development, then their estimates are going to get blown up and you're never going to launch anything on time.

Kevin: There is also something I know that we touched on with maybe some of the lower stakeholders. Like say, for us, it may be the accessibility team or the performance team. And especially in 2005 we were really good as far as *us* bringing them to the table. And I think that built a lot of trust too.

I want to go back to that in a minute. Michael mentioned it earlier about anticipating both consequences and people that we need to go and talk to. But just to finish the wrap-up on the getting involved—so, as the tech manager, you are involved really early.

Kevin: Yeah. I help manage swirl and help refine requirements, and then, when they are a little more solid, Michael comes in and he can poke and prod a bit but they are pretty well vetted.

Then the same thing happens with design. I get involved early on with sketches and then Michael comes in when things are little more baked. And I think being a developer has helped tremendously.

So if you weren't a developer before you were a manager, would you have Michael involved earlier in the process?

Kevin: Yeah, I would have to bring him in a lot earlier on. I don't know how much of that kind of parallel stuff we could do if that were the case, though, because Michael would be stretched too thin.

That's true. You would need another.

Michael: You would almost need, like, tag team leads, so that one person could be leading the current development cycle while the next lead is working on the design and brainstorming stages.

Kevin: And I don't know if I am writing myself out of a job. [laughter] But I am kind of doing that, and cultivating that, for other reasons, like bringing Jason up as another type lead.

From an advantage perspective, I want him to grow. I want all the members of my team to grow for their own careers' sake. I am self-interested, of course. I'm looking out for the company. I also want redundancies. But that also helps with, in this perspective, if I weren't able to technically evaluate things on my own, I could have Jason lead.

Well, it almost doubles your capacity at that point. You can be involved in two projects extremely early on and then bring them in and you don't really mess up a current development cycle, you can just do more because you have more resources.

Now I want to go back. I think it is really important to be able to anticipate problem spots. This is going to be really hard to answer. It's a skill. I think anyone can do it. It's just a skill. So how do you develop that skill? Is it just experience, or are there other things that you can do?

Kevin: Like share tips.

Michael: And like the skill of anticipating the future requests and having that influence how you implement current requests.

Yes, all of that. I've called it "cheating ahead"—Mark Robinson's term—where you can see a requirement and you know the kernel of it. You can distill and synthesize it quickly and turn it into something that you can do before maybe it's absolutely final. I think you've both mentioned that. How do you do that? How do you learn to boil those down?

Kevin: One of the things I do—and I did actually even in the very first beta—was early prototyping. And I know there's other people on the team. Michael has done that as well. Even just now. Right? With the "draggable" make this-my-home-page kind of thing.

So, we do a lot of that. A request will come in. I worked on prototypes for AIM, supertab, video. Those are ones that we knew, even before the DRD was complete, getting that done so you can scope it when you do your LOEs. You'll be able to anticipate some of how it would work and feed that back to the product people with advice on how you think it should probably work, technically as well as program-full.

I think that helps a lot, especially with some of the more meaty problems that are going to be hard to LOE. Some of these easier ones we've got down and any experienced developer knows. Some little piece-of-the-page widget with 10 links is going to take them a number of hours.

But some advanced AIM supertab, integrating in a new API you've never really looked at, it's going to be a complete SWAG unless you've done prototyping beforehand.

DEFINITION

SWAG, in case you are curious, stands for Stupid Wild Ass Guess.

Michael: In terms of implementing requirements, implementing features in such a way that leaves the door somewhat open for future aspects of them, one of the things that that makes me think of is the whole...Two different ends of the spectrum are the person who has developed the skill to do that really well, and I don't know if you want to use the AOL.com team as an example of that or not, I don't know. We do it pretty well.

So compare that to the other end of the spectrum. I always think of, like, the outsourcing teams, right? Not to bash India, but the biggest problem that I've had working with developers in India is usually that they need letter-by-letter instruction on how to implement things, and they don't stray from it.

And they need letter-by-letter instructions on the details, like implementation details, which is really what you're talking about. We're talking about how you implement something, which decisions you make to lead you down one path versus another.

Like, Path A will be a very limiting path for the future but will still fulfill the requirements. Whereas Path B will fill the requirements and leave you open.

Kevin: One example that came to mind that you always do and the team does well, is published parts on the page. Take for example that link-list module. The list of links. They'll say, "OK, we just want the links. And we want six." So, [our response is] usually, "They want six. Let's put 10." For when that one more or two more come in, as well as, "Let's make the title publishable."

Because, yeah, even when they say they want it to be the "happy, fun module," tomorrow it might be the "extremely happy, fun module."

Michael: Yeah. That captures the whole mantra that we have that nothing is hard-coded. We hard-code nothing. If we can, we make the configuration publishable. We make everything tweakable and publishable through a tool.

My goal, as I always state it, is to write myself out of the process. That's always been my goal. And maybe it comes from the fact that the best developers are the laziest developers. Right? In a way. Because I want to do the least amount of work in the future.

So, the better I write the thing today, the less I have to do later. And when the requests come down the pike for things, I can say that's publishable, and everybody's happy. So, definitely, the "hard-code nothing" mantra is a big one.

Kevin: There's a danger here, though, and I've seen it: over-engineering.

Michael: Sure, yeah. There's definitely the balance. You definitely have to keep the balance.

So, is that purely experience? To develop...what's that line?

Michael: I think in a way that it's a continuum of experience and intuition. And if you don't have the intuition, you need more experience to make up for it.

Probably, some people can come out of their development training and start on day one, and since they're a very intuitive person on this level, they can make guesses as to how to do things. But if you don't have that, you need to use the past experience to build that up.

So, a lot of it just is having the experience to develop that intuition and say, "I've seen this before..."

Michael: Yes, exactly.

"...And this is what worked last time and this is what didn't." I think the other part is creativity. I find this in hard-core computer science guys who come out of college with a master's in computer science, where everything is a [xx]. It's all the same solution, it doesn't matter what the problem was.

Where if you have some creativity, you can find a different solution that may be more...And part of that is knowing when to shut the creativity off, too.

Michael: Yeah. There is definitely the art aspect of it. I mean, that's why it's hard. It's not like you can apply a formula to it and make it work. I just keep coming back to the whole outsourcing thing, when you have a cultural difference between the majority of the developers that we run into from India, who really do need that lock-step set of instructions.

And there isn't necessarily that learned behavior from the last project to the next project. It's like, you finish one project—and this is not just India, this is anybody—there are some people who...A project is very discrete. You have your requirements, you do your requirements, you're done with that project, and you forget it.

And you go on to the next project. And you have those requirements and there is no relationship between those requirements and the ones in the last project. Even though those are two completely different projects, you have to bring...

I think, in order to achieve this kind of creativity, intuition, and learned behavior thing, you have to bring forward everything you learned from the last project—what went wrong and what went right, and what they wanted after it was done, to say how should I have done that—to every future project.

It's the way you can keep honing the skill and the direction.

Treating Web Development as a Craft

There's as much art to Web development as there is science. In several discussions about Web development, it's come up that the best developers consider what they do a craft to be honed instead of just a job. Some attributes of a craftsperson are

- ❖ passion
- ❖ dedication
- ❖ curiosity
- ❖ creativity
- ❖ intuition
- ❖ problem-solving

All are skills that can be developed, even if you don't have an innate talent for them. When you start thinking of your code as art, something should fundamentally change in how you do your job. Code is created to get something from one point to another. Art creates pleasure. When you get true pleasure from creating artful code, you've successfully joined the guild of Web craftspeople. The skills learned along the way help make even the most troublesome projects easier to manage, and are all you need to find at least something in each one to get excited about.

Hopefully, you became a developer because you're passionate about the Web and building things on the Web (sites, applications, widgets, Web services, or whatever). Sometimes, that passion wanes, or moves, and that's OK. But, if you're passionate, you're more likely to explore and spend your time looking for the most elegant, simplest solution possible to every problem. As you develop your problem-solving skills, you move beyond solving problems just in code, and start thinking about and solving problems for the entire project, even if it's not in your discipline or your responsibility. The willingness to look outside of your own domain is a good indication that you've crossed the line from "assembly-line worker" to craftsperson.

A large part of problem-solving is the ability to take previous experience and apply it to current problems. Being able to think about past problems and see how they apply to the current problem is a key skill. Craftspeople rarely make the same mistake twice, and develop the intuition necessary to know which direction to head. Part of applying past experience is introspection and being honest about assessing how well you've accomplished something. Without that, you won't be able to apply those lessons to future problems, because you won't have understood what exactly you learned from a problem.

There is a challenge here for managers to give their people opportunities for development, and empower them to develop the skills of a craftsperson. It helps a great deal if management encourages developers to feel ownership over their small piece of the project. They may be given a fairly limited task but they should be given the freedom to solve that problem in their own way. Depending on the experience level of the developer, there may need to be some more mentoring or validation of code, but giving developers freedom to explore possibilities and choose the best one for themselves can help them develop that sense of ownership. Also, the more developers know about where their tasks fit into the big picture, the more likely they are to feel like what they're doing matters and the more likely they are to develop that sense of ownership.

Part of my discussion with Michael Richman and Kevin Luman centered around coming up with a definition of *craftsman* and how they develop passion, ownership, and empowerment in developers on their team.

Kevin: I guess it's the difference between thinking of yourself, too, as a craftsman or an assembly-line worker. If you're a craftsman and you really care and you're really into what you're doing and the products you create and your output, I think that sort of mind-set leads more towards wanting to explore other avenues and different levels, or different ways of approaching problems. And introspection and reflection on what things worked and what things didn't.

Michael: Developers are problems-solvers, right? The more line-worker developers are problem-solvers only on the code level, but the more expansive, craftsman developers are problem-solvers for all aspects of the project, and that's where you get the people aspect.

So, anticipating future requests and future needs is about problem-solving for your customers. And you have to think about all possible customers, product QA, ops, performance, accessibility, the users, the publishers, and the dev team.

You've got to think of everybody and try to solve everybody's problems. That also may mean trying to think of what the problems are around that project for each of those groups.

But the craftsman ideal isn't just a skill, it's an ethic. How does that assembly-line developer become a craftsman and treat his or her work as not a science but an art?

Kevin: Part of it, they have to be empowered to be able to do so. And treated like a craftsman and not an assembly-line worker. And that's where you are more of a team, and you feel a vested interest in a product. I think that helps, certainly.

I think we've probably seen that in Big Bowl (a publishing system used on a lot of AOL content channels). You can do the opposite, where you take craftsmen and turn them into assembly-line workers.

By removing any creativity?

Kevin: Yeah. You take a person and you say, "Today you're going to work on pets. And you're going to get this feature in. Here it is, the requirements." I'm tech manager and I'm just doling out requirements that have come in this pipeline. Like, never-ending feature requests or enhancements. And I'm responsible for this N number of channels, and my team, I just plug in different developers into different requests.

And there's no care or concern. Code needs to be nurtured too. I mean, it's living, especially if you have multiple developers working in that code. At some point, it'll become unmanageable.

If people aren't stopping and saying, "It's time for a re-factor," they'll just keep cutting and pasting the same stuff over and over again, or repeating the same errors over and over again.

Or, even worse, they have a myopic view of the product itself, and the code base. And they don't see what impact their changes may have.

That small set of requirements is sort of the product as a whole.

Kevin: Yes, the only person they're trying to please is their manager, the tech manager. And that's it, because they are an assembly-line worker. And there's the manager. You clock in, you clock out, you just do what you're told to do. You could be replaced easily by a WYSIWYG editor.

Michael, what's your definition of a craftsman?

Michael: This is a hard question. I try to think about the people on the dev team that I work with, who I've seen evolve into more craftsmen-like developers. And I'm asking myself, "Why? Did I have any influence on that?" Possibly. And if so, how?

What I think of is, it's just that I try to communicate in every meeting the process of thinking about something that leads me to suggest the way that they do it. I don't just say, "Do it this way." We have a conversation about, "This is something that I want to make publishable and here's why. Why don't you do it this way, because it'll leave the door open in the future for this request that's going to come down the pike."

For me, it's about trying to solve everybody's problems with the particular implementation. That's not really a definition of a craftsman but it's the way I think about it from a coding point of view.

I haven't mentioned this, but I definitely engage it and feel it: I love coding. And I love coming up with the creative and elegant and simplest solution to the problem, in code, that does all of these things for everybody. This is starting to sound super-geeky, but I really do love opening up VI and getting the code.

In fact, that's one of the first things I do when "architecting." I do think about it, but documentation for architecture doesn't work for me. I actually code to architect.

And you doodle.

Michael: Yeah.

Kevin: I think one of the key defining factors for a craftsman is passion. If you don't have a passion for what you're doing, it's going to reflect in your code. And everything you do. It's going to reflect in your interactions with the people you work with, your customers, QA, Ops, whoever it might be.

It'll permeate throughout, and it will be reflected throughout. So, a passion for what you're doing is one of the must-haves of a craftsman. I don't know if it's the whole definition of a craftsman, but it's definitely a requirement for becoming a craftsman.

And I don't think people necessarily come with a passion. There's some people who get in the field with passion, some people get into it because they think it's a high-paying job—and, hey, that's fine—it doesn't mean that they can't be passionate or become passionate.

And the organization can help in that respect. Or it can hurt, as we've seen. It can take that passion away, just as easily.

How do you figure out what that passion is, and how to take assembly-line workers—or people who may have at one time had that spark—and reignite it? Because you're right, being a craftman is all about being passionate about what you do, whatever it is. And when you have that passion, you want to get better at it.

Kevin: And please the people, the stakeholders involved.

That's the difference between creating code and creating art. Code is to get something from Point A to Point B, and art is to create pleasure in something, whatever it is. So, I think we have a definition. It's passion—that's all good. But how do you ignite it? Michael mentioned empowerment.

Michael: Yeah, Kevin mentioned empowerment too. But I was going to echo it, because I think that's one of the key ways. If you let someone get in on the ground floor and have some kind of stake in the thing they're going to be developing, then they'll definitely care about it more.

As opposed to just kind of doling out the requirement at the end of the line, saying, "You're the last cog in the widget." That's wrong…"The last cog in the line to spit out the widget." [laughs]

I think that's definitely one way of doing it, giving people a voice in the whole process.

Kevin: And to be honest with AOL.com, in the "what you see" we really don't have a lot of say or empowerment.

So, it's really finding the spot where you can empower people within the process.

Kevin: Exactly. That's what I said. But it doesn't mean that you're powerless. So, what are the spots where you can effect change? For instance, we're proud of what we've done in maintainability of code, in performance, and in accessibility. Because those are the things we can instill and we can succeed in, regardless of the feature.

So, part of empowerment is ownership. How do you make people feel that they own their piece of it? Is it freedom to fail, freedom to experiment? What is it? How do you do it?

Michael: How do we do that, Kevin? [laughter] I'm not sure we *do* do that. Do people feel like they do have ownership over their pieces? I think some people do and some people don't on our particular team.

And in a way, that's like the people who do are the ones who choose to. And the people who don't, choose not to. Now, are we asking how do we "make" or encourage the people who don't feel the ownership to feel it? I don't know. I mean, there's a certain limit. Some people just don't want it.

Right. And I don't think we're saying there's not a place for the assembly-line worker.

Michael: I guess it comes down to the style in which you manage and lead the team. Because if you leave it open and leave it as a...

Kevin: I don't micro-manage.

Michael: Right. There's no micro-management and there's no dictation of how things should go.

Kevin: Michael! I don't micro-manage! Repeat after me! "Kevin Luman does not micro-manage." [laughter]

Michael: Right. And I don't micro-architect.

Kevin: Yep, it's true. Even when you're telling people, in the end, that you're right. Everyone gets assigned a task to do but it keeps going down. They still have freedom within that to be creative.

I try and psych people up: "Hey, this is a really good, meaty problem." Like, it's going to be interesting. Here are some of the problems and it's going to be interesting finding how we do this in an elegant, maintainable way.

And as a manager, I at least try to spark that. "OK, do they think it's cool?" Can you at least drive that?"

And if they don't, you give them a carrot for the next one... You say, we just have to get this done, the next thing will be...

Kevin: I have to do that too. If there's some people who don't want...Like, take the CSS, like some of the Web developer or Web technologist types, now engineers, who have had to take on the ownership of a lot of the CSS.

One of the things I've tried to do with the team is make sure all the engineers write their own CSS. But we still have our gurus, who shoulder bigger burdens of it. And it's like, some releases there's a lot more of it; others, less. But I still try to give everyone on the team something challenging and interesting when I can.

And if things are crunched, we might, of course, have to move it off to someone else.

So, you guys let your developers give their own estimates, right? Do you guys LOE everything?

Michael: Yes, and it works. I think we're pretty cognizant of when we're utterly insane. We try to keep in mind how long it will take a particular person to accomplish something.

Kevin: We definitely give the LOE with that in mind. As a manager, I have to be thinking, what's the acceptable max? And part of doing that would be knowing that if it gets to a certain limit, someone—like maybe a Michael—will have to lead, to step in and help out. But you also hope that's part of the training.

You set them up for success.

Kevin: Yeah. And learning, and growth.

Which is great, because that encourages the craftsman development. "I'm not a hired gun to just do this one thing. I can branch out. And now I know, even if I don't necessarily like this and I'm not passionate about that kind of development or whatever, I've got the experience and I can speak the language." So that's a really good thing.

Kevin: And they own more of the project.

Right. And you get more coverage. So, if somebody gets hit by a bus, you've got backup. [laughter]

Kevin: Which goes both ways. It's not just on the harder stuff. It's also why I want—and I've tried to push—all the engineers to be doing the CSS. It's something they should know as well. For a throughput, as well. And I think it is growth, if they like it or not. I think, as a developer, if you're in this, you should know that.

Right. Definitely. So, anything we missed? Anything else you guys want to share?

Kevin: A wrong turn for me—they're not major ones, but minor ones that I constantly try to catch myself on—is not communicating enough. Forgetting to make sure, oh, yeah, I should have put QA on that mail, got them involved earlier on this.

Or even right now when I'm doing prototyping, make sure to cc: Michael (lead software design engineer) or Jason (senior software engineer), so they're up to speed, as much as they want to be. If they're really busy, Michael and I kind of do this, have this agreement: If I see him and he knows, it's not a priority, I'm not looking for a response, it's informational only. If he's really busy, he won't look at it. If he's not, he has time.

This has highlighted that your relationship is as important as almost any of the other parts to the success of anything you do. If you don't have a good relationship with whoever's in charge of managing or requirements and resourcing, you're sunk.

Michael: Yep.

Kevin: Yeah, relationships are crucial.

Well, it goes back to the communication in the end. The reaching out early and knowing who to pull in, and when, is essential.

Kevin: And that helps to build the trust.

Right. When you don't surprise people at the last minute with stuff, that really helps. Because they're more likely to cut you some slack the next time that there is an emergency.

Kevin: Well, and there's a give and take that goes back to what Michael was saying. There's this balance with everything you have to weigh. And if accessibility digs in their heels, they could make life really tough for us.

But if they trust us, and when we say, "Hey, this is going to be really tough. Can we go this step and work on addressing that feature release?" a lot of times they say, "Yeah." Because they trust us, that we're not just going to keep punting it off down the road. Then you've got to follow up and do what you've promised.

This comes up a lot. So you don't say "No," you say, "We can't do it now. And here's why. But we can do it here. Is that OK?" And nine times out of 10 they'll say it's fine. Because you have to make sure that you tell them, "Well, if we stop everything we're doing, and do this one thing that you want, it's going to cost you. If we wait, you get it just a little bit later than that. But you still get everything you asked for."

Kevin: Again, teams want to succeed. Teams want to win. And if everyone's on the team, they're focused on that goal of winning, more so than their own particular fiefdom or agenda.

Hopefully, you can see throughout the interview that Kevin and Michael have a great relationship, and that helps them a great deal in dealing with the stress of the day-to-day challenges of working on AOL.com.

Designing for Performance

The design goal for AOL.com was to create something that looked and felt like AOL, but was cutting-edge and differentiated the site from its competitors. To that end, before there were even any specific requirements set down for this project, and just to get an idea of what the product team was looking for, the design team came up with several dozen initial concepts for the look and feel of the site—extremely creative and beautiful designs. Unfortunately, most of them contained several elements that just couldn't be implemented in modern Web browsers, or would cause major performance problems.

And therein lay the rub: performance. The site needed to load and be usable over a dial-up connection in less than 10 seconds. This meant that everyone involved had to compromise: Designers had to let go of some visual flair, and development had to come up with some new ways of doing things.

Fortunately for AOL.com, they were able to do all of that. Development was involved from the very beginning of the design process, and worked with the designers to make sure that what was designed could be faithfully created in "real life."

David Artz and I were involved very early on in the process, brought in to comment on how things could be implemented and to find performance problems in the designs. We worked with the designers on each revision, providing comments, suggestions, and, in some cases, prototypes to show how each design element impacted performance. This meant a lot of revisions from the designers until we got to the final design for the product.

DESIGN IS A TEAM EFFORT

For many projects, design happens in a vacuum, without feedback or input from development. This leads to unreasonable requirements, broken expectations, and missed deadlines. There's absolutely no reason for this to happen if design and development work together from the start.

Estimating Performance Before You Write a Line of Code

David and I wanted to see if we could estimate the page size before we started development, and came up with a couple methods for doing so that ended up working quite well.

Before we get into that, we need to take a step back and talk a little bit about tools. I love tools, and have built several over the years to help me determine how well I was doing my job (building Web pages). One of these was a script that ripped pages apart and told me what percentage of the document was markup. This became a personal guidepost for how well I was marking things up. The percentage goal was based on how complex the design was, of course, but I tried to keep my documents to less than 50% markup. Unfortunately, the more complex the design and data, the more markup you need to represent that data. A complex data table is going to have far more markup than a blog, for example.

My original script was a page built for AOL's server, and no longer exists. But I've recreated the basic methodology here as a JavaScript bookmarklet (remove all the line breaks if you actually want to use it):

```
javascript:
function recurseNodes(node) {
    var total = 0, kids=node.childNodes, n=kids.length, i=0;
    for (i=0;i<n;i++) {
        t = kids[i];
        if (t.nodeType == 3) {
            total+=t.nodeValue.length;
        } else if (t.childNodes.length > 0) {
```

```
        total+=recurseNodes(t);
      }
   }
   return total;
}

function pageSize() {
   var d=document;
   var h=document.getElementsByTagName("html")[0];
   var text=recurseNodes(h);
   var markup = h.innerHTML.length;
   var p = (text/markup)*100;
   var m=h.innerHTML;alert("Text: "+text+", HTML: "+markup+", text
percentage of whole: "+p+"%");
}
```

```
pageSize();
```

If you create a bookmark in your browser with that code in it (again, with line breaks removed), you can click that bookmark on any page, and it will throw an alert with the size of the "text" content of the page, the size of the markup, and the percentage of the whole document that's textual content. It's not perfect, but it's a fun, quick test to see if you're meeting your goal.

TABLE 7.1 shows the results from some popular commercial sites.

TABLE 7.1 Amount of Text Content on Selected Popular Sites

Web Site	Amount of Text (in bytes)	Total Content (in bytes)	Text % of total content
Amazon.com	37,322	141,481	26.4%
AOL.com	13,808	62,233	22.2%
CNN.com	20,281	117,459	17.3%
eBay.com	28,427	70,772	40.2%
Google.com	1,385	5,136	27%
MSN.com	7,482	43,335	17.3%
MySpace.com	12,435	47,178	26.6%
Yahoo.com	85,176	115,704	73.6%

Steve Chipman has also written a bookmarklet called "Page Info" that does that, and more. You can find it at his Web site: http://slayeroffice.com/?c=/content/tools/pagenfo.html.

David and I did a quick spin around the Web looking for comparable portals and did some checks to see how they were doing with their markup and what percentage of the whole it was. From that unscientific assessment, we concluded that if we could hit 1:5 ratio of text to markup (that's 20%), we'd be OK.

It all starts with content. Early on, our design team produced wireframes with example content provided by the editorial group. We took those, copied all the text out into a blank text file, got the size of it, and then multiplied it by five to get what we thought the markup size would be. That gave us our initial load time estimate. We knew that we couldn't be any faster than that initial number.

Once we left the markup, we had to start guessing about images, CSS, and JavaScript. There were some scripts we knew we had to include for reporting and advertising, but we also knew that we'd need a certain amount of JavaScript for actual functionality. We assumed that the site would have about half as much JavaScript as it had markup, and the CSS would be about one-third the size of the markup. These were just guesses. We ignored most of the art (because we assumed it would be pulled in through CSS after the page had loaded) except the photos. We found photos that were roughly the same dimensions, optimized them, and then added their size to the total.

Once we had all those numbers, we could come up with an estimate for how large the page would be once it was built, based solely on the design mockup. We did this for each of the designs, presented them to the designers and product owners, and made our suggestions.

Having numbers is always good—even if they're only for comparison—and they helped us back up our opinions about each feature's piece of the overall performance picture.

To illustrate, here's an example "worksheet" for figuring it out:

1. Enter the number of characters in the document: _____

2. Markup size = line 1 $\times$ 5: _____

3. List known required JavaScript and CSS files and their sizes: _____

4. Application JavaScript = line 2 $\times$ .5: _____

5. Application CSS = line 2 $\times$ .33: _____

6. Combined size of photos: _____

Just fill in the data as you get it, and you can get a pretty good estimate of how long it's going to take for a user to load your page.

If you take just line 2, that's the number of bytes users have to download if they have all the other content in their cache. This is a user who comes back using the same browser and either just reloads the page or comes back the next day.

If you take the numbers from the lines 2 through 5, you have the number of bytes that the user without any of your content in their cache has to download in order to get to "first render" (when content is first displayed in the browser), as long as all your JavaScript files are in the <head> of the document.

Performance Concerns

There are several things to keep in mind when dealing with performance. There are many compromises to be made between the different pieces of content on the page, and many things that can be done to make sure the most important content on your page shows up first while the rest of the page loads. The first step is to determine which sections of the page are the most important. Usually, they're near the top left corner of the page. Let's look at AOL.com as shown in **FIGURE 7.2**:

FIGURE 7.2 The AOL. com homepage: Most important content near the top left. *(©2007 AOL LLC. All Rights Reserved. Used with permission.)*

The first thing you see is the AOL logo, and then the search box. The next section is the "dynamic lead" that rotates through five different editorial mini-pages. To the right of that is a small toolbox with the six most popular activities on AOL. Then, you see the first ad. All of these things are "above the fold," meaning that 90% of the audience will be able to see them without needing to scroll.

When you bring up AOL.com in a browser over a slow connection, you get usable content fairly quickly—as quickly as your browser can download the HTML and initial CSS and JavaScript. As shown in **FIGURE 7.3**, everything else loads as it comes in, but the page is usable as soon as that initial chunk of content comes in.

FIGURE 7.3 HTML text-based content loads in fast.

The user isn't waiting for an ad to render or any onload events to fire in order to use the page. Everything is functional as soon as the first render happens.

Getting to this stage isn't easy. It means a lot of work up front to make sure that all of that important content is actually in the document, and sometimes breaking some principles of "progressive enhancement." It all depends on the goals of your site. If you're a portal and you want to drive people to your content, and allow them to get to what they want to do quickly, maybe this is the right approach for you.

All content on AOL.com is delivered compressed. Take a look at total amount of data that is ultimately delivered:

❖ 44 kilobytes of HTML

❖ 62 kilobytes of JavaScript

❖ 40 kilobytes of CSS

However, when it's compressed, you'll see that it's actually only

❖ 12 kilobytes of markup

❖ 24 kilobytes of JavaScript

❖ 9 kilobytes of CSS.

That means the browser will render the content a *lot* faster, because it spends less time waiting for content to download.

Compression is great for text content. As you can see, you can greatly reduce the size of markup, JavaScript, and CSS. The same can't be said for compressing images or other binary files; you'll get some benefit there but the big win is for text.

> **NOTE**
>
> Please see Appendix C for more information on compression.

Let's go through how AOL.com has maximized performance by looking at what has to download in order for the most important content on the page to be usable before all of the art has downloaded and before the onload event has fired. We'll walk through the pieces of content downloaded and when things happen in the browser. **FIGURE 7.4** illustrates the process outlined below.

1. Markup is downloaded, decompressed, and turned into a DOM.

2. JavaScript and CSS files in the <head> of the document are downloaded, decompressed, and parsed.

3. The browser starts rendering, stopping as it hits <script> elements in the document to either run or download scripts. The first script outside the <head> the browser finds on AOL.com is for reporting; it shows up right after the <body> tag, so no content is rendered until that file is downloaded, parsed, and run.

4. The browser renders the header, which contains the logo and the search box.

   It encounters another script element. This one puts focus on the search box, so users can search right away without needing to click in the field first.

5. Minor scripts write out the Sign In/Sign Out links.

6. The Dynamic Lead is loaded—first all the markup, and then the three script elements that start the rotation.

7. The rest of the content in the left column is loaded.

8. The right column starts rendering. The "Communication Center" renders first, followed by a script that sets a class on the dropdown arrows next to "Money," "Music," "My AOL," and "Video."

9. Several placeholders for advertising render, but not until after all the content on the page is displayed. (We'll talk more about this later.)

10. The rest of the right column renders.

11. The footer renders.

12. The scripts that call the ads are run. Once the ads render, they're moved into the correct spots in the right column.

Among those familiar with progressive enhancement, that list may raise an eyebrow or two. That's fine, because AOL.com is also accessible—since all the important content is on the page, screen readers easily handle it. All of the JavaScript has accessible alternatives. We'll talk more about accessibility later on.

AOL.com is a site that people come back to—to check mail, read the news, hear the latest albums, or get stock quotes. To improve their experience with the site, files are *cached*, meaning users don't have to download the files every time they request the page. Now, because the content of the page changes so frequently, the HTML is never cached. But all JavaScript, CSS, and images are cached, for variable amounts of time. For example

❖ HTML: never cached

❖ Images: 24 hours

❖ JavaScript: 30 days

❖ CSS: 30 days

This is great, because as long as someone uses the same browser and doesn't empty his cache, he'll never need to go back to the server to download those files—greatly reducing the amount of time it takes to load the page.

All of this caching introduces a problem: What if you need to make a change to the CSS or JavaScript? There's a chance that users won't see that change for a month. AOL.com solves this by versioning all JavaScript and CSS files in the URL. If you look at the page, you'll see a URL that looks like this:

```
http://www.aolcdn.com/_media/aolp_v21/main.css
```

The "v21" piece is the version. There's a configuration option to tell what version the page should load. This gets around the caching problem easily; since it's a brand new file, all users should see the changes as soon as the file's published.

One last tip on reducing load time: Reduce the number of files you make the browser download. Your overall file size might be OK, but if that's split up over a couple hundred files, your page will feel a lot slower than it should. There are several reasons for this:

❖ In Internet Explorer, only two files at a time will be downloaded from any one domain.

❖ Every file you download has anywhere from one-half to several kilobytes of HTTP headers that come along with it. This can greatly increase the total amount of data users have to download to see your page. HTTP headers aren't compressed, so there's very little you can do to reduce this size.

❖ All the JavaScript and CSS files you put in the <head> of your document *must* be downloaded before the browser will try to render the page. Since all CSS, link, and style elements have to be specified in the <head> anyway, it should all be one file.

❖ JavaScript "blocks" page rendering (meaning the browser won't display any content below that <script> tag until the script is done downloading *and* running), even when the scripts are pulled in inside the body of a document. This means that the browser will stop rendering when it gets to a <script> element and wait for that to download or execute before continuing.

Performance is an ongoing process. Especially for legacy projects, you'll want to start small and make incremental improvements. If you're starting with a clean slate, you'll want to do as much as you can up front to make sure your page is as fast as possible. Just because more users are on high-speed connections doesn't mean they're getting more patient. If anything, they're less patient—expecting everything to load instantly. The closer you can get to "instant," the more satisfied users will be with your site.

Interview: David Artz

David Artz leads AOL's Optimization team, which looks at AOL products and provides feedback on how to make them faster, in addition to tools for measuring a site's performance. He did a lot of work with the AOL.com team to make sure the page loaded as quickly as possible.

What's your role at AOL?

AOL's Optimization team is focused on improving the speed and accessibility of AOL's Web sites. We do this by providing clear, measurable standards in Web site optimization and by documenting and evangelizing best practices and solutions in achieving a more "optimized" experience. We also consult and provide real-time feedback and analysis on high priority products such as AOL. com throughout the entire design process.

What's the difference between "perceived" and "real" performance?

When you start digging into performance, you quickly realize there's a blurry line when it comes to deciding when a page is "loaded." Do you count the stuff loading below the fold? What about objects and scripts engineered to load last?

Perceived performance is the user's perception of the speed of the page, and when it's ready enough for them to start using. Though this can vary for different users, I generally say it's when all graphics, text, and essential functionality above the fold (browser window without scrolling) is ready to use.

Real performance is much easier to measure, which is typically why it serves as our benchmark when managing performance-improvement efforts. It's when all objects on a page are loaded in, no matter where they load in the document or if the user even needs them.

Our team places much emphasis on perceived performance, and uses techniques such as moving scripts from the <head> element to the bottom of the body, system text and CSS for design elements, load status messages, strategically ordering HTML content, and loading content only when the user scrolls to see it.

What tools do you use?

We use HTTPWatch and a homegrown tool lovingly named "PAT" (Performance Analysis Tool) that generates charts and reports based on data from HTTP-Watch. PAT will parse HTTPWatch's logs, and give us the opportunity to classify objects as advertisements, code, graphics, etc., so we have a good idea of where our KB and requests are going, and then estimate load time based on that data for various connection speeds.

We also have a tool that is a hit with our execs called Webometer, which quickly loads a site and its competitors in a Web browser, giving instant data on comparative performance.

What should developers do first when judging a design for performance?

If you want to truly estimate, you have to imagine the outcome of the resulting build, which may be tough on new projects or if you're new to Web development. Also, a more experienced developer (especially one who's been through my training) will have an arsenal of tools that can make any design perform well.

This could be a chapter in itself, but the steps I would follow are

1. Get a spreadsheet; you'll want to tally up K size and number of objects.

2. Based on the amount of text and the complexity of the layout, calculate how big the CSS and HTML will be (this is one of those experience-dependent ones).

3. Look at the design and think through how many and how heavy the graphics and photos will be when sliced.

4. Estimate the client-side JavaScript file size you will need—this can get big if you need to use shared libraries.

5. Tally up the results, and divide total KB by the speed you're targeting (DSL = 768 kilobits = 96 kilobytes per second).

6. Account for object requests by multiplying by 40ms per object for JavaScript and 20ms for CSS and images.

In general, all a developer can do is push for lighter design and less functionality, and think where we can be clever by moving requests later in the page.

How do you keep track of performance over time?

On the Operations side of the AOL house, we have automated tests that run over the week, which we use as a pulse on our top sites and their competitors. Our goal at AOL is to be faster than the competition, and be optimized for performance using the latest techniques regardless.

Repeatable Steps

There are concrete steps you can take during the design process to make sure your site will perform when you're done with development. We talked about them fairly quickly, so here's a quick list of things to make sure you do whenever you start the design process:

❖ Involve development early.

❖ Use available tools to get the numbers from competitors or comparable sites.

❖ Use those numbers to set performance goals for your project.

❖ Scrutinize each revision of the design for potential performance pitfalls.

❖ Measure and get numbers—the more "real" you can make those numbers, the better.

❖ Think about performance up front. The more work you can do during the design phase, the better you'll be in the long run.

Performance is a process. The last point in the list above is really important, so I'll repeat it: The more work you can do up front, the better. The time you spend finding problems early in the process will save hours and hours of debugging and hair-pulling later on when the design's been agreed upon and you *have* to get it working.

System Design and Architecture

On large projects like AOL.com, no one is ever working alone. There are Web services to integrate, databases and Web servers to set up, repositories to create, art to cut, and various other tasks that have to get done before you can flip the switch and launch something. On a project this large, no one person does all of these things. This section's not going to discuss most of these in detail but will address how you can approach the monumental integration and technical design tasks associated with building something this large.

The Buddy System

When it comes to developing Web applications, the buddy system is definitely the way to go. Pairing up your backend/middleware developer with your front-end developer as a team to work very closely together is a great way to get things done quickly. They should work together to design Web services and tools so you end up with a seamlessly integrated product instead of a bunch of duct tape.

There are several benefits to this way of working:

❖ The producer and consumer of Web services (JSON, XML) for the page are on the same page. This means the services and the code to interact with them will be as efficient as possible.

❖ No one person has to worry about everything. Dividing responsibilities between the front end and middleware is a nice clean line. You can have some crossover, but you know who "owns" each piece.

❖ Although there's an owner for each piece, there's also backup. Having someone close by to bounce ideas off of and answer questions is always helpful.

❖ Two is a small enough number that there's not a lot of communication over-head. Most problems can be solved over an instant message or a quick phone call. There's no need to schedule big conference calls with dozens of people and juggle schedules.

Two seems to be the right number when working on a project of this size. You'll need to have many more folks working on other pieces, like publishing tools, managing other projects that feed pieces of the main one (Web services, integration points, etc), designers, operations, database administrators, etc. But, pairing the developers on the project works well.

Get the Stubs Out

The days of flat Web pages are over. For the most part, no one writes just HTML and publishes it as a single document, at least not for large sites like AOL.com. That means Web services, scripting languages, and integration with other systems.

When it comes to designing Web services, there is no such thing as a vacuum. A Web service should never be designed without thinking about how a developer would go about consuming that service. That means thinking in terms of simplicity, what steps someone will have to take to interact with your service, and making those steps as simple as possible. The easiest way to do this is to create *stubs*—example responses or processes that take a request and return a canned (fake) response. This gives the consumers of your Web service a chance to play around with it and give you feedback before you go through the trouble of actually hooking it up with any backend systems. This is a good way to make sure your "buddy" (the one we paired you up with in the last section) will be able to work quickly and with confidence once the "real" service is ready.

Things to think about when creating stubs:

❖ Don't just think about what happens when things work—think about when things aren't going so well. What does an error response look like? How can you tell the consumer of your service whether to try again or give up?

❖ What kinds of data can be returned? Can you get more than a set number of items back? For example, if your service returns search results, what does it look like when you get two results back? Three? Ten? None?

❖ Do you need to provide more than one "flavor"? How do you provide both XML and JSON responses?

❖ Can any programming language consume your services? Validate your assumptions and make sure that you're not tying yourself to a single way to consume the service.

Stubs allow for integration to happen before all the pieces are ready. This means each party responsible for a piece of infrastructure or any front-end developer could be finished with their work long before you're ready to integrate with them.

If you've done your job correctly, and the real service matches the stubs, it's just a small configuration change to point from the stub to the real thing.

Stubs also give you something to test against. When you have the real service ready to go, you should always go back and compare it to the stubs to make sure you've remained consistent. There isn't much point in creating stubs if the end result is totally different.

Creating stubs for all of your Web services not only saves you time, it gives you a reference implementation you can give to other folks who might need to integrate your services. You don't need to give them access to a live production machine to develop with. They can develop and test against the stubs and then test against the live service once they're done. It saves load on your production environment, and means a lot less hassle for folks who may work remotely or outside of your corporate firewall.

Thinking About Workflow

Consumers (we call them "users") aren't the only ones who interact with your product. In the case of AOL.com, there's an entire army of folks who do editorial work on the individual pieces of the page. They're spread across organizational units, and they all have their own concerns and requirements for the tools they use to publish content. These requirements may include licenses for photography, content that needs to go live and come down at a particular time, different methods for formatting, different feeds they need to integrate, or ways to track contractual obligations. All of these requirements need to be addressed and handled by the publishing tools you create to drive the site.

In many cases, the tools are the last things to be built because they're seen as the least important. They're not. When you think about all the hours that each of those editors spends in those tools, and all the times they do the same thing over and over again, any wasted steps or broken tools could end up costing your company thousands, if not millions, of dollars in lost productive time.

One way to go about building tools is to first gather information from the editorial staff:

❖ What do you need to do to get from "nothing" to a finished product you can publish on the site?

❖ Are there concrete, reproducible steps you can document?

❖ What tools do you use now?

❖ What do you like about them?

❖ What's wrong with them?

❖ How often will you be using the tool?

That's just a sample. There are some questions you might want to avoid. Don't ask about flexibility or uptime. No matter if they need it or not, the response is always "100% flexible and available 100% of the time." No one needs a tool that's 100% flexible, and most publishing tools don't need to have 99.999% uptime. Flexibility is expensive. The more flexible a tool is, the more options it needs to have, which cuts down on how quickly you can do the things you do most often.

There's also a danger in asking people what they want. They may not know, or may not know quite how to ask for the thing they really need. How do you get around the fact that human beings are unreliable? Watch them work. This may seem uncomfortable, but having someone walk you through exactly how they do their job is a much more enlightening process than asking them questions. Spend an hour or two watching them do their job and take notes. This will give you a lot of insight into what they *really* spend their time doing and what the tool needs to do in order to help them do it more efficiently.

Often, tools are designed by the developer, which can lead to problems. It's a good idea to have a designer spend some time on the workflow around tools. They shouldn't spend their time making it "pretty," but a good interface designer spending an hour or two making sure the tool makes sense is a good investment. Developers have a habit of thinking of what a tool is doing underneath the interface, which leads to some strange interactions for the people using the tool. The input of a thoughtful designer will help will make the tool's "user experience" a lot smoother.

Being considerate of the users of the tools used to publish the site will almost always lead to better content, and the cost savings can be pointed to as a real win, no matter how big the company is.

Front-End Wizardry

You can have the fastest Web server, database, and cache server, and you may be connected to the Internet with the fastest pipe possible—and your users may *still* think your site is slow. There is a tendency in technology organizations to give less time or discipline to front-end code, even though the vast majority of time between when a user makes a request and when content is displayed is spent downloading and rendering that content. No amount of performance optimization on the backend will improve that experience; the only way to make things feel faster is to show the same discipline on the front end that you use in your server-side code. This section will introduce the basics of standards-based development, and some best practices you can use to whip your markup and CSS into shape.

Making Your Markup Sing with DOCTYPE

Early on in the process of designing and developing AOL.com, the team met often to discuss markup best practices, performance, and to make sure that all of them were on the same page. Prior to this, my work on improving performance for AOL Search taught me that one of the best ways to improve performance was to use semantic markup, and a DOCTYPE that put modern Web browsers into "standards mode." We chose that same approach for AOL.com.

But before we get into that, let's take a step back. Some of the words in the previous paragraph may be English but might not make any sense unless you're already a part of the Web standards "club."

What Came Before

In the old days, everyone used HTML tables to determine the layout of their pages. This worked, but created bloated, hard to maintain documents that took a long time for browsers to download and then render.

This model was OK. It mostly worked, and allowed people to build complex layouts on the Web. Unfortunately, it wasn't very flexible or maintainable, and it punished users because their browsers had to try to figure out how to draw gigantic mazes of nested tables (according to several people who work on browser rendering engines, rendering tables is one of the hardest things they have to do).

The lingua franca of the Web, HTML, was also a problem. HTML 4 didn't enforce its rules. To write valid HTML 4, you could leave tags unclosed, have both unquoted and quoted attributes, use both upper- and lower-case tags, and there was no need to provide a DOCTYPE, telling the software consuming the document what specification the document conformed to. This meant that browsers had to guess about where a particular tag ended, which led to a gigantic set of tests the browser had to do before it could even consider rendering the document.

Thankfully, no one has to live with that pain any more.

DOCTYPE Switching

The advent of XHTML 1.0 and CSS 2.0 gave browsers a chance to break from the old rendering model of HTML 4 (now called "quirks mode"). XHTML took some of the rules of XML and applied them to HTML's vocabulary. The rules are simple but allow browsers (or any other parser) to very quickly decipher the document's structure and move on to rendering. For a document to meet the standards of valid XHTML, it has to

❖ Use a DOCTYPE as the first content of the document. The DOCTYPE for XHTML 1.0 transitional is:

```
<!DOCTYPE html PUBLIC "-//W3C//DTD XHTML 1.0 Transitional//EN"
"http://www.w3.org/TR/xhtml1/DTD/xhtml1-transitional.dtd">
```

❖ Have an opening and closing `<html>` element as the root element of the document.

❖ Have an opening and closing `<head>` element as a child of `<html>`.

❖ Have an opening and closing `<body>` element as a child of `<html>` and as a sibling of `<head>`.

❖ Have an opening and closing `<title>` element as a child of `<head>`.

❖ Set all tags in lowercase.

❖ Have closed tags. For example, if you create a paragraph tag, it should look like this: `<p></p>` instead of just `<p>`.

❖ Set all attribute names in lowercase.

❖ Enclose all attribute values in quotes.

These rules are fairly easy for browsers to enforce, and, equally good news, there aren't that many of them, which means browsers can render that content faster.

Browsers were able to introduce a feature called *DOCTYPE switching*, which allowed them to very quickly decide what kind of document they were dealing with and change the rendering mode appropriately. The two modes are called *quirks mode* and *standards mode*. (Firefox has a third mode, but it's not different enough to talk about.) Quirks mode is the old model, where the browser goes through all of the different tests it used in the "old days" to create something to render. Standards mode does away with most of those tests and gets to something renderable much faster. In many cases, just changing from quirks to standards mode can provide a 10x improvement in rendering speed.

How do you tell the browser to render a document in standards mode? By using a DOCTYPE! It's highly recommended that you use XHTML 1.0 Transitional (see the rules list above for the exact text). This provides the same vocabulary of available tags while giving you the benefit of standards mode. XHTML 1.0 Strict removes several elements (most importantly, `iframe`) that limit its usefulness.

Once your document is rendered in standards mode, you're not done. You need to then make sure it's valid, using either a built-in validator (most good text editors and WYSIWYG editors have them built in now) or by using the W3C's validator at http://validator.w3.org. Having a valid XHTML document is just the first step to producing a good product, but it's an important one. It's a good initial test of quality. If the document validates, it means you can be reasonably sure that the CSS you write will find the right elements and do what you expect it to.

Semantic Markup

Even with a valid XHTML document, it's still possible to use HTML tables for layout and continue creating bloated, unmaintainable pages. But part of the benefit of having your document render in standards mode is that you need less markup to handle your layout, because most of the instructions for how the browser should display your document is in an associated CSS file (which we'll get to in a little bit).

Instead of relying on tables, it's now possible to use the entire HTML vocabulary to express so much more than how a document is supposed to look. It's now possible to express what the content of a document *means*. If there's a list of items, it should be marked up with list elements. For example, in the old days, lists might be marked up like this:

```
&#0149; Oranges<br/>
&#0149; Apples<br/>
&#0149; Grapes<br/>
&#0149; Pears<br/>
```

But, today, you should use HTML lists:

```
<ul>
    <li>Oranges</li>
    <li>Apples</li>
    <li>Grapes</li>
    <li>Pears</li>
</ul>
```

By default, that gives you the default styling of a list, but it also opens up a lot of possibilities. If you want to take that list and turn it into a navigation bar, or maybe just a comma-separated list on a single line, you could accomplish it with CSS. Compare that to the fate of the previous, old-timey example—what you see is all it's ever going to be, and no amount of CSS is going to save you.

This new way, HTML lists, will also result in less markup (not in that example, but there will be a better one in a minute). Because you're now able to use the entire vocabulary that HTML has to offer, you can use the "right" element for content instead of using meaningless elements like <div> or <span>. For example, most sites have a navigation bar at the top of their sites that contains a list of links. Many sites have something very close to the following to represent that list of links:

```
<div id="navigation">
    <div id="link-one"><a href="/">home</a></div>
    <div id="link-two"><a href="/about">about</a></div>
    <div id="link-three"><a href="/help">help</a></div>
    <div id="link-four"><a href="/login">login</a></div>
</div>
```

Many sites don't even use links there but use <spans> with onclick events. Why they do this boggles the mind, but it certainly exists out there in the wild. A better, smaller, and more semantic way to represent that list might be:

```
<ul>
    <li id="home-link"><a href="/">home</a></li>
    <li id="about-link"><a href="/about">about</a></li>
    <li id="help-link"><a href="/help">help</a></li>
    <li id="login-link"><a href="/login-link">login</a></li>
</ul>
```

The first snippet contains 272 characters. The second contains 247 characters, a savings of almost 10%. Over an entire document, especially when replacing layout tables with more semantic elements, that savings can grow to as much as 50%.

Using semantic markup instead of table-based layouts or using <div>s and <span>s for everything can greatly reduce the amount of markup in your document, which means your users have a better experience with your products.

CSS Best Practices

Cascading Style Sheets were introduced to the Web in 1996. Until Netscape 4.7 and Internet Explorer 4 came out, CSS was only good for setting fonts and maybe text color, because the browsers hadn't implemented it fully yet.

Thankfully, today's modern browsers have reasonably interoperable implementations of CSS, which gives developers and designers a lot of freedom when it comes to styling semantic content.

AOL.com had very aggressive performance targets for broadband and dial-up users, which meant that the more style information that could be pushed into cached CSS files, the better.

CSS Goes First

Before a browser renders any part of the page, it will download all CSS and JavaScript files in the `<head>`. Once those files are downloaded and parsed, the browser will usually try to render as much of the HTML document as it has.

It's a good idea to put the link to your CSS file as the first thing in the `<head>` after the `<title>` element. This gives your browser a head start (no pun intended) on downloading it and building out the CSS DOM. The fewer CSS files the browser has to deal with, the simpler that CSS DOM, and the faster the browser can render the page.

One Style to Rule Them All

One of the things the team learned during performance testing, especially for broadband users, is that as bandwidth goes up, the browser's CPU and connections-per-host become the largest bottlenecks for performance. According to the HTTP 1.1 specification, a browser is only allowed to open two connections for each domain. That means if you have two style sheets on the same domain, your browser can't download anything else while it's working on those two files. The fewer files you make your users download, the faster your page will load, no matter how much bandwidth the user has available.

What that means for your site, as it did for AOL.com, is you should put all your CSS into one large style sheet. It may seem like a pain, but there are several tricks you can use to keep yourself sane while working with one large file that contains all your styles.

The best place to start is to have good markup, which we talked about in the previous section. This will help you write less CSS, and CSS that's easier to keep organized. By giving yourself logical hooks to style by, and semantic classes and IDs, you'll be able to navigate the different sections of your CSS much like you navigate through the HTML that makes up the document.

You should pick a structure for your CSS document that works for you. You can use the one below, or pick one of your own, but keep it consistent. The closer you can keep your CSS selectors to the order they appear in the document, and the more specific your selectors are, the easier it will be to find things when you need to change something.

Here's a sample:

```
body {
    width:80%;
    margin:0 auto;
```

```
    padding:0
    font:76% arial, helvetica, sans-serif;
    background:#fff;
    color:#000
}

h1, h2, h3, h4, h5, h6 {
    margin:0;
    padding:0;
}
#header {
    margin:0;
    padding:1em;
}

#header h1 {
    padding:1.5em
}

#header h1 a {
    display:block;
    color:#333;
    text-decoration:none;
}

#content {
    margin:0 1em 0 0;
    padding:1.2em;
}
```

There's no HTML document to refer to but here's the basic order:

❖ Generic HTML selectors

❖ General use class selectors

❖ ID selectors for major sections of the document

❖ Descendent selectors for that section

The properties within a declaration are also kept in order, just to keep things clear when reading the file. This helps for documentation purposes and troubleshooting. Pick an order that makes sense to you and that you can stay consistent with. Here's one possibility:

1. Width

2. Floating

3. Margins and padding

4. Borders

5. Fonts

6. Colors

7. Text styles

If you can keep your CSS files in sync with your HTML document, you'll be better off when you need to troubleshoot those styles, or if you need to hand that document off to someone else. Whoever takes it over should easily be able to figure out your convention and make sense of it.

Accessible CSS

One of the coolest accessibility features that AOL.com has is how it handles resizing fonts. It resizes not only the text on the page, but the entire layout and major images as well. This section will show you how that's done, by building a much simpler document and applying the same principles.

The Document

As you'll see, this is a much simpler version of the layout that AOL.com uses. Here's the markup:

```
<!DOCTYPE html PUBLIC "-//W3C//DTD XHTML 1.0 Transitional//EN"
    "http://www.w3.org/TR/xhtml1/DTD/xhtml1-transitional.dtd">

<html xmlns="http://www.w3.org/1999/xhtml" xml:lang="en" lang="en">
<head>
    <title>Accessible CSS Example</title>
    <link rel="stylesheet" type="text/css" href="accessible.css"/>
</head>

<body>
    <div id="header">
        <h1><a href="http://aol.com">AOL.com</a></h1>
    </div>
    <div id="content">
        <h3>This Section's Title</h3>
        <p class="image"><img src="example-image.jpg" alt="This image
is just an example."/></p>
        <p>Welcome to my example document. What do you think? Isn't
it swell?</p>
    </div>
```

```
<div id="navigation">
    <h3>Tools</h3>
    <ul>
        <li><a href="">mail</a></li>
        <li><a href="">money</a></li>
        <li><a href="">music</a></li>
        <li><a href="">AIM</a></li>
        <li><a href="">MyAOL</a></li>
        <li><a href="">video</a></li>
    </ul>
</div>
<div id="footer">
    AOL LLC | AOL International | Terms of Use | Privacy Policy |
Trademarks | Customer Support
    Accessibility Policy | AOL Unsolicited Bulk E-Mail Policy |
Advertise With Us | Download AOL | Beta | Site Map
    </div>
</body>
</html>
```

FIGURE 7.5 shows what it should look like in a browser.

Right, not the most attractive thing you've ever seen. That's about to change.

AOL.com

This Section's Title

Welcome to my example document. What do you think? Isn't it swell?

Tools

- mail
- money
- music
- AIM
- MyAOL
- video

AOL LLC | AOL International | Terms of Use | Privacy Policy | Trademarks | Customer Support
Accessibility Policy | AOL Unsolicited Bulk E-Mail Policy | Advertise With Us | Download AOL | Beta |
Site Map

FIGURE 7.5 The basic AOL.com, stripped of styles.

Initial Styles

Let's start by putting in some generic styles and styling the major sections of the site, and see where that gets us.

Here's the CSS:

```
body {
    margin:0 auto;
    padding:0;
    font: 76% arial, helvetica, sans-serif;
    background:#fff;
    color:#000;
}

h1, h2, h3, h4, h5, h6 {
    margin:0;
    padding:0;
}

#header {
    background:#036;
    padding:1em;
}

#header h1 a {
    color:#fff;
    text-decoration:none;
}

#content {
    float:left;
    padding:1em 0;
}

#content h3 {
    padding:.5em;
    background: #036;
    font-size:1.2em;
    color:#fff;
}

#navigation {
    float:right;
    padding:1em 0;
}
```

```
#navigation h3 {
    padding:.3em;
    font-size:1.1em;
    background:#063;
    color:#fff;
}

#footer {
    clear:both;
    padding:1em 0 .5em 0;
}
```

FIGURE 7.6 shows what it should look like now in your browser.

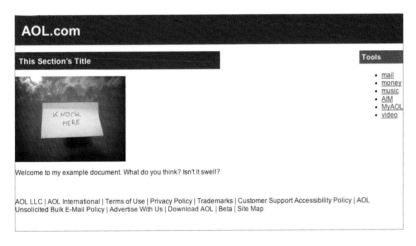

FIGURE 7.6 The basic layout of the AOL.com page forming.

The Tricky Bit

Now comes the fun part! AOL.com pulls off its trick by using em values for content and image widths, so that's exactly what we're going to do. If you look at the initial styles we created for our example document, you should see the following declaration:

```
body {
    margin:0 auto;
    padding:0;
    font: 76% arial, helvetica, sans-serif;
    background:#fff;
    color:#000;
}
```

DEFINITION

An em is a unit of measurement that is set relative to the font size of the current element.

Since modern browsers all set their default font size to 16 pixels, 76% of that is 12px. Everything we do from this point on will be relative to the font size we set on the <body> element. For example, to get a width of 755px at the default font size, the browsers set the width of their containing <div> to 62.5em (because 755 ÷ 12 = 62.5). All of the other elements that are resized when the user changes font size are set up using this formula.

Taking the CSS we had from the previous step, we'll add widths to the <body> element, the content and navigation <div>s, and the example image.

Here's the CSS:

```css
body {
    width:62.5em;
    margin:0 auto;
    padding:0;
    font: 76% arial, helvetica, sans-serif;
    background:#fff;
    color:#000;
}

h1, h2, h3, h4, h5, h6 {
    margin:0;
    padding:0;
}

#header {
    background:#036;
    padding:1em;
}

#header h1 a {
    color:#fff;
    text-decoration:none;
}

#content {
    width:40em;
    float:left;
    padding:1em 0;
}

#content h3 {
    padding:.5em;
```

```
    background: #036;
    font-size:1.2em;
    color:#fff;
}

#content p.image {
    float:left;
    padding:0 .25em .25em 0;
}

#content p.image img {
    width:16.66em;
    height:12.5em;
}

#navigation {
    width:22.5em;
    float:right;
    padding:1em 0;
}

#navigation h3 {
    padding:.3em;
    font-size:1.1em;
    background:#063;
    color:#fff;
}

#footer {
    clear:both;
    padding:1em 0 .5em 0;
}
```

Looking at the widths, **TABLE 7.2** shows what we have.

TABLE 7.2 Converting to Em-based Measurements

Region	Width em/px	Height em/px
body	62.5/755	auto
#content	40/480	auto
#content p.image img	16.66/200	12.5/150
#navigation	22.5/270	Auto

FIGURE 7.7 shows what it should look like in any modern Web browser (tested in IE6, Opera 9.5, Firefox 2.0, Safari 2.0, and Firefox 1.5).

And **FIGURE 7.8** shows it with the font one step larger.

This approach gives you a lot of flexibility; more importantly, it gives your users a lot of flexibility. When they resize the text in their browser, it's not crammed into a tiny little space. The container grows with the text, instead of staying the same size and ruining the visual look of your site.

FIGURE 7.7 Setting up the columns.

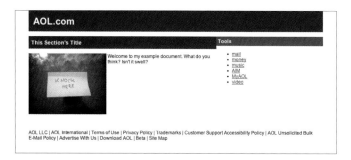

FIGURE 7.8 Resizing the fonts.

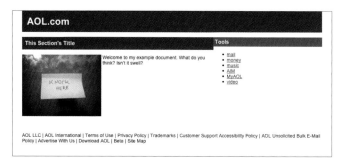

Performance in the Real World

One of the biggest challenges in any site is performance. We talked at the beginning of this section about the work you can do up front to give yourself the best opportunity to have a well-performing site. Now it's time to talk about what you do with the live product to make sure your users have the best possible experience. The three most important things you can do to maximize performance for your users, no matter their connection speed, are caching, compression, and reducing the number of objects users have to download. We'll discuss best practices and pitfalls around each.

Caching

We've talked about caching before, but it's important enough to repeat when it comes to real-world performance.

There are very few things that users really need to download every time they visit your site. Usually, the large majority of content users have to download won't change every time they view the page. To give your users the best possible performance, it's a good idea to cache the content that doesn't change frequently. This usually includes CSS, JavaScript, and images. Since the HTML for dynamic sites is just that—dynamic—there's no good way to cache it.

The easiest way to tell a browser to cache a file is to set the "Expires" HTTP header to some far-distant date. Setting this depends on your Web server and programming language. If you have a CDN (Content Delivery Network), it may do this for you. Let's look at a couple examples from AOL.com. All of the CSS and JavaScript files have an Expires date set 30 days in the future. So, for a whole month, users will use the cached version of the CSS. The navigational images also use the same Expires date. All of the programmed images have an Expires time of only 24 hours in the future, since those change frequently—potentially several times a day. If you use Apache as your Web server, you can use the following in your `.htaccess` file to do the same thing:

```
ExpiresActive on
ExpiresByType "text/css" "now plus 1 month"
ExpiresByType "image/jpeg" "now plus 1 year"
ExpiresByType "image/png" "now plus 1 year"
ExpiresByType "image/gif" "now plus 1 year"
ExpiresByType "text/javascript" "now plus 1 month"
```

This does raise one problem: What if you have to make a change? Currently, AOL. com will publish a file with a whole new URL and change the HTML to point to it. This gets around users having the file cached and makes sure they get the updates.

There are many different ways to handle caching and updating content, but this approach has worked well for AOL.com.

Compression

One of the best things you can do to improve performance is to compress all your non-binary files. There are several points where you can do this compression: by hand on the file system, in the Web server, or in your router. AOL.com currently uses the router to do the compression, but most modern Web servers have compression either built in or provided by a plug-in.

Compressing text content (HTML, CSS, and JavaScript) can provide a savings of up to 50% in the amount of data sent over the Internet. There's a little overhead on the user's machine when the content is decompressed, but 90% of the time it is much faster to decompress the file than download it, even over a high-speed connection. Compressing binary files such as images, though, usually provides no benefit, and creates files larger than the original.

Reducing Objects

As connection speeds increase, the bottleneck for users displaying your page moves from downloading the content to parsing and rendering. There is also a hard limit on the number of files that browsers will download at a time. Internet Explorer (all versions) will only download two files per host at a time. This means that if all your files are on the same domain (like www.aol.com), IE will only download two of those files at a time, no matter how fast the connection is. The default for Firefox is four files per domain (although this is easily tweaked either by using the preferences or the FasterFox extension). Also, the more complicated your CSS and JavaScript, and the more files they're split up across, the more work the user's browser has to do to create the initial Document Object Model and the CSS Object Model, and to decide what the Cascade and Inheritance for all those styles are.

The more you can combine CSS and JavaScript into single files, the better. Currently, AOL.com has one main JavaScript and CSS file. There are a couple of other JavaScript files, but they're for external advertising and reporting systems. All of the JavaScript, Flash, and CSS files downloaded by ads aren't loaded until after the browser's "onload" event has been fired.

Conclusion

The team behind AOL.com is a first-rate group of developers and designers working in a very closely watched fishbowl and under a lot of internal pressure. AOL.com is the front page not only of that domain but of *all* AOL products. That means everyone wants a piece of them and their every move is scrutinized. Under this pressure, this world-class group turned out a world-class portal—not only in how it looks and works but in accessibility, performance, and in ease of adding new features. I'm proud of the very small part I could play in the process of developing AOL.com, and to have worked with such an amazing group of professionals.

AOL.com isn't perfect—no site is—but the things it does well, it does very well. Those are the parts I felt were important to share: the way the team works together, Web standards, accessibility, and performance. Hopefully, you can take the lessons we learned on this project and apply them to your own.

Cascade and Inheritance

CSS Inheritance

For some CSS properties, the child elements inherit the properties of their parents. A paragraph element, for example, is the child of the body element (i.e., the paragraph is "contained" inside the body). As such, it inherits certain CSS rules that we might define for the body. For example, consider the following style sheet:

```
body {
  font: 13px sans-serif;
  color: #555;
}
p {
  color: red;
}
```

By default, the paragraph element inherits both the font and color settings of its parent: the body element. So, any text within a paragraph tag is also a 13-pixel sans-serif font—we need not duplicate that rule by putting it in the paragraph selector. If we want to style the text inside of our paragraphs differently than the parent element, we can override the inherited values.

So, here, while we colored the text of the body element gray, we've overridden that color in the paragraph element by specifying that its text should be colored red.

The Cascade

A wonderful benefit of CSS is the Cascade. Think of a large site that has different sets of content, just as a large company would have different departments, each with its own unique issues and jargon. Think of how much would work would get done if Human Resources department employees could only talk shop with Product Marketing employees.

To accommodate the presentation of this large site's different content, we can write two or more style sheets for each department's section, and import them into a master style sheet—in essence, layering the styles rather than maintaining one large style sheet that would encompass the entire site. This gives developers the freedom to create and adapt the presentation layer as they see fit.

Afterword

Inspiration Never Arrives in a Vacuum

Sometimes inspiration comes as a serendipitous lightning bolt, arriving through a programming trick from a book, a color scheme seen in a restaurant ad, or an online chat with a colleague.

More often it comes from experience—the well-earned lessons from past mistakes, put to good use for current and future projects.

However, experience can sometimes be a handicap. Time-tested, well-used advice can become glaringly obsolete in an instant, especially in an industry in which communication happens as rapidly across the ocean as across the office.

The maturing of browsers led developers to move away from Web pages bloated with way too much presentational HTML and toward semantically lean, elegantly marked up pages.

The late arrival yet quick distribution of Microsoft Internet Explorer 7 for Windows finally allowed CSS developers to broaden their designs.

Google Maps showed programmers that JavaScript could be used to redefine surfing habits. With Ajax-enabled sites, gone are the days when a quality Web experience involved a full-page refresh after every click of the mouse.

Developments like these prove that the Web design industry has matured but, by nature, is never static.

Professionals must continually learn and relearn their trade, casting aside old Web development dogma when it becomes necessary to do so. As the set of Web standards becomes better, so too do the designers and developers improve their craft.

Web professionals like you and the people featured within these pages, helping to create the shape of Web standards, are the true inspiration. Keep up the fantastic work.

Christopher Schmitt
July 2007
Cincinnati, Ohio

Appendix A

Targeting Web Browsers

Every Web site has different types of visitors. A Web standards-based approach is by its nature more forgiving of the differences in Web browsers because standards-compliant sites are based on open standards, not proprietary technology. Additionally, Web standards professionals make fewer assumptions about the types of visitors who come to their sites and don't assume that all of them will be using the same browser.

That said, every organization is going to have a different type of audience, be it a business-to-business audience, business-to-consumer segment, students, government, or just a cross-section of society at large. It can be very useful for a Web team to know what Web browsers to "target" while working.

Just about every Web server keeps logs of the visitors it serves, and this information includes data on what Web browsers and operating system (OS) platforms those visitors are using. This is done by inspecting the HTTP_USER_AGENT header of every HTTP request.

Web standards experts all agree on at least one important rule: Never assume a single browser is the only audience of the site. Attempt to cater to all, using the open standards instead of proprietary technologies.

Web Log Analysis

Most major Web sites and companies have made some form of commitment to a software package that can help analyze their server logs. This is critical information for any professional Web team. Every project and every business is going to have different needs. If there has been no commitment to a software package, there are volumes of free, commercial, and open-source tools that can analyze logs from a variety of Web servers.

Some software packages are free or affordable. Even the free (or almost-free) packages provide robust reporting features. Often analysis packages require code (which, keep in mind, is not always compliant with Web standards) to be inserted in the documents on a Web site for enhanced statistical data that typical logs don't provide. Tools like these are particularly valuable if a developer does not, for whatever reason, have access to his or her own raw Web server logs.

One such toolkit is Google Analytics (www.google.com/analytics). Google's service (**FIGURE A.1**) provides reporting data over time on a number of key design- and UI-related areas, including

❖ Browser and OS platform versions

❖ Screen resolution

❖ Screen colors

FIGURE A.1 Google Analytics offers many useful features for Web designers. (http://analytics. blogspot.com/2007/05/ new-version-of-google-analytics.html)

❖ Languages

❖ Plug-in support (Java and Flash)

❖ Connection speeds

Modern Web Browsers

Professional Web designers and developers have been able to embrace Web standards because the vast majority of users are surfing the Web with a modern browser. These browsers support enough of the standard that Web teams can effectively code to it while keeping the content and critical features of the site usable and accessible by browsers that may be using a text-only version of a site. For instance, Netscape Navigator 4 typically is served usable, accessible text due to its inability to support enough of the Web standards in use today.

Modern Web standards-compliant browsers are typically considered to be anything greater than or equal to

❖ Internet Explorer 5+ on Mac

❖ Internet Explorer 5+ on the PC

❖ Safari on Mac OS X

❖ Konqueror (uses WebCore/KHTML like Safari)

❖ Netscape 6 (any Gecko-based browser, including Netscape Browser 8)

❖ Opera 6

❖ Mozilla Firefox on PC/Mac

Since the Web standards-aware browsers have been available for some time, there are sets of Web standards-based browsers that are considered to have troubling (or buggy), if not impossible to cope with, levels of Web standards support. These include:

❖ Konqueror using KHTML code base (basically Safari)

❖ Internet Explorer 5.x on both Windows and Mac OS

❖ Safari 1.x

❖ Netscape 6 and 7

❖ Opera 6 through 8

TIP

An excellent, modern, and forward-thinking resource example for setting browser policy is the Yahoo! UI Graded Browser Support system developed at Yahoo!. These standards are based on Yahoo!'s browser's statistic data, which is an excellent cross-section of the Web. This can be referenced online at http://developer.yahoo.com/yui/articles/gbs/.

Alternative Devices

A professional Web team needs to assume that an unpredictable variety of non-traditional devices will be used to browse its site. Some of these include

❖ Text-based browsers such as Lynx

❖ Assistive technologies like screen readers, such as JAWS or Window-Eyes

❖ Game consoles

❖ Mobile or handhelds such as PDAs (Personal Digital Assistants) and cellular and smart phones

Web teams should become familiar with these alternative devices and learn how to support them (**FIGURE A.2**).

FIGURE A.2 Opera Software produces Opera Mini, an exceptionally powerful mobile Web browser for handhelds and cell phones.

Company Policy

Whatever degree of browser support an organization chooses, it should be an educated decision that is regularly evaluated, at the very least once a year. It should be documented and integrated in the Web team's Quality Assurance (QA) process. This requires software and hardware configurations being made available to test with. Not having access to testing software or hardware can mean lost customers, opportunities, and revenue—and even, in some cases, open up the potential for legal action.

At the same time, unless you are working in a controlled environment where the users' software can be guessed or controlled (such as a corporate intranet), even browsers that are "not supported" should be given something that can be accessed or information about what software *is* supported.

Appendix B

Accessibility

The W3C has created a number of best-practice recommendations with regards to Web standards-based approaches to accessibility. Traditionally, terms like *Section 508* (government regulations around accessibility) have left many a designer with feelings of dread, believing that they will have to seriously hold back their designs.

Happily, with the little effort it takes to follow professional best practices, Web designers or developers can get their code closer to purely accessible than ever before. A team needs only to make reasoned decisions and produce thoughtful markup, CSS, and in particular scripting (which should not be 100% required for a site to work) in order to come fairly close. Accessibility should always be in the back of a designer's mind when creating the UI and when a developer is programming backend software. The main areas of concern—the ones in which it's most challenging to attain accessibility successes—are the one-off scenarios, integration with third parties, potential CMS or other software issues, and multimedia.

In addition to the W3C, governments worldwide are also defining standardsfor acceptable levels of accessibility. Some of the accessibility guidelines include:

❖ United States Federal Government Section 508, www.section508.gov/

❖ W3C Web Accessibility Initiative (WAI) Web Content Accessibility Guidelines 1.0 (WCAG), www.w3.org/TR/WAI-WEBCONTENT/

❖ W3C WAI WCAG 2.0, www.w3.org/TR/WCAG20/

❖ W3C Accessible Rich Internet Applications (WAI-ARIA) Suite, www.w3.org/WAI/intro/aria

Each set of guidelines defines different levels of accessibility. Typically, an organization should decide which of these levels to shoot for and begin plans to test and evaluate based on that target as part of its QA process.

Resources

In addition to the accessibility standards listed above, here is a list of resources to start developing more accessible Web sites for your audience:

❖ Adobe Accessibility Resource for Acrobat and Flash Design, www.adobe.com/accessibility/index.html

❖ Six Principles of Accessible Web Design: An Introduction to the WAI Page Author Guidelines, www.hwg.org/resources/accessibility/sixprinciples.html

❖ Dive into Accessibility. A 30-day primer on Web site accessibility, http://diveintoaccessibility.org/

❖ Know Your Users: Web Accessibility from the User's Perspective. A video featuring demonstrations of assistive technologies for the Web, www.fresnostate.edu/webaccess/users/default.html

❖ Communicating With and About People with Disabilities. A handy resource with tips on how to talk to people with intellectual, cognitive, or developmental disabilities, www.dol.gov/odep/pubs/fact/comucate.htm

❖ Screen Reader Simulation, www.webaim.org/simulations/screenreader/

❖ Low Vision Simulation, www.webaim.org/simulations/lowvision.php

❖ *Countering Design Exclusion: An Introduction to Inclusive Design* by Simeon L. Keates and P. John Clarkson. ISBN: 1852337699.

❖ *A List Apart*'s Accessibility section. A Web design magazine containing expert-written articles on current topics of accessible Web design, www.alistapart.com/topics/userscience/accessibility/

Appendix C

Web Site Performance Tips

When Web teams consider performance, they usually think of server-side issues such as server hardware performance, application software performance, and bandwidth considerations. The main thing that they associate with performance as it relates to client-side considerations is...a few graphics, and that's about it.

The truth is, there are a number of client-side performance issues, many of which are quite effective in affecting the user-perceived speed of a Web site. The "time to display" in the browser and the time for the page to be ready for the user to interact with it is possibly the most important aspect of performance from a user perspective. User perspective is everything.

UI coders have to take a lot into account when creating the UI layer of a site, and they are fortunate if they have opted for a Web standards-based approach, because it is more efficient than the older methods. Modern pages are lighter weight, and there is some evidence they are rendered faster in the browser. Certainly, leveraging the browser's cache for presentation and scripts can be beneficial because that information does not have to be downloaded every time.

The usual design rules apply about keeping file sizes to a minimum. But this applies to graphics, CSS files, JavaScript, Flash files, and anything else that a Web page has to load. However, the actual structure of the page, the way it's put together, where it is requesting the files from, and the way artwork is cut can all have tremendous impact on the load time in a Web browser.

A number of industry experts, including the Yahoo! UI team (www.yuiblog.com) in particular, have published research on page-loading and the way browsers make requests to the server (see the links at the end of this section for more of the research). Their and others' research is of immense value to front-end developers looking for optimizations. Of particular interest is how Web browsers request files, in what order, and what they can and cannot do in parallel.

Some interesting performance tips from Yahoo! UI and others include

❖ Fewer files mean faster load times, even if some of those files are larger than smaller sets of smaller-sized files. This is because each HTTP request the browser makes and the server responds to is exceptionally time-intensive.

❖ Combining images and using CSS to position and clip the graphics to show parts of them at a time can speed up load times, because of fewer HTTP requests. These images are frequently referred to as "CSS Sprites."

❖ Consider, either as part of a build process when deploying a Web site or in real time, merging numerous CSS and JS files into their own single file in order to reduce HTTP requests. Another way to dynamically merge files is to use server-side scripts.

❖ A browser can load CSS files simultaneously; however, once it hits a `<script>` tag, the browser suspends other load operations and loads each `<script>` individually in sequence. Once the scripts are completed, the browser then proceeds with loading the page. This can seriously skew load times.

❖ To help mitigate multiple `<script>` tag load impacts, consider placing `<script>` tags just before the closing `<body>` tag to allow the page to load before the scripts.

❖ Execute page-building JavaScript when the document has completed loading, as opposed to when the whole page loads (also known as `window.onload`). For more information, see the performance experiment section following this, and the sidebar "Execute on Page Load, or Event on DOM Document Load" in Chapter 3.

❖ Spread images or scripts out over multiple DNS names so the browser can request more files simultaneously. These can be simple DNS CNAMES, as the IP address doesn't matter. There is a limit to this benefit, so reading the research on this technique is recommended (see notes below).

❖ Enable gzipping or compression of HTTP served content. Almost all Web servers today and Web browsing clients can serve and accept compressed content; this can shave a lot of size off the downloaded files.

❖ Where there are large numbers of scripts required but selectively used, authors should consider investigating a technique called "Lazy Loading" or "On-Demand" script loading, which allows only basic scripts to be loaded until extra libraries are needed, which are then loaded dynamically without a page refresh.

❖ Modern JavaScript can get fairly bloated, so consider using one of several online tools that strip unnecessary code and white space from scripts to make the files smaller. Two examples are Douglas Crockford's JSMin (crockford.com/javascript/jsmin.html) or Dean Edwards' Packer (http://dean.edwards.name/packer/).

> **NOTE**
>
> For the above and more, including additional tips and further explanations, please see some of the following original research and resources online:
>
> Performance Research, Part 1: What the 80/20 Rule Tells Us About Reducing HTTP Requests
> http://yuiblog.com/blog/2006/11/28/performance-research-part-1/
>
> High Performance Web Sites: Rule 1—Make Fewer HTTP Requests
> developer.yahoo.net/blog/archives/2007/04/rule_1_make_few.html
>
> Optimizing Page Load Time
> www.die.net/musings/page_load_time/

A Performance Experiment

How do some of these techniques fare in the real world? Where can the savings actually happen? It's important to remember that different types of sites will fare differently based on their makeup and what techniques are employed on them. For example, large news or e-commerce sites and the typical Web designer's blog are different types of sites altogether, with diverse server needs and volumes of traffic. Additionally, a number of other variable factors also affect performance, from the quality and type of Internet connection to the speed of the computer being used.

To get real-world examples, metrics must be pulled from large sites with hundreds of assets and thousands of users. These sites can be literally hundreds of kilobytes in file size. You can also extrapolate large-site performance benefits from small-scale examples, such as blog pages, which are often 100KB or smaller. That's the test we're going to try here.

The Basic Setup

Using a dial-up connection and the excellent Mozilla Firefox extension Firebug (www.getfirebug.com), you can inspect the download requests of a given Web page using its networking tools. These tools display a graph of each object, its file size, and the time to download it in comparison to other objects on the page.

Firebug is free, open source, and a highly recommended tool for debugging everything from CSS to JavaScript and Ajax.

Starting with a small-scale blog that features 112KB of files, Firebug shows that these files are broken down into 22 unique requests that take roughly 20.44 seconds to download over a dial-up connection.

Consider also that the JavaScript, when building advanced page effects, typically is loading a number of scripts onload—when the document has finished loading—and that will not happen until 20 seconds after the page is initially loaded.

The site features

❖ Four CSS files: a 47-byte file, a 13KB file, a 5KB file, and a 738-byte print style sheet

❖ Three JavaScript files in the document's <head>: one 18KB file, one 2KB file, and a 20KB file from an external site for statistics tracking

❖ Three other 20KB JavaScript files from external sources for small advertising promotions

Examine the initial, out-of-the-box graph from Firefox. The same graphic and list of files would be almost exponentially larger on an enterprise-scale site, and so would the download times and numbers of files (**Figure c.1**).

Looking at the graph, you can add up the times and see the point at which the CSS and JavaScript in the document's <head> are loaded, the document itself, and also the point at which the artwork and other files are loaded:

❖ The HTML document itself takes 2.5 seconds to load.

❖ The CSS files are loaded with some overlap to the document, but with a little extra time compared to the HTML document.

❖ As expected, the three JavaScript files in the <head> are loaded one file at a time, in sequence, while nothing else is loaded; however, this process does not start until after 2.5 seconds or so.

❖ By the time these JavaScript files are loaded, almost six additional seconds have passed.

❖ Roughly eight seconds pass before the first graphic is loaded, due to waiting on these other requests.

❖ It can be safely assumed that at a certain point, the document is rendered in the user's window, and colors and layout are applied from the CSS, at least after 2.5 seconds for the CSS to load, although no artwork is displayed in those first eight seconds.

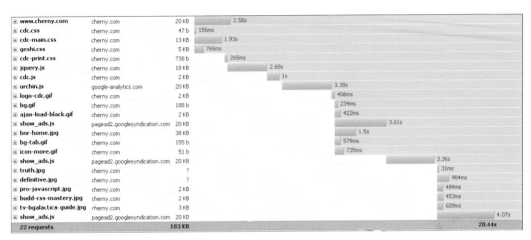

FIGURE C.1   The base page load performance graph in the Firebug Firefox add-on.

Far from a scientific analysis, but an interesting story nonetheless, in particular the portion where the scripts are loaded one at a time and in sequence.

Now, consider for a moment that there has been some optimization already at this point. The first, 18KB JavaScript file is a white space-packed JavaScript file that was compressed from 50KB to 18KB. A 50KB file on a 56Kbps dial-up connection would take a full *six seconds to download, all while nothing else is happening.* This alone would push out the time to display any artwork to something like 11 seconds.

Finally, this script actually queues up several JavaScript events and actions unobtrusively and loads the scripts, not at the end of the page load as per usual, but once the HTML document's DOM has loaded, cutting that time down from 20 seconds to eight seconds. This is a huge performance boost (read more about it in the JavaScript sidebar "Execute on Page Load, or Event on DOM Document Load" in Chapter 3).

Merging Files and Moving Scripts

A first pass through can easily optimize the files' linking and placement inside the document with a couple of easy steps:

❖ Merge the CSS files.

❖ Merge the JavaScript files.

❖ Move the JavaScript files to the bottom of the document just before the closing `<body>` tag.

Before merging the files, the script and link tags looked like this:

```
<link rel="stylesheet" type="text/css" href="/-/css/cdc.css" />
<link rel="stylesheet" type="text/css" href="/-/css/cdc-print.css"
    media="print" />
<script type="text/javascript" src="/-/js/jquery.js"></script>
<script type="text/javascript" src="/-/js/cdc.js"></script>
<script src="http://www.google-analytics.com/urchin.js"
type="text/javascript">
</script>
```

Additionally, the cdc.css file used @import to bring in two further CSS files, cdc-main.css, and geshi.css. The @import directive is a common technique to screen out old browsers that don't support more modern CSS commands. Combining the CSS files is a fairly straightforward process of taking the content of cdc.css, main.css, geshi.css, and cdc-print.css, and saving them off into a single linked file called cdc.css.

One immediate problem is that the CSS links to a print-specific CSS file, cdc-print.css, and if that content is pushed into cdc.css then there has to be a way to specify that its rules are print-specific. The CSS specification solves this dilemma through the use of inline media handlers. Using an @media declaration, which is wrapped around the rules that apply, means that the cdc.css file looks like this:

```
/* content from the other css files here */
@media print {
   /* content from the cdc-print.css file such as: */
   #nav { display: none; }
   #content { position: static; }
}
```

It seems odd because it's not typical to see curly braces {} inside of other curly braces {} in CSS. Now, with a single file the media type is set to all, which, much like @import, can help screen out older, unsupported browsers:

```
<link rel="stylesheet" type="text/css" href="/-/css/cdc.css"
   media="all" />
```

Beyond this, the JavaScript files (the ones that can be combined) are combined and moved out of the document's <head> and placed just before the closing <body> tag:

```
<script type="text/javascript" src="/-/js/cdc.js"></script>
<script src="http://www.google-analytics.com/urchin.js"
   type="text/javascript"></script>
```

```
</body>
</html>
```

So, the `cdc.js` file contains both `jquery.js` and `cdc.js`. Unfortunately, the last file is from another source, and can't be combined.

Combining the CSS and JavaScript files reduces the number of HTTP requests on this page to 18 requests—down from 22. There is now one main CSS file and one main JavaScript file, which replaces the three scripts that used to be in the document's <head>.

The results can show how these simple steps can speed up the user's experience. First, the download time is reduced, albeit only about a second on a site as small as this. It is, however, interesting that even a small page can have a small performance boost. One can imagine the effect on a large site, with a server having to respond to thousands of users. Here, reduction to four fewer requests made for a small savings in terms of download time, however, the server itself has less work to do. The busier the site, the more that will add up (**Figure C.2**).

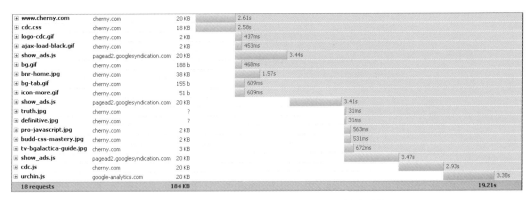

Figure C.2   The base page load performance after reducing the number of linked files and moving the JavaScript before the closing **<body>** element.

Another item worth noting is that it is now only roughly 2.5 seconds before the page is downloading the attached artwork—vividly increasing the user's perception of how responsive and well-performing the site is. The main page's scripts being downloaded at the end of the body document has not delayed the loading of the artwork and other assets, because (as has been noted) loading scripts prevents other files from loading. Now, this operation happens at the end of the document.

HTTP Compression

HTTP 1.1 file compression has been supported by most Web browsers for years. Unfortunately, for years common Web browsers such as Netscape 4 had exceptionally buggy implementations. With that said, Web servers had some questionable implementations as well. Today, most major Web browsers have shaken the bugs out and server technology has also caught up to some degree. With Apache there is mod_deflate, mod_gzip, and even PHP has some built-in real-time compression options. Microsoft's Internet Information Server (IIS) also supports compression, although it is complicated to set up, and often third-party add-ons can assist or even augment its features.

For demonstration purposes, the last step in the experiment is to enable HTTP compression on the server side for the JavaScript and CSS files. Note that in this demonstration, the HTML document has not been compressed, although document compression is almost more common and can yield spectacular results as well, sometimes on the order of a 60% savings. These are all text-based files, which are easy to compress and produce wonderful savings that really pay off.

How compression can be enabled is complex and beyond the scope of this discussion; however, many resources online are available and should be read carefully.

Loading up the test page and tracking the Firebug graph shows some impressive results (**FIGURE C.3**):

❖ On a dial-up connection, the page now loads in 16 seconds (a three-second gain for a user is exceptional).

❖ 20KB in CSS has been reduced to 5KB.

❖ 20KB in JS has been reduced to 10KB.

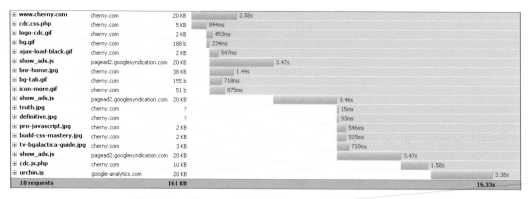

FIGURE C.3 The page with HTTP compression enabled.

This is a benefit in terms of both server-side bandwidth costs and downloads for users, and the impact on page document weight is obvious. Note that one of the JS files could not be merged or compressed because it was hosted on an outside server.

Remember that these experiments were performed on a small-scale site with low traffic. The results on enterprise sites—with high bandwidth costs, a greater quantity of assets, larger file sizes, and more users—can provide an exceptional payoff.

TIP

Compression can be tricky for many reasons, in particular due to its sordid history and inconsistent support by browsers. Attempts to configure or implement HTTP compression should be performed carefully and with ample research, experiments, and lots and lots of testing. The tests should be tested. And then tested again. Search online for help with regard to PHP compression, Apache `mod_deflate`, `mod_gzip`, or IIS utilities.

Appendix D

CSS Selectors Reference

Obviously, browser support for CSS selectors varies, so testing is critical. What follows is an overview of just some of the available CSS selectors. These and more can be found in the CSS specifications, as described at www.w3.org/TR/REC-CSS2/selector.html.

Selectors

E	Type or Element selector	Matches any E element

```
p {color:red;}
<p>This text is red</p>
```

E.warn	Class selector	Matches element E with class of warn

```
div.warn {color:red;}
<div class="warn">This is red</div>
```

Classes can be used by themselves to apply to any element:

```
.warn {color:red;}
<div class="warn">This is red</div>
<p class="warn">So is this</p>
```

#myid	ID selector	Matches any E element ID equal to myid

```
#myid {color: red;}
<div id="myid">Text inside will be red.</div>
```

E F	Descendant selector	Matches any F element that is a descendant of an E element

```
div p {color:red;}
<div><p>This text is red.</p></div>
<p>This text is not.</p>
```

E > F	Child selector	Matches any F element that is a direct child of an element E. White space around > is optional.

```
li > p { color: red; }
<ul>
 <li><p>This text is red.</p></li>
</ul>
<p>This text is not.</p>
```

E + F	Adjacent selector	Matches any F element immediately preceded by an element E

```
h1 + p { color: red; }
<h1>Header</h1>
<p>Paragraph is red.</p>
<p>But not this one!</p>
```

E:first-child	The :first-child pseudo-class	Matches element E when E is the first child of its parent

```
li:first-child { color:red; }
<ul>
<li>this will be red</li>
<li>this will not be</li>
</ul>
```

E:link	:link pseudo-class	Matches elements E that are links, typically a anchor links in (X)HTML

```
a:link {color:black;}
a {color:blue;}
<p>
 <a href="#link">This is black.</a>
 <a id="link">This is blue.</a>
</p>
```

E[foo]	Attribute selector	Matches any E element with the foo attribute set (whatever the value)

```
a[href] {color:green;}
<p>
 <a href="#link">this, is a green link</a>
 <a id="link">this, is not</a>
</p>
```

E[foo=val]	Attribute selector	Matches any E element with the foo attribute set exactly to "val"

```
a[rel=external] { color: green; }
<p>
 <a rel=external>this matches, and is green</a>
 <a rel=internal>this is not green</a>
</p>
```

E[foo~=val]	Attribute selector	Matches any element E with an attribute matching foo exactly in a space-separated list

```
a[rel~=example] {color: green;}
<p>
 <a rel="copyright example">this is green</a>
 <a rel="copyright">this is not</a>
</p>
```

E[foo|=val]	Attribute selector	Matches any element E with the foo attribute set where the first part of a hyphenated value is "val". This is typically for language attribute matching.

```
a[lang|=en] {color:green;}
<p>
 <a lang="en-US">this matches, and is green</a>
 <a lang="fr-FR">this is not green</a>
</p>
```

*	Universal selector	Matches any element, any rule applied here applies to any and all tags, including forms, etc.

```
* {color: red;}
```

Everything will be red. Typically avoided.

A better use of the universal selector is inside of something; however, the same caveats apply:

```
#box * {margin: 0;}
<div id="box">
 <p>Everything in this div will have no margin.</p>
 <ul><li>Everything!</li></ul>
</div>
```

Index